# Conflict and Dev

Since the late 1990s, a new awareness of the relationship between conflicts and development has grown. Developmental factors can act as a trigger for violence, as well as for ending violence and for triggering post-conflict reconstruction. This book explores the complexity of the links between violent conflict (usually civil wars) and development, underdevelopment and uneven development. It emphasises the connections between stable developed economies and civil wars in other parts of the world, and examines how structural factors (such as the organisation of the global economy) virtually condemn some regions to conflict and underdevelopment.

This valuable introductory text explains, reviews and critically evaluates this complex relationship. It focuses on intrastate conflicts and complex political emergencies that combine transnational and internal characteristics. Attention is also given to interstate conflicts. Chapters emphasise how the relationship between conflict and development traverses many scales (macro, meso and micro) and dimensions (economic, political and cultural). Furthermore it explains how different developmental challenges and opportunities emerge along the full life cycle of conflict. Specifically, the role of poverty, state, market, civil society, globalisation, humanitarian aid, refugees, gender and health within conflict dynamics are examined. The book also investigates specific developmental issues emerging during conflict management and post-conflict reconstruction. Both authors have a background in conducting research in deeply divided societies, and argue that many of the processes connected with war and peacemaking deliberately write people out of the equation. This book attempts to 'write people in'.

By drawing on contemporary theoretical debates and examining current policies and events, the text unpacks the difficult and complex aspects of the relationships between armed conflict and development and makes them accessible, interesting and policy relevant. It considers how peacemaking, peacebuilding and post-war reconstruction are usually more sustainable and successful if politicians, policymakers, entrepreneurs and those working for international NGOs take on board local opinion and capacity. Written in an accessible style, the book considers the main contemporary theories and arguments on conflict, development and the interactions between the two. The text is illuminated throughout with case studies drawn from Africa, the Balkans, Asia and the Middle East.

**Roger Mac Ginty** is a Reader at the School of International Relations, University of St Andrews. He specialises in the study of peace, conflict and conflict management. His publications include *No War, No Peace: The rejuvenation of stalled peace processes and peace accords* (2006).

**Andrew Williams** is Professor of International Relations, University of St Andrews. He specialises in the study of conflict and international history. His main research interests include international conflict resolution, international history and international organisation. He has had a great deal of experience of the practice of conflict resolution and has worked as a consultant for United Nations organisations such as UNDP and UNITAR. He has published widely in key journals. His book *Liberalism and War* was published by Routledge in 2005.

# Routledge Perspectives on Development

**Series Editor:** Professor Tony Binns, *University of Otago*

The *Perspectives on Development* series will provide an invaluable, up-to-date and refreshing approach to key development issues for academics and students working in the field of development, in disciplines such as anthropology, economics, geography, international relations, politics and sociology. The series will also be of particular interest to those working in interdisciplinary fields, such as area studies (African, Asian and Latin American Studies), development studies, rural and urban studies, travel and tourism.

If you would like to submit a book proposal for the series, please contact Tony Binns on j.a.binns@geography.otago.ac.nz.

## Published:

David W. Drakakis-Smith
*Third World Cities*, 2nd edition

Kenneth Lynch
*Rural-Urban Interactions in the Developing World*

Nicola Ansell
*Children, Youth and Development*

Katie Willis
*Theories and Practices of Development*

Jennifer A. Elliott
*An Introduction to Sustainable Development*, 3rd edition

Chris Barrow
*Environmental Management and Development*

Janet Henshall Momsen
*Gender and Development*

Richard Sharpley and David J. Telfer
*Tourism and Development*

Andrew McGregor
*Southeast Asian Development*

Cheryl McEwan
*Postcolonialism and Development*

Roger Mac Ginty and Andrew Williams
*Conflict and Development*

## Forthcoming:

Jo Beall and Sean Fox
*Cities and Development*

Tony Binns, Christo Fabricius and Etienne Nel
*Local Knowledge, Environment and Development*

Andrea Cornwall
*Participation and Development*

Janet Henshall Momsen
*Gender and Development* Second Edition

Tony Binns and Alan Dixon
*Africa: Diversity and Development*

Michael Tribe, Frederick Nixon and Andrew Sumner
*Economics and Development Studies*

David Lewis and Nazneen Kanji
*Non-Governmental Organisations and Development*

Clive Agnew and Philip Woodhouse
*Water Resources and Development*

David Hudson
*Global Finance and Development*

Hazel Barrett
*Health and Development*

W.T.S. Gould
*Population and Development*

Andrew Collins
*Disaster and Development*

# Conflict and Development

Roger Mac Ginty and Andrew Williams

Routledge
Taylor & Francis Group

LONDON AND NEW YORK

First published 2009
by Routledge
2 Park Square, Milton Park, Abingdon, Oxon, OX14 4RN

Simultaneously published in the USA and Canada
by Routledge
270 Madison Avenue, New York, NY 10016

*Routledge is an imprint of the Taylor & Francis Group, an informa business*

© 2009 Roger Mac Ginty and Andrew Williams

Typeset in Times New Roman and Franklin Gothic by
Keystroke, 28 High Street, Tettenhall, Wolverhampton
Printed and bound in Great Britain by
TJ International Ltd, Padstow, Cornwall

*British Library Cataloguing in Publication Data*
A catalogue record for this book is available from the British Library

*Library of Congress Cataloguing in Publication Data*
Mac Ginty, Roger, 1970–
Conflict and development/Roger Mac Ginty and Andrew Williams.
p. cm. — (Routledge perspectives on development)
1. Civil war—Economic aspects.   2. Economic development—Political aspects.
I. Williams, Andrew, 1951–   II. Title.
HB195.M195 2009
338.9—dc22
2008041929

ISBN 13: 978–0–415–39936–4 (hbk)
ISBN 13: 978–0–415–39937–1 (pbk)
ISBN 13: 978–0–203–88000–5 (ebk)

ISBN 10: 0–415–39936–X (hbk)
ISBN 10: 0–415–39937–8 (pbk)
ISBN 10: 0–203–88000–5 (ebk)

This book is dedicated to Charlie Williams, Private, RAMC, 1896–1916, a working man who lost his life in a war over power and resources, like so many others before and since.

# Contents

# Plates

# Boxes

# Abbreviations

| | |
|---|---|
| ADB | African Development Bank |
| ADB | Asian Development Bank |
| ANC | African National Congress |
| AU | African Union |
| CNN | Cable Network News |
| CPA | Coalition Provisional Authority |
| DDR | disarmament, demobilisation and reintegration |
| DFID | Department for International Development |
| DRC | Democratic Republic of Congo |
| EAR | European Agency for Reconstruction |
| EBRD | European Bank for Reconstruction and Development |
| ECHO | European Commission Humanitarian Aid Office |
| ECOWAS | Economic Community of West African States |
| EU | European Union |
| GDP | gross domestic product |
| GNP | gross national product |
| GOS | Government of Sudan |
| ICC | International Criminal Court |
| ICRC | International Committee of the Red Cross |
| IFI | international financial institution |
| IGO | intergovernmental organisation |
| IMF | International Monetary Fund |
| INGO | international non-governmental organisation |
| INSTRAW | (UN) International Research and Training Institute for the Advancement of Women |
| JEM | Justice and Equality Movement |
| LDCs | least developed countries |
| MDGs | Millennium Development Goals |
| NATO | North Atlantic Treaty Organisation |
| NGO | non-governmental organisation |

| | |
|---|---|
| NICs | newly industrialised countries |
| OCHA | Office for the Coordination of Humanitarian Affairs |
| ODA | Official Development Assistance |
| OECD | Organisation for Economic Cooperation and Development |
| OSCE | Organisation for Security and Cooperation in Europe |
| PA | Palestinian Authority |
| PIOOM | Interdisciplinary Research Programme on Root Causes of Human Rights Violations |
| PLO | Palestine Liberation Organisation |
| PRT | provincial reconstruction team |
| R2P | responsibility to protect |
| RUF | Revolutionary United Front (Sierra Leone) |
| SAP | structural adjustment programme |
| SPLA | Sudan People's Liberation Army |
| SSR | security sector reform |
| TRC | truth and reconciliation commission |
| UN | United Nations |
| UNCTAD | United Nations Conference on Trade and Development |
| UNDP | United Nations Development Programme |
| UNHCR | United Nations High Commissioner for Refugees |
| UNIDIR | United Nations Institute for Disarmament Research |
| UNMIK | United Nations Mission in Kosovo |
| UNRRA | United Nations Relief and Rehabilitation Agency |
| UNTAC | United Nations Transitional Authority in Cambodia |
| UNTAET | United Nations Transitional Administration in East Timor |
| USAID | United States Agency for International Development |
| WCT | war crimes tribunal |

# Introduction

*Development Studies = Developing States focused*

*Development theorists largely ignored conflict + just recently had something to say about development issues*

One of the oddities of social science research has been that theories of development and theories of conflict have largely evolved in isolation from one another. This was especially odd since development economics as an academic subdiscipline and area of policy expertise emerged in a post-Second World War context defined by violent conflict. Moreover, the lens of development studies was firmly focused on the developing states, many of which were prone to conflicts relating to decolonisation, post-independence power struggles and proxy competition among Cold Warriors. The few development economists who considered the matter saw war as an interruption of development and surmised that development could not begin until war had ceased in a particular location (Thomas 2006: 186). As a result, most development specialists excluded countries experiencing violent conflict from their studies. In effect, conflict was written out of development.

We must be careful not to be too harsh on the development theorists: many were economists more at ease with the study of a state's fiscal levers than its political machinations. Moreover, the vast majority of development research was country-specific and thus poorly placed to observe regional or international patterns, including those that contributed to violent conflict. Just as development theorists largely ignored conflict, the emerging subdiscipline of conflict studies had little to say – until relatively recently – about development issues. There were a few honourable exceptions among the conflict theorists (Gurr 1970; Azar 1990), but by and large their lenses of inquiry overlooked the potential of

*[Handwritten annotation at top: "sole interest of many theorist - interstate war - interplay between military + political leaders"]*

development (and de-development, underdevelopment and uneven development) to contribute to both war and peace. The sole interest of many theorists was interstate war and the interplay between military and political leaders in different states. Economic conditions within states were important only in terms of how they could sustain a state's ability to pursue war. Alongside the macro-level lens that examined the war potential of states and the international system, other conflict theorists adopted a micro-level of analysis by using social psychology to explain the conflict potential of individuals (Deutsch 1973; Cairns 1996). The mezzo-level lenses, and particularly ones which would examine the condition of identity groups, were largely overlooked.

The not so splendid isolation of development and conflict studies from one another was no longer sustainable when the end of the Cold War witnessed an initial upsurge in civil wars. Not only were these civil wars more visible than their Cold War predecessors, but also the international system was in flux and there was a scramble to find national, regional and international mechanisms to deal with civil war. In this context, there was a rush to explain the phenomenon of civil war, and the corpus of academic, policy-related and journalistic work exploring the linkages between conflict and development began to grow. Crucial in this process was a more sophisticated understanding of the nature of conflict and the long-term and often unsatisfactory nature of pacification strategies (Kaldor 2006). The orthodoxy that development was an integral part of peacebuilding spread very quickly and was notably promoted by UN Secretary General Boutros-Ghali's 1992 *Agenda for Peace* text. There was also a growing realisation of the links between the outbreak of violent conflict and underdevelopment and uneven development (Collier 2000b; International Development Committee 2006: 8). As a result, many academics, policymakers and political leaders came to see development as a key to conflict prevention. The concept of human security, which gained prominence from the mid-1990s onwards, was highly influential in broadening conceptualisations of security to encompass issues traditionally regarded as germane to development or social improvement (United Nations Development Programme (UNDP) 1994; Shaw *et al.* 2006: 3–18).

*[Handwritten annotation in left margin: "rush to explain civil war bk flux of resources to see how to deal w/ civil wars"]*

This book is published at an exciting time in the evolution of our understanding of the relationship between conflict and development. The situation is not unlike that faced by seventeenth- or eighteenth-century cartographers upon 'discovering new territories' in the Pacific: they were able to map the coastline and principal features visible from the coast, but a more detailed map of the interior required exploration of the unknown. In a similar way, we have a good understanding of the outlines of the relationship between conflict and development, but there is less clarity on the precise nature of this relationship, particularly in terms of how it changes according to circumstances and context. Moreover, the adoption of critical and historical lenses make it clear that conflict and development policy interventions are attended by a raft of ethical and practical problems.

There is a further similarity with the situation facing early cartographers: they were seeking to understand and represent a territory in a particular way, compressing a society, its peoples and environment onto the western format of the printed page that conformed to increasingly regularised cartographic norms. We need to be aware that many of our discussions of conflict and development use peculiarly western tools of analysis and occur at a level of abstraction far removed from the lived experience of those facing the challenges of conflict and development. The fact remains that most development and peacebuilding policy (and the research that underpins it) is designed in the global North but is directed at the global South (Scholey 2006: 179–80). Moreover, western analyses of developing world and conflict contexts can be prone to stereotyping that overwrite a more complex reality. Thus we are all familiar with African women portrayed as '[a]lways poor, powerless and invariably pregnant' or African men as aggressive (Win 2007: 79).

Just as early cartographers were anxious to curry favour with their patrons and anxious not to offend powerful interests, contemporary analyses of peace, conflict and development operate in environments conditioned by politics and funding. Funding bodies tend to prioritise research with practical relevance. Often this is for understandably good intentions, but it risks shoehorning research into limited directions so that it is in service to technocratic 'solutions' and avoids critical or innovative thinking. Thus, for example, the UK government is more likely to fund an evaluation of a development project it is carrying out, rather than a study of the structural factors that are likely to limit the success of the wider development programme. Sometimes powerful interests mean that the study of peace, conflict and development is severely constrained. Arms manufacturers, governments, international organisations, international financial institutions and NGOs find external scrutiny a burden and may take steps to manage or thwart it.

Perhaps the most prominent example of hypersensitivity to research and critical scrutiny concerns Israel. Mearsheimer and Walt's (2007: vii–xii) study of the pro-Israel lobby in the United States was dropped by its publisher and met with astonishing hostility when eventually published. Former US President Jimmy Carter and Nobel peace laureate Archbishop Desmond Tutu also came in for criticism (much of it personalised) for likening Israeli treatment of Palestinians to 'apartheid'. The effect of this hypersensitivity to criticism is a self-censorship among many academics. For example, few will use the term 'Israeli state terrorism' when Israeli actions meet the criteria for such a label. These intellectual danger zones are by no means restricted to scholarship and policy analysis on Israel. Early cartographers would annotate their maps with the legend 'here be dragons' on areas deemed too dangerous to map. In a similar way, there are issues and areas that modern researchers of peace, conflict and development find controversial or inconvenient to study.

Controversies abound in the study of conflict and development: Are internal or external factors primarily responsible for a state's underdevelopment? Should aid agencies cooperate with warlords to distribute humanitarian goods? How can the post-9/11 security demands made by western states be reconciled with human rights, social inclusion and political liberalisation in developing world states? What are the implications for humanitarianism of growing civil–military cooperation? Can increasingly intrusive western means of development programming and good governance be reconciled with indigenous and traditional norms? How can increasingly technocratic development and peace-support interventions address the affective or emotional dimensions of development and peacebuilding? These questions, and many more, form the basis for this book.

The essential purpose of the book is to chart our understanding of the complex relationship between conflict and development. The book is written from a largely critical perspective: critical in the sense that it questions orthodoxy, but not so critical as to forget that academic sophistry is of little help to those facing the very real hardships that attend the problems of conflict and development. At heart, development and conflict revolve around people, yet social scientists (along with government planners, non-governmental organisation (NGO) log-frames and financial models) have been particularly successful in writing people, and especially the affective dimension integral to human life, out of its analyses. This book recognises that humanity red and raw plays an essential part in stories of conflict and development. Hate, rage, revenge, hopelessness, bitterness, ignorance, love, joy and mercy are as relevant to analyses of processes of conflict and development as academic conceptualisations.

The book is based on five assumptions about development that help with our understanding of the connections between conflict and development:

- That development is not necessarily a good thing; it can have negative and unintended consequences.
- That development can trigger and sustain violent conflict.
- That development, by its very nature, is an uneven process.
- That development is not just about economic growth.
- That development can be targeted in ways that aid post-war reconstruction and reconciliation.

The first assumption (that development is not necessarily a good thing) may initially seem Luddite or somehow antithetical to human advancement, especially since development is regarded by many as the means through which public goods (education and health care) and personal liberty (freedom of expression and action) can be attained. 'In everyday usage "development" is virtually synonymous with "progress"' (Thomas 2006: 187). Moreover, in the western political mind, the continuation of economic development is a fundamental assumption of political and economic life. The shelf-life of the western political leader who advocated limits on growth would be very short indeed. Jimmy Carter's emphasis on American fuel dependency is believed to have been a major factor in his 1980 electoral defeat to Ronald Reagan. Indeed Reagan's 'It's morning in America again' television commercial for his 1984 re-election campaign is regarded as a modern masterpiece in light and fluffy electioneering that shied away from pressing issues such as accelerating economic disparities. Despite the tremendous political, economic and moral power behind the orthodox position that development is always a 'good thing', critical observers must be prepared to judge development according to its actual impact and ambition. Such normative judgements will depend on the moral-ethical-political framework held by the individual, community or institution that makes the judgement, and the vantage point from which they make their judgement. Put simply, where one sits will determine how one judges development. If development is demonstrated to inflame conflict, degrade environmental conditions and have profoundly negative social and cultural consequences, then it is entirely reasonable that observers reflect this in their judgements. It is unreasonable to brand those who are against 'bad' or unjust development as being against all development.

This leads to the second assumption, that development can trigger and sustain violent conflict. This is by no means always the case. Indeed, as will be demonstrated in later chapters, development can help prevent conflict or aid post-conflict reconciliation. Yet is it important to recognise the conflict-promoting potential of developmental processes whereby intergroup resource competition, population displacement, environmental degradation and the erosion of social structures that may have once restrained conflict may all contribute to violent conflict. These issues will be explored in detail in Chapter 1.

The third assumption, that development, by its very nature, is an uneven process, contributes much to explanations of the initiation, maintenance and ending of violent conflicts. A complex array of structural and proximate economic, political and geographical factors accounts for the uneven nature of development. Many of these factors will be discussed in later chapters. The unevenness of development (and resources and approaches to development) suggests that conflict will be 'inevitable', but as we will see it is often the management of resources and development that matters. As important as unevenness is the *perception* of unevenness. This is particularly salient in societies with identity-based divisions in which groups may interpret their share of resources through an ethnic, religious or racial lens.

The fourth assumption, that development is not just about economic growth, stems from the tendency of many observers (not just development economists) to overlook the social, political and cultural dimensions of development. Crucial in this regard is the type of development strategy pursued and the relative importance attached to redistribution and market freedom, as well as political and cultural development. A narrow economic lens could examine China's astounding economic growth rates (averaging at just over 10 per cent between 2001 and 2007) and declare it a development success (Asian Development Bank (ADB) 2006: 137). But a more holistic approach might take account of the state's poor human rights record. Amnesty International's (2008) *State of the World's Human Rights* report observed that

> [g]rowing numbers of human rights activists were imprisoned, put under house arrest or surveillance, or arrested. Repression of minority groups, including Tibetans, Uighurs, and Mongolians, continued . . . the death penalty continued to be shrouded in secrecy and was used extensively.
>
> (Amnesty International 2008)

The final assumption is to recognise the potential of development to contribute to post-war reconstruction and reconciliation. In an ideal situation a mutually reinforcing relationship can be established between development and reconstruction. Formerly divided peoples can come together for the joint pursuit of economic growth and social progress. This is not always the case, and poorly managed post-war reconstruction often has profound consequences for the nature of the post-war society, some of them negative.

Alongside these assumptions on development, it is worth noting that the main focus of this book is on civil war, rather than interstate war. This is primarily because war between states is a rare phenomenon, while civil war (albeit often internationalised) is more common. In 2006, for example, although thirty-two armed conflicts were ongoing, none of them could be classed as interstate (Harbom and Wallensteen 2007: 626). Importantly our interest in conflict extends beyond the direct violence of overt war. Indirect or structural violence plays a key role in contexts of conflict and development. Such violence is often deeply embedded in the socio-economic and politico-cultural behaviour of a society. It can be insidious, barely visible and taken for granted. It takes the form of discrimination in the provision of public goods and opportunities, the militarisation of society and the prevalence of societal attitudes

**Plate 1  A child's shoe in rubble in Beirut: one of the aims of this book is to write people back into accounts of conflict and development**

(sometimes encouraged by the state or other institutions) that certain groups are inferior to others. So this book proceeds by adopting holistic views of both conflict and development. Neither concept constitutes a neatly compartmentalised category. Instead they are messy, ill-defined and there is little agreement about the best way to pursue development and conflict transformation. Above all, both concepts relate to the most contrary and awkward species of all: humans. People don't always say what we want them to; they don't always believe what we say; they don't always behave as we expect them to; and they're not always as grateful to us as we feel they should be. As a result, people are often written out of analyses of conflict and development.

An array of factors help write people out of many studies of peace, conflict and development: the media's need to compress thousands of individual experiences into a single narrative; the technocratic bias of policymaking in which units and spreadsheets are more manageable than people; and social sciences' move towards large-scale studies and its inability to deal with the affective dimension of human behaviour. Indicative of this 'writing out' of people is development and conflict-sensitive 'programming' as practised by many donor governments and agencies. The term 'programming' suggests a machine-like process whereby carefully regulated inputs are expected to have particular outputs. Just as war is often criticised for dehumanising individuals and objectifying them into a lumpen enemy, there is a real danger that responses to conflict and underdevelopment have a similar effect. Most studies, apart from biography, cannot hope to convey individual experiences. In terms of academic studies, anthropology has perhaps had most success in recognising that people in conflict zones do not constitute an undifferentiated mass and that individuals often experience events and processes in very different ways.

This chapter proceeds with brief overviews of the evolution of theories of development and conflict so as to provide a context for subsequent chapters. In relation to development studies, it is particularly important to understand the contemporary dominance of neo-liberalism and market-led 'solutions' and the consequences of this for internationally sponsored development and peace-support interventions. The evolution of conflict studies shows how a more complex understanding of the causes and maintenance of conflict has emerged, and how this has shaped contemporary conflict transformation interventions. The chapter concludes by outlining the basic structure of the book.

# The evolution of development theory

Summarising a multidisciplinary endeavour such as development studies is a difficult task, especially when the ultimate purpose of development, and the optimum means of achieving it, are hotly contested. Kothari (2005: 1) is rightfully critical of surveys of the discipline that 'articulate a singular theoretical genealogy'. Development studies has been peculiarly faddish, seizing upon theories and techniques at particular moments, only to discard them in favour of a new saviour theory or technique. Kothari (2005: 2) also warns against interpretations of development studies which regard 1945 as Year Zero, as though no development or thinking about development occurred before that year. Scrutiny of the means to achieve economic development has a long intellectual pedigree (Meier and Rauch 2000). J.M. Keynes was particularly prescient of the need for peace negotiations to take seriously the issue of long-term economic development. Dispirited after his ringside seat at the Treaty of Versailles negotiations following the First World War, he observed that 'Peace has been declared at Paris. But winter approaches' (Keynes 1920: 235). According to Keynes:

> The Treaty includes no provisions for the economic rehabilitation of Europe, – nothing to make the defeated Central Empires into good neighbours . . . nothing to reclaim Russia; nor does it promote in any way a compact of economic solidarity amongst the Allies themselves; no arrangement was reached at Paris for restoring the disordered finances of France and Italy, or to adjust the systems of the Old World and the New.
>
> (Keynes 1920: 235)

As will become clear in later chapters, lessons seem to have been learned, in that it is well recognised that the ending of wars provides unique opportunities for international political and economic intervention. Less clear, however, are the optimal types and extent of any intervention.

Although 1945 was not Year Zero, it was the year in which the contours of the modern international financial architecture were established. The World Bank and the Bretton Woods exchange rate mechanism (which facilitates international trade) date from this era. The Second World War also saw the United States re-establish itself as the predominant state in the world economy. The decade and a half after the Second World War was the highpoint of economic planning during which development economists were convinced that '"good" scientific analysis would generate the "right answers"' (Harriss 2005a: 19). This was the period of positivist orthodoxy, in which the primary aim of development was accelerated economic growth, the primary agent was the state (mediated by the Bretton Woods institutions) and the primary means of achieving growth was careful analysis followed by a precise plan. The plan often involved raising rural productivity and transferring underutilised labour from the agricultural to industrial sectors (Leys 1996: 8).

By the late 1950s and early 1960s, it was becoming clear that economic growth was difficult to achieve in many developing world contexts, and that the fruits of any growth were rarely shared fairly. There was no shortage of economic theories, but as J.K. Galbraith (1964: 38) observed, 'it would be a mistake to identify complexity with completeness and sophistication with wisdom.' The failure of the initial post-war development planning led to a new emphasis on modernisation and technology transfer. The key here was the adoption of 'modern' forms of administrative and political organisation in imitation of western states and businesses, the transfer of western knowledge and skills through education programmes, and a 'green revolution' of increased agricultural productivity through the use of western farming methods (Rostow 1960). This, in turn, sparked a radical critique in the late 1960s and early 1970s as it became clear that, in many cases, modernisation strategies had made few appreciable differences to citizens in the developing world (Harriss 2005a: 19–25). According to left-wing critics, the '"modernising elites" were really . . . lumpen-bourgeoisies, serving their own and foreign interests, not those of the people; world trade perpetuated structures of underdevelopment' (Leys 1996: 12). According to this view (usually called 'dependency theory'), modernisation was a recipe for further immiseration and a structural dependence on western economic powers (Frank 1967).

Global political trends, and specifically the Cold War, had a profound impact on development strategies. A number of states, including Cuba, Ethiopia, Tanzania and Vietnam, adopted socialist development programmes, usually under the tutelage and protection of the Soviet Union. To differing degrees, 'scientific socialism' was mobilised in the service of development. This often involved the nationalisation of industry, restrictions on foreign capital, land reform, and an enhanced role for the state in directing economic exchanges and initiatives (Clapham 1987). In most cases, the results were not good: the socialist 'reforms' tended to be disruptive and often reliant on state coercion, the global economy offered a poor fit for those not willing to reform, and socialist experiment states such as Angola, Mozambique and Ethiopia were often the scenes of violent civil war. The true fragility of these states' economic models did not become apparent until the collapse of the Soviet Union and the withdrawal of subventions. Both dependency theory and the socialist model of development paled into the background with the coming tide of neo-liberalism.

The neo-liberal revolution of the 1980s and beyond was in sympathy with wider political and economic changes. The political right was on the ascendant in the United Kingdom and the United States, and globalising market forces meant that national and international controls over capital had been severely eroded. Traditional responses of state-directed development policy were no longer effective in an economic climate characterised by economic shocks, unstable commodity prices, international capital flight and increasingly powerful and mobile multinational corporate interests. The end of the Cold War meant not only the collapse of the Soviet Union as a material supporter of alternative models of economic development, but also the collapse of the notion of 'an alternative'. Former Soviet satellites proved to be in no position to resist aggressive economic reform interventions (often called the 'shock doctrine') by international financial institutions. The rise of neo-liberalism was also assisted by abundant evidence of state incompetence and corruption throughout the developing world. Deepak Lal (1998: 65) noted how the 'old development economics . . . implicitly assumed that the state was benevolent, omniscient, and omnipotent.' The 'Chicago School' (who claim intellectual authorship of neo-liberalism) were pushing at an open door at the headquarters of the World Bank, the International Monetary Fund (IMF) and rightist governments. The essential neo-liberal argument was that the dead hand of the state and an invariably bloated public sector acted as a brake on economic development, while an unfettered market could act as an engine of development. In this view, the benefits of market-driven growth would trickle down and benefit all.

According to James Dorn (1998: 13), 'the real plight of underdeveloped countries is not market failure but government failure – that is, the failure of government to protect property rights, enforce contracts, and leave the market alone.' Champions of neo-liberalism were forthright in what needed to be done: the state must be pared back, the market freed from regulation, state assets should be privatised, and exchange controls and industrial licences should be lifted. The salvation for underperforming economies lay in more exposure to the market, not protection from it. Peter Bauer (1998: 36) had little time for 'unfounded

notions about Western responsibility for Third World backwardness.'
For him it was

> abundantly evident throughout the Third World [that] the poorest and
> most backward societies and areas are those which have fewest
> commercial contacts with the West, and the most advanced are those
> with the most extensive and diversified contacts, including contacts
> with those bogeymen, the Western multinationals. Throughout the
> Third World the level of economic attainment declines as one moves
> away from regions with most Western contacts to the aborigines and
> pygmies at the other end of the spectrum.
>
> (Bauer 1998: 28)

Neo-liberal prescriptions, which were enthusiastically endorsed by global
capital and the leading international financial institutions, were rolled out
in former Soviet-bloc states, often with catastrophic social consequences
(Klein 2007: 180–4). Western governments, and by extension their
development aid institutions, increasingly adopted market-led 'solutions'
to all aspects of governance.

Cloaked in a populist mantle of the empowerment of entrepreneurs and
the cutting of public sector waste, neo-liberal truisms became the new
orthodoxy. According to David Harvey,

> Neo-liberalism has, in short, become hegemonic as a mode of
> discourse. It has pervasive effects on ways of thought to the point
> where it has become incorporated into the common-sense way many
> of us interpret, live in, and understand the world.
>
> (Harvey 2005: 3)

The intellectual dominance of neo-liberalism is essential to our
understanding of the responses of leading states, international
organisations and international financial institutions to the problems of
conflict, development and peacebuilding. Market-led 'solutions' have
been hardwired into the organisational culture and policy responses
of donor governments and NGOs. Whether this manifests itself in
micro-credit schemes to further women's empowerment, or in the
privatisation of state resources as part of a post-war reconstruction
programme, it has had a profound impact on the ethos of
humanitarianism, development and conflict amelioration policies.

Under the guise of 'good governance', massive programmes of social,
economic and political engineering have taken place in societies emerging
from conflict and economic crisis. In many cases, relationships between
citizens and the state, the state and the market, and the state and other

states have changed radically. For example, neo-liberal wisdom may demand that a state cuts its bureaucracy at the conclusion of a civil war in order to keep down inflation and achieve international competitiveness. Yet, the political loyalty of particular sections of the population may have been dependent on patronage from the state in terms of employment or access to public goods. Neo-liberal interventions may thus radically alter political bonds and have far-reaching consequences for political participation and stability, and public perceptions of political processes and institutions.

Unsurprisingly, neo-liberalism has attracted immense criticism, particularly in relation to its inability to address poverty and social exclusion. The near deification of the market and corporate power has, according to its critics, reconfigured the balance of power in many states, with public interests being demoted. Harvey (2005: 19) regards neo-liberalism as a 'system of justification and legitimation' aimed at reinforcing 'the capitalist social order'. In this view, it is a potentially authoritarian political model: 'The neoliberal state is necessarily hostile to all forms of social solidarity that put restraints on capital accumulation' (Harvey 2005: 75). While Dorn (1998: 14) regarded 'Chile's free market revolution' of 1973 as 'an example for the rest of Latin America', Harvey (2005: 8–9) was excoriating of Pinochet's US-backed coup on 'little September 11th' and the widespread suppression that followed in the name of libertarian ideas. It is true that many champions of neo-liberalism are agnostic of the social and political costs of an unfettered market. Deepak Lal (1998: 68, 70) observed that 'The characteristics of good government are more important than its particular form' and 'it is by no means self-evident . . . that Western democracy necessarily promotes a market-friendly culture.' Critics remain unconvinced of the redistributive potential of the market and believe that politics do matter, particularly in relation to political commitments to social inclusion (Harriss 2005b: 228).

Certainly there is a widespread understanding of the potentially pernicious effects of market-led programming in development and peacebuilding contexts (Chua 2004). As Moore (2005: 263) notes wryly, 'Intellectuals have a generic tendency to explain.' But analysis and explanation, no matter how erudite, are not the same as policy alternatives. The problem for critics of neo-liberalism is that their opponents have created a self-reinforcing *system* based on widely accepted norms of efficiency, cost-effectiveness and enterprise. The neo-liberal system is promulgated by corporate interests and international financial institutions, chimes with populist causes, has reconfigured the ethos of public sector institutions (from hospitals to universities) in the developed and developing world, and is in alignment with the strategic interests of leading states. Critics are perfectly correct in pointing to the spectre of 'predatory disaster capitalism' that profits from the misery of others (Klein 2007), but the structures of the contemporary international political economy have been captured by neo-liberal forces and the system seems able to sustain itself (or at least defer or pass on the costs) for the foreseeable future. Even the 2008–2010 global credit crisis did not fundamentally alter government faith in the market.

The predominance of neo-liberalism does not mean that development assistance aimed at emancipating populations, increasing opportunities and promoting redistribution in the developing world has come to an end. Certainly, neo-liberal structures and principles guide much development activity, but the development sector is flourishing. In 2007, worldwide overseas development assistance was $103 billion (though in true free-market style, much of that was creamed off by western consultants) (Mathiason 2005; Blanchflower 2008). The United States alone spent almost $22 billion on development aid in 2007, and oil-rich Gulf and Arab states are fast becoming major development donors (Harmer and Cotterrell 2005). Increasing emphasis is placed on integrated development interventions, so that the economic, environmental, political and social dimensions of development are interlinked and mutually supporting (Baker 2006). Sustainability, local participation and ownership, and pro-poor initiatives are a common vein through contemporary development thinking and practice. The UN Millennium Development Goals (MDGs), as agreed by 189 governments in 2000, have crystallised development priorities:

- eradicate extreme poverty and hunger
- achieve universal primary education
- promote gender equality and empower women
- reduce infant mortality
- improve maternal health
- combat HIV/AIDS, malaria and other diseases
- ensure environmental sustainability
- develop a global partnership for development.

Reflecting the target-driven nature of development programming, a number of international organisations and leading donors (for example, the Asian Development Bank) now explicitly organise their programmes around the Millennium Development Goals.

Although development activities have been subject to immense faddism since the late 1940s, and although there have been broad shifts in emphasis (from planning to the market-led initiatives), a number of constants are worth noting. The first is that development is still largely a North to South enterprise: intellectually, practically and financially. The second constant is that macro-economic structures are still biased towards the global North and there are few indications that this situation will change. The third constant factor is that many of the states that were in the most need of development in the 1940s and 1950s (during the peak of development planning optimism) are still grossly undeveloped.

There is no great mystery about the causes and cures of under-development. As Jeffrey Sachs (2008) observed,

> Reaching the MDGs won't take miracles – we know how to keep children alive in malarial regions, we know how to increase food production . . . In simple terms, the limiting factor holding back our progress towards the Goals is the richest countries coming up with the money they have promised.
>
> (Sachs 2008: 6)

## The evolution of conflict theory

Like development studies, attempts to understand conflict and peace have attracted theorists and practitioners from a diverse range of disciplinary and ideological perspectives. Both Adam Curle (1971: 1–3) and John Groom (1988: 105–8) have identified a tripartite division between strategic studies (concerned with state attempts to gain or maintain dominance over other states), conflict studies (which regards conflict as an unintended outcome of conflicts of interests and is concerned with regulating harmful competition to minimise the outbreak of conflict), and peace studies (a critical endeavour convinced that the structures of the international system require radical overhaul in order to achieve pacific relations). These strands of research have shown considerable overlap, particularly in terms of their concentration on the causes of conflict. As Chapter 1 contains a detailed explanation of the dominant theories of conflict causation, this section will give a more general account of the evolution of thinking on conflict.

It is worth noting that for many writers, violent conflict was regarded as a given (a mere by-product of great power interplay or the consequence of natural or primordial inclinations), and its causes were not subject to serious scrutiny. Military history, which depicted war as 'a deplorable necessity' (Creasy 1876: xi), thrived, but did little to advance our understanding of the precipitants of conflict, or its wider social or cultural impacts. More considered deliberations on the nature and causes of warfare occupied scholars from Sun Tzu (544–496BC) and Thucydides (460–395BC) to Saint Augustine (354–430) and Hugo Grotius (AD1583–1645), but their work did not constitute a united or recognisable field of conflict studies (Jacoby 2008: 8–12). Real world 'traumas' such as the First World War (over 35 million casualties, the industrialisation of warfare and the militarisation of societies), or the unleashing of nuclear weapons gave renewed impetus to those attempting to systematise knowledge of conflict (Wallensteen 2007: 6). For example, Lewis Fry Richardson (1950), a Quaker conscientious objector who served with the Friends' Ambulance Unit during the First World War, sought to apply mathematical analysis to warfare, particularly the propensity of armament programmes to lead to conflict. Yet Richardson, and other pioneers of the study of conflict as a generic phenomenon such as Quincy Wright (1942) and Georg Simmel (1955), were a distinct minority. Indeed, many of those who pursued 'peace studies' were derided as cranks, cowards, unpatriotic or 'religious nuts' (Rooney 2000: 16).

The tendency of researchers to compartmentalise their research agendas and thus separate domestic conflict from international conflict, or dichotomise violent conflict and structural forms of violence, meant that attempts to find a general theory of conflict were few and far between (Azar 1990: 5). The subdiscipline of international relations, for example, has been mainly concerned (until relatively recently) with wars between states and showed little inclination to investigate sub-state conflicts. It was not until the 1950s and 1960s that a recognisably modern strain of conflict research emerged. Miall (2007: 27) notes how much of this research attempted 'to capture the generic characteristics of conflict', stripping conflicts of their context in order to better examine the relationships between actors and the dynamics of conflict processes. Much of this research was influenced by game theory, behaviouralism and the application of social psychology to conflict (Axelrod 1990; Boulding 1990: 37–8). Indeed, rational choice and bargaining theory approaches to the study of conflict are particularly popular (particularly among North American and Scandinavian academics) and are prominent in leading journals of peace and conflict. These approaches have helped scholars to concentrate on key issues such as the credibility of antagonists in their commitments to peaceful outcomes, asymmetries in the information available to conflicting parties, and 'issue indivisibility' or the extent to which parties are amenable to compromise or a division of resources (Fearon 1995).

Over time, more holistic understandings of conflict have emerged. This has been complemented by the 'mainstreaming' of peace and conflict research, with the establishment of research institutes, specialist journals and a greater acceptance of the systematic study of conflict in policymaking circles. There has been something of an intellectual emancipation of peace and conflict. No longer is it the preserve of a few pacifists and the closed shop of military and foreign policy officials. Indeed, after decades of being on the margins, the study of peace and conflict has even become popular. Christopher Mitchell (1994: 128) recalls how, as a reaction to the rash of civil wars in the 1990s, 'a range of scholars . . . discovered that they have "really" been doing conflict resolution "all along"'. 'Ex-strategic theorists, military security experts, Sovietologists and area specialists' suddenly turned their attentions to the problems of civil war. As will be outlined in Chapter 1, the rush to 'explain civil war' has variously focused on the importance of identity, regional factors and econometric indicators. The modern evolution of conflict studies has reflected real world conditions. The post-Cold War upsurge in conflicts, greater interventionism by international organisations and international NGOs (INGOs), and the impact of globalisation on public awareness of conflicts on the other side of the planet, demanded a better understanding of conflict. The failure (or limited success) of some immediate post-Cold War international interventions demanded a further refinement of our understanding of conflict.

Specialist subfields in the study of conflict developed in the 1990s and beyond, with the comparative study of negotiated peacemaking processes (Darby and Mac Ginty 2000), reconciliation (Hayner 2002) and disarmament (Wulf 2000) gaining particular attention. A number of conflict resolution 'gurus', or respected practitioners such as John Paul Lederach, Roger Fisher, William Ury or Ben Hoffman, also gained greater prominence (Fisher and Ury 1991; Lederach 1995). There was a growing consensus on the multidimensional nature of conflict, its increasingly transnational nature in a globalised context, the need to see beyond conflict manifestations to examine conflict causes, and – crucially – the importance of development issues in explaining conflict (Azar 1990: 2). Research on conflict has also recognised the protracted nature of many conflicts, the tendency of violent conflicts to reignite following periods of calm, and the difficult, long-term and costly nature of post-peace accord peacebuilding. Indeed, 'no war, no peace' situations have become common in which parties agree to a ceasefire but fail to push for a comprehensive peace process (for example, in Sri Lanka, Israel/Palestine and Colombia at various times in the 1990s and 2000s), or reach a peace agreement but fail to move towards a widespread reconciliation (for example, Northern Ireland or Lebanon) (Mac Ginty 2006).

The increased research on peace and conflict did not occur in a vacuum. Instead, a real world laboratory of civil war and post-civil war contexts was available. Indeed, much research has been sponsored by governments, international organisations, and development agencies as they struggle to understand the complexities of contemporary conflict. A (mainly European) critical strain emerged in the growing corpus of conflict-related literature. The critics, such as Chandler (2000), Pugh and Cooper (2004), Richmond (2005a) or Mac Ginty (2006), dismissed much of the orthodox literature as being merely 'problem-solving'; that is focused on specific functional tasks related to peace negotiations or the implementation of peace accords without asking wider questions about power relations and international structures that help perpetuate conflict. According to the critics, peace-support operations sponsored by leading states and international financial institutions amounted to a 'liberal peace' or 'peace as governance' (Richmond 2005a: 63) whereby western norms and institutions were extended. In effect, according to this view, internationally supported peace interventions were an exercise whereby states emerging from civil war were compelled to conform to western strictures, particularly in relation to their adoption of neo-liberal economic models and western forms of governance. The notion of the 'liberal peace' will receive more attention in Chapter 2. For the time being it can be defined as the dominant system of peace favoured by leading states, leading international organisations and international financial institutions.

Importantly, there has been an elision of international strategies to deal with conflict and underdevelopment. According to many intervening parties, development is the answer to conflict and underdevelopment. Thus many of the same strategies that are deployed in societies emerging from civil war can also be found in societies free from civil war but suffering from underdevelopment. Development strategies in societies emerging from civil war might be modified so as to be 'conflict sensitive', but they essentially amount to the same thing: the promotion of the orthodoxy of neo-liberalism, 'good' governance reforms, and the use of aid conditionality or selectivity to encourage conformity.

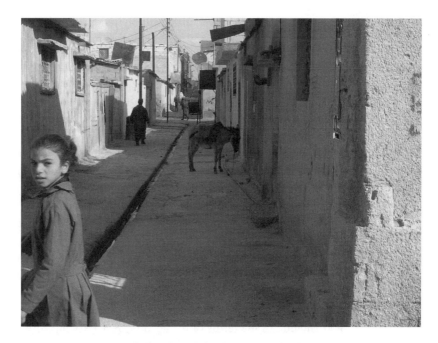

**Plate 2  A refugee camp in Jordan: in recent years there has been a greater understanding of the interconnections between conflict and underdevelopment**

Alongside the critical strain to the literature on peace, conflict and development, other scholars and policymakers have been vexed at how to 'win' the War on Terror and subjugate opponents in Afghanistan, Iraq and elsewhere. The United States and UK increasingly see development and post-war reconstruction as a key means of winning 'hearts and minds' in the support of their conquest of Iraq and Afghanistan. Thus we have seen the securitisation of development or the incorporation of development into security strategies. This has been most visible in the provincial reconstruction teams at work in Afghanistan and Iraq whereby soldiers become 'armed humanitarians', with obvious consequences for ideas of neutrality and impartiality which some associated with humanitarianism. Critics say that western states are more interested in order and security than development and reconstruction. For example, in early 2007, the United States committed an additional 28,829 troops to its war effort in Iraq. Over 21,000 of these were combat troops and just 129 were tasked with provincial reconstruction (*Guardian* 2007; see also Tisdall). Such militarised development results in highly contradictory international interventions: in less than a year British troops fired over 4 million bullets in Afghanistan *and* spent over £100 million in development assistance (Harding 2008).

A conflict-specific nomenclature has developed, with a battery of prefixes and suffixes fine-tuning our understanding of the concepts of peace and conflict. Thus 'peacekeeping' denotes traditional United Nations (UN) 'blue helmet' troop deployments, usually to police an agreed separation between antagonists. 'Peacemaking' suggests a more active form of intervention or activity, possibly including force to compel parties to negotiate or make concessions. 'Peacebuilding' was originally regarded as an activity that occurred after a peace accord was reached in order to support that accord. It covered a range of political, social, economic and cultural activities and so was cognisant of the links between conflict, peace and development. The strict delineation of peacebuilding as an activity that occurs after a violent conflict ceased no longer holds. 'Peace implementation' usually refers to both the fulfilment of the provisions of a peace accord and attempts to provide an environment (for example, security, minority return, a tax base to fund social spending) to enable the implementation of the terms of the accord. 'Peace fixing', if we may be permitted to coin a new term, is the common activity of internal and external parties to a peace accord returning to the negotiating table to modify the accord to react to problems. In the post-9/11 period, there has been a slight draw back from the use of the word 'peace' by a number of leading states as they promote security agendas (often under the term 'stabilisation').

There has also been a transition in the suffixes used in relation to conflict. 'Conflict resolution' was overtaken by 'conflict management' when some critics suggested that conflicts could not be definitively resolved. Instead of finding solutions, societies had to recognise the integral nature of conflict to human societies and thus find non-violent ways of managing the conflict. But the term 'conflict management' was criticised for assuming that some actors would be managers (often powerful or well-resourced external actors), while other actors would be managed (often indigenous, less powerful actors). The term 'conflict transformation' is now current (doubtless to be supplanted by another term in the coming years). Conflict transformation again recognises that conflict is part and parcel of human existence, but aims at transforming relationships between individuals, groups and institutions from destructive to constructive bonds.

## Structure of the book

About
Ch 1

Chapter 1 advances our understanding of conflict and development by examining the links between poverty, profit and violent conflict. It outlines the main theories that explain the escalation and maintenance of conflict and discusses the political economy of violence whereby conflict becomes a profitable activity and therefore – in some cases – sustainable. The chapter also examines the connection between the presence and exploitation of natural resources and conflict. Chapter 2 provides an overview of the institutional architecture that shapes contemporary peace and development: states, the market, international organisations and international financial institutions. Contemporary conflict and development takes place in a context of complex multilateralism and hyper-globalisation in which multiple actors can be involved in the same conflict and/or development process, often using proxies and sometimes acting in contradictory ways. Thus, for example, the UK government may be investing heavily in the economic and military pacification of Afghanistan through the North Atlantic Treaty Organisation (NATO) and the UN, while UK consumer demand fuels poppy cultivation and the warlords associated with its trade (Coghlan 2006).

In contrast to Chapter 2 and its focus on top–down institutions, Chapter 3 deals with people, as citizens, the displaced, victims, antagonists, consumers of public goods, men or women, unified in civil society or fragmented into particularistic groups. The elixir for those who wish to promote conflict, peacebuilding or development is popular participation as a means of legitimising their enterprise. This chapter will explore the impact of conflict and development on people, and the strategies that ethnic entrepreneurs, political leaders, aid agencies and others use to mobilise and connect with groups.

Chapters 4, 5 and 6 are essentially intended to show how policymakers and academic students of conflict alike have tried to conceptualise the problems that arise after conflicts have arisen and, in some cases, 'ended'. We have summed it up as 'transitions' from conflict and war to a kind of 'peace' (Organisation for Economic Cooperation and Development (OECD) 2007: Foreword). Chapter 4 looks at thinking on conflict resolution (though we prefer the term 'transformation') and the techniques and methods that have emerged since the end of the Cold War to try to damp down conflicts and deal with their psychological, social and other 'deficits', as Miall et al. (1999) and Ramsbotham et al. (2005) have put it. This will encompass an examination of different approaches to ending conflict, including newer approaches such as truth and reconciliation commissions. Chapter 5 looks at the evolving notion of 'reconstruction' after wars, and in particular takes issue with the belief that we can have a 'one-size-fits-all' approach to such efforts. It will in particular flesh out what we called above the 'increasingly technocratic [nature of] development and peace-support interventions'. The alphabet soup of reconstruction now includes acronyms like DDR (disarmament, demobilisation and reintegration) and SSR (security sector reform) that have to be understood by any neophyte (or advanced) student of conflict and development. We will attempt to sieve the soup in such a way as to make clear both the underlying rationale for such terms and practices, but also their implementation. In this chapter we will also look in more detail at some of the human and structural problems involved in 'reconstructing' a society. What are the problems to do with the health of the population that need to be considered after a war, for example? Finally, Chapter 6 comprises an overview of the difficulties of using 'aid' as a panacea during, but mainly after war. The focus here will be on those delivering aid, and the reaction of those to whom it is delivered, which is not always positive. We consider that this dilemma is one of the keys to understanding what is both wrong, and right, with current development policies in the developing world. Along the way, text boxes are used to illustrate points. Chapters will end with summaries, discussion questions and suggested further reading. Since many of the organisations and issues mentioned in the chapters have content-rich websites, e-resources are annotated at the end of each chapter.

## Summary

- Theories of conflict and development have largely evolved in isolation from one another.
- More recently, there has been a greater cross-fertilisation between ideas and policy approaches to conflict and underdevelopment.
- Particular worldviews have dominated thinking about conflict and development. At the moment, neo-liberal economic ideas influence development thinking and, in the aftermath of 9/11, security and order is playing a prominent role in peace promotion.
- There is a growing realisation that there are no 'quick fixes'.

## Discussion questions

1 How could 'success' in development be defined? Conflict
2 How can we make sure that development and peace-support prevention
interventions do not become a new form of imperialism?
3 Consider if there are realistic alternatives to neo-liberal development
models.

## Further reading

Excellent surveys of the evolution of development theory and practice can
be found in Leys, C. (1996) *The Rise and Fall of Development Theory*,
Oxford: James Currey, and Kothari, U. (ed.) (2005) *A Radical History of
Development Studies: Individuals, institutions and ideologies*, London: Zed
Books. A neo-liberal assault on Keynesian or state-led development strategies
can be found in Dorn, J., Hanke, S. and Walters, A. (eds) *The Revolution in
Development Economics*, Washington, DC: Cato Institute; Ramsbotham, O.,
Woodhouse, T. and Miall, H. (2005) *Contemporary Conflict Resolution: The
prevention, management and transformation of deadly conflicts*, 2nd edition,
Cambridge: Polity provide an excellent survey of literature and approaches to
conflict.

## Useful websites

A goldmine of material on conflict and conflict transformation can be found at
Beyond Intractability: www.beyondintractability.org/, while the Humanitarian
Practice Network provides online reports on development and humanitarian
issues: www.odihpn.org/. On Israel's sensitivity to criticism, the Mearsheimer
and Walt article is available from the *London Review of Books* at www.lrb.
co.uk/v28/n06/mear01_.html and Mearsheimer can be seen making his case on
YouTube at www.youtube.com/watch?v=HSAqNuf55k0. Criticisms of the
Meirsheimer and Walt thesis are abundant. See, for example, a letter from Alan
Dershowitz at www.lrb.co.uk/v28/n08/letters.html#letter1 or an article by the
Anti-Defamation League at www.adl.org/Israel/mearsheimer_walt.asp.
Dershowtiz was also critical of Jimmy Carter's use of the term 'apartheid' in
relation to Israel, see www.huffingtonpost.com/alan-dershowitz/the-world-
according-to-ji_b_34702.html.

# **1** **Poverty, profit and the political economy of violent conflict**

## Introduction

In the first years of the new millennium, the intellectual champions of the free market were riding high. They were buoyed by the election of a US president who promised small government, greater freedoms for entrepreneurs and an end to extensive nation-building programmes abroad. Rather than government intervention, the market, in conjunction with personal liberty, offered the solution to many of the world's problems. This view (usually known as neo-liberalism, or neo-conservativism in its more authoritarian form) was attractive as it tapped into commonsensical homespun truths: through hard work, self-reliance and personal freedoms, individuals would be able to make their own choices in life. Since individuals were likely to behave rationally they would avoid conflict and violence and would encourage their political leaders to avoid conflict. Rational individuals would see economic development as a ladder out of conflict. In short, 'free markets made free men' and free men would not be foolish enough to become involved in war (Mandelbaum 2002). As President George W. Bush (2007) put it, 'prosperous nations are less likely to breed violence' and the way to defeat violence is to 'advance peace and prosperity across the world.'

The view that liberalism and free trade offered a universal balm against the scourge of violent conflict has an impeccable intellectual pedigree. Thinkers such as John Rawls (1999) and Francis Fukuyama (1989) have championed the power of individual freedoms, open markets and rational choice to guide individuals and communities away from violent conflict. The claim that free trade prevents violent conflict is reinforced by empirical evidence. Krause and Suzuki's study of postcolonial states in the 1950–92 period demonstrates that 'trade openness significantly reduces the likelihood of civil war onset' (Krause and Suzuki 2005: 38). This indicates a virtuous circle whereby trading partners require a stable environment; the more they trade, the more they profit and the more they are aware of the disincentives attached to conflict.

However, just as there are strong arguments that champion the market as a guarantee against violent conflict, there are equally strong arguments that make connections between market-induced inequality and the causation, escalation and maintenance of violent conflict (Pugh and Cooper 2004: 2). John Harriss (2005a: 38) observed that 'war was obviously the world's greatest industry in the period of neo-liberal ascendancy.' Amy Chua (2004) provides a devastating account of how free trade, in conjunction with perceptions of ethnic difference, has led to the persecution of minority groups around the world. Chinese traders in Indonesia, Lebanese merchants in west Africa and Jewish business families in Russia, all have been targets of mobs and political campaigns that identify them as profiting from the poverty of the majority. Naomi Klein (2005) identifies how 'predatory disaster capitalism' profits from both war (arms sales, capital flight) and post-war reconstruction (lucrative reconstruction contracts and opportunities to establish new markets). Many authors, and indeed protagonists in armed conflicts, identify poverty as a key factor in tipping discontent towards violent conflict. For example, Subcomandante Marcos, the leader of the 1994 indigenous rising in Chiapas (Mexico), defended his actions as a way of bringing 'justice when now there is not even minimum subsistence' (Marcos 1994).

So, opinion is polarised on the role of economics (saviour or villain?) in the outbreak of civil war. This chapter will examine the often contradictory literature on conflict and development, using examples to illustrate the linkages between conflict, poverty and profit. One explanation that will be referred to throughout the chapter is the 'greed thesis', which suggests that economic motives are the most reliable indicators of the behaviour of protagonists in the outbreak and continuation of war (Collier 2000b). This has been much criticised, but it has also been incredibly influential (finding favour with governments and international organisations) and so it deserves serious scrutiny.

The chapter is divided into three sections. The first section examines the various economic and development-related arguments on the causation and escalation of violent conflict. There is little consensus on the precise linkage between the market, development, poverty and profit on the one hand, and conflict on the other, so this section will attempt to summarise the main arguments. The second section examines the factors behind conflict maintenance and pays particular attention to the political economy of violent conflict, or the peculiar economic dynamics that sustain war. Often dismissed as symptoms or manifestations of war, the politico-economic ecology of contemporary warfare deserves our attention. An anthropological lens is particularly useful in illustrating the ways in which individuals, communities, armed groups, businesses and states variously prosper, starve or 'get by' during war. The third section concentrates on the resource environments often found in the sites of violent conflict and considers the extent to which the presence, absence and distribution of resources such as diamonds or water can fuel or calm violent conflict.

## Conflict causation and escalation

Despite the assertions of some authors, there is no universal theory of conflict causation. The idea of a 'one-size-fits-all' theory is attractive, not least because a general theory of conflict causation may lead to a general theory of conflict management. But the sheer variety of conflict actors, environments and dynamics complicates matters for conflict analysts. Each conflict has a peculiar 'conflict DNA'. This may be a partial match with other conflicts, but will contain factors specific only to that conflict. Moreover, there is no unilateral cause of conflict. Instead, conflicts have multiple causes that interact in highly specific ways according to the context. Certainly conflicts can have primary causes that take precedence over secondary causes, but the variegated nature of human polities, economies and societies means that a single factor cannot spark a conflict in a vacuum. Different factors will have different weight at different stages of a conflict trajectory. For example, a single atrocity or grievance may prove inflammatory at the outbreak of a civil war, but it becomes overtaken by other factors that sustain the conflict in the longer term. The task for the conflict analyst is first to identify conflict causes (plural) and then establish the connections between them. This is rarely an easy task, since the public rhetoric used by protagonists may mask truer motives, or because protagonists (such as the Lord's Resistance Army in Uganda or Shia and Sunni militias in Iraq) may be secretive and offer few public clues as to their motivations.

Complicating matters even further is that antagonists may have different motivations for engaging in conflict. This applies within and between groups. Consider the Israeli–Palestinian conflict. At the intra-group level, recruits may be motivated to join Islamic Jihad for any number of reasons: spiritual fulfilment, to avenge a grievance, peer pressure, family tradition, belief in its political and strategic aims, to boost personal esteem or to make a private profit. Israelis may join the Israeli Defence Forces because of a desire to defend their state and community, to gain new skills and further their career, to continue family tradition and fulfil conscription obligations or to avoid being branded deviant or cowardly by not joining up. At the intergroup level it can even be argued that Islamic Jihad and the Israeli Defence Force are engaged in different conflicts. Although they share the same 'battlefield' and pledge themselves to the destruction of the other, their conflicts have very different aims. For Israel, the conflict is largely justified in terms of defence and security. For Islamic Jihad, it is about righting grievances and promoting a religiously inspired worldview. The conflict analyst is faced with a bewildering array of 'evidence' and, ultimately, must make a judgement call on which factors they believe to be most significant in the escalation of a conflict. Box 1.1 illustrates, with reference to Colombia, how multiple factors compete for the attention of the analyst. Rather than a science, conflict analysis is an art and involves human – and therefore potentially frail – judgement.

---

## Box 1.1

### *Colombia: a confusing conflict stratum*

A single word explanation is often given for the long-running war in Colombia: drugs. Drug money fuels both the legal and illegal economies with anti-state guerrillas, pro-state paramilitaries and elements of the state all implicated in the drugs trade. In 2000, Colombia was responsible for 74 per cent of world coca production (Guáqueta 2007: 438). But scratch the surface and a more complex conflict stratum is revealed. Certainly the drugs trade is important, but its primary significance has been in maintaining the conflict once it had already begun and creating a political economy of war that provides a disincentive to most antagonists to explore serious and comprehensive peace initiatives. At the heart of the conflict is the contested legitimacy of the weak Colombian state. From the nineteenth century it has been attempting to assert control over all of its territory and has faced a series of failed peasant revolutions for the past 150 years (Richani 2002: 23). At each stage of its development, the state has attempted to reform itself so as to protect the interests of an expanding and increasingly urban middle class. Right-wing paramilitaries (often linked with large landowners) have provided the state with a private (but poorly controlled) security force while left-wing guerrilla groups have sought to exploit the grievances of the dispossessed. World Bank studies have found that the size of large farms is increasing and the land tenure system makes it 'nearly impossible for productive small farmers to acquire land through the land sales market' (Deininger *et al.* 2004: 3). The weak state has been prone to regional influences from leftist ideologies, interventions from the United States and a ready supply of arms through porous borders. So, are drugs the cause of the Colombian conflict? No, but drugs money has become a fuel for a pre-existing conflict with long-term roots.

Sources: Richani (2002), Deininger *et al.* (2004), Guáqueta (2007)

Given that the focus of this book is on conflict and development, the bulk of this section will dwell on development and economic-related explanations for conflict causation. Yet there are entire subfields of literature on conflict causation that make little reference to development, economics, profit or poverty. Non-economic or non-development-related explanations for the outbreak of violent conflict include the often overlapping categories of biological disposition (Simmel 1955), psychology (Tajfel 1978), religion (Appleby 2000), identity (Sen 2006), ethnicity (Connor 1994; Young 2003), nationalism, ideology, history and ancient hatreds, bad neighbours, manipulative leaders (Brown 1997), the security dilemma (Posen 1993), cultural dysfunction (Kaplan 1994), the nature of the state (Tilly 1985) and incompatible worldviews (Huntington 1998). Many of these explanations regard economic factors as contingent, or providing a context in which the primary factor operates. Thus, for example, an ethnic group may develop an elaborate self-narrative of grievance, how its rights are denied, and how it is distinct from other identity groups. Declining economic conditions, in which the competition between identity groups becomes more intense, may provide the backdrop or even tipping point for a slide into violent conflict. A group may become convinced of its own 'relative deprivation', especially if inequality is visible along religious, ethnic or racial lines (Jacoby 2008: 103–13). But, in this explanation, economic and development-related factors are secondary and only come into play when stimulated by other factors or if a prior existing condition (entrenched ethnic or religious difference) is in place.

The important point to bear in mind is that conflicts are caused by a combination of factors. Those who promote economic or development-related explanations for the outbreak of violent conflicts, need to take account of non-development-related explanations and how these interact with development-related factors. Amartya Sen makes the point that poverty on its own is not enough to cause conflict. He recalls his own childhood memories from Calcutta during the 1943 Bengal famine and 'the sight of starving people dying in front of sweetshop windows with various layers of luscious food displayed behind glass windows, without a single glass being broken, or law and order being disrupted' (Sen 2006: 143). Other factors, especially 'the illusion of singular identity . . . in a world so obviously full of plural affiliations', were required to transform inequality and destitution into violent conflict (Sen 2006: 175).

Conflicts do not just happen. Just because a society is ethnically, racially or religiously fissured does not mean that conflict will follow. Seattle (a diverse multicultural city) is a more common model than Sarajevo (one riven by ethnonational conflict). Indeed, given the multiplicity of identity groups that claim to be distinct from others, there is remarkably little violent conflict on the planet (Brubaker and Laitin 1998). This suggests two points. The first is that many human societies have developed systems

Plate 3  A Muslim cemetery in Bosnia: just because a society is ethnically fissured does not mean that conflict will follow

that manage or suppress difference, often in non-violent ways. The second is that violent conflict requires active instigation agents, particularly if latent tensions are to be escalated into overt violence. These instigation agents may take the form of political leaders or ethnic entrepreneurs who purposively inflame and mobilise their supporters, or circumstances – such as an assassination or shock election result – that agitate already tense group sensibilities (Zartman 2005: 268–73).

## Economics and civil war

Unsurprisingly, economists have been at the forefront of arguments that conflict causation can be explained by economic rationalism. Paul Collier and a number of collaborators have produced a corpus of studies that link the onset of civil war to economic factors (Collier and Hoeffler 2002; Collier *et al.* 2003). Many of these studies are based on econometric modelling and are attractive because they allow analysts to avoid considering nebulous and difficult-to-define potential conflict contributing factors such as identity or historical grievances. Two main arguments have been advanced under what has been termed the 'greed thesis' or economic explanations of violent conflict:

- that economic factors can act as predictors of violent conflict (or help identify civil war prone societies)
- that combatants are motivated by economic predation.

The first argument identified economic factors – usually at the national level – that make a society prone to civil war. In particular, the level of per capita income, its rate of growth and the structure of the economy (especially its dependence on commodity exports) were identified as the key risk factors for the onset of civil war (on a dataset of fifty-two civil wars in the 1960–99 period). Collier and colleagues found that a doubling of per capita income halved the risk of civil war, and that when commodity exports account for 25 per cent of gross domestic product (GDP) the risk of civil war is 33 per cent, as opposed to an 11 per cent risk of civil war if commodity exports are at 10 per cent (Bannon and Collier 2003: 2–3). Findings such as these have encouraged governments and policymakers to promote poverty reduction and economic diversification programmes – often based on free market remedies – as part of conflict prevention strategies (International Development Committee 2006).

The second argument identified the profit motive – or 'greed' – as the primary motor behind civil war. Collier noted that 'conflicts are far more likely to be caused by economic opportunities than by grievance', but that rebel organisations will engage in a public discourse of grievance 'since they are unlikely to be so naive so as to admit to greed as a motive' (Collier 2000a: 91–2). Thus, 'civil wars occur where rebel organizations are financially viable', with the ability of antagonists to generate revenue being the principal reason why civil wars break out in some locations and not in others (Collier 2000b: 2). Münkler (2005) reinforces the view that civil war is economic rationalism taken to the extreme: the availability of weapons and untrained young men makes contemporary civil war 'downright cheap' and 'highly lucrative'. 'In the short term the force used in them yields more than it costs and the long-term costs are borne by others' (Münkler 2005: 74, 77). In this view, civil war conforms to a straightforward business model that seeks to maximise resource extraction through banditry, 'taxation', or the trafficking of diamonds, timber or people. It also aims to reduce costs by overlooking social responsibilities to citizens and cutting the costs of running a regular army. By boosting income and cutting costs, profit will be maximised. 'The entrepreneurs of the new wars' often emerged from the criminal underworld and used nationalist or ethnic movements as convenient vehicles from which to pursue their business interests (Münkler 2005: 80). William Reno's analyses of the civil wars in Sierra Leone and Liberia paint a dystopian picture in which political leaders drop all pretence of maintaining a functioning state that offers basic public services and protection to citizens (Reno 1997a, 1997b). Instead, leaders formed alliances with business organisations (often from overseas) to extract mineral resources. Ultimately, the civil wars in both territories resembled privatised conflict, with control of mineral resources the key aim (Keen 1998).

The claim by Collier and others that economic motivations must be given precedence over non-economic issues (such as identity) amounted to an intellectual cruise missile aimed at scholars who held that ethnicity or religion held the key to the onset of civil war. They responded in kind, and were particularly annoyed that the economic rationalism arguments found favour with the world's main international financial institutions (IFIs) which were playing an increasing role in the management of conflict and post-war reconstruction. The econometric methodologies favoured by the greed theorists matched the bias of the IFIs towards rational quantifiable explanations for social phenomena and the technocratic, free market remedies they favoured. Critics of the greed thesis pointed out that societies experiencing civil war were a poor environment for the collection of statistics, and so urged caution over the datasets employed to suggest that certain countries offered a permissive economic context for the onset of civil war (Cramer 2002). Collier was also criticised for using proxies, using high male unemployment as a proxy for greed rather than grievance (Kandeh 2005: 96). But those who rejected the greed thesis or the economic explanations for civil war had two more serious objections. The first was that the greed thesis located the causes of war inside states and conveniently absolved external (mainly western) actors from any blame (Pugh and Cooper 2004: 2). This was especially the case in relation to the iniquitous international trading regimes that condemned many developing world states to prolonged economic retardation. The single state lens also tended to ignore regional dynamics, such as the flow of weapons and people across a border or interference from a neighbouring state, which often contributed to violent conflict. The second objection to the greed thesis was that its proponents mistook correlation for causation (Mac Ginty 2004). Few denied that a permissive economic environment could encourage conflict or that a self-sustaining political economy of war could develop. What they did object to was the argument that economic factors were the *primary* engine of war. Instead, they argued that political and identity factors were the key initiation agents of war and that economic factors often subsequently came into play to change the nature and aim of the conflict.

Over time, the greed *or* grievance academic debate has given way to an emerging consensus that greed *and* grievance are responsible for the outbreak of civil war (Ballentine and Nitzschke 2003). The precise weight to be afforded to each is still contested, though since this weighting will change from conflict to conflict it is sensible to avoid building a general theory of conflict. We can say that most civil wars take place in poor countries, though poverty and inequality *per se* are not sufficient factors in the outbreak of civil war. Moreover, certain economic characteristics (such as low growth and a dependency on commodity exports) predispose societies to civil war. But a permissive environment does not amount to a causation factor. Certainly economic factors can enable civil war, but for combustion to occur, the economic factors need to spark with other factors (Homer-Dixon 1994).

It is also important to note that development, rather than offering a ladder out of conflict, can contribute to conflict. Many of the social processes associated with development create conditions in which conflict is less easily restrained or is more easily escalated. As Box 1.2 and the example of cattle-raiding in Kenya and Tanzania show, urbanisation, environmental degradation, the breakdown of family structures and a lessening of respect for traditional sources of dispute resolution may all create conditions permissive for violent conflict. Yet, to some, these social processes may simply be the by-products of social progress. China's rapid economic development illustrates the potential of development to contribute to conflict. An aggressive state-led development programme has resulted in the displacement of millions of people (well over 1 million people were displaced as part of the Yangtze Dam project: Aird 2001: 24), severe environmental degradation, land confiscations, and the perception among many rural peasants that they are the collateral damage in the country's economic liberalisation. The Chinese regime admitted to 87,000 riots and demonstrations in 2005, despite a 9 per cent economic growth rate (Cody 2006). The key point is that development often produces community dislocation and uncertainty, and may materially disadvantage some groups, encouraging them to view their status in relation to other groups. In such circumstances the restraints on conflict may lessen.

## Box 1.2

### Cattle-raiding in Kenya and Tanzania: development escalating conflict

Pastoral communities in Kenya and Tanzania have a long history of inter-tribal cattle-raiding (Fleischer 1998). Traditionally, the cattle-raiding was sustainable in that relatively small numbers of cattle were taken and casualty figures were low because traditional weapons were used. Often cattle raids were linked with rites of passage ceremonies, with adolescents using the raids as an opportunity to prove their valour (Hendrickson *et al.* 1998). In recent years, however, development-related changes in society have transformed the character of cattle-raiding. As a result, the fall-out of cattle-raiding – in terms of casualties and displacement – has increased markedly. There has been an increasing monetisation of exchange, with the result that cattle-raiders are stealing cattle to sell to urban-based criminal gangs rather than for the traditional reasons of individual/group esteem and subsistence pastoral farming. An increasingly urban and aspirational population is fuelling a demand for a meat-based diet, a demand that entrepreneurs are keen to satisfy. Meat consumption in the developing world has doubled between 1987 and 2007 (Bittman 2008). In addition to these development-related drivers, the intensity and effect of cattle-raiding have escalated as traditional weapons are being replaced by firearms (readily available from conflicts in the region).

Sources: Fleischer (1998), Hendrickson *et al.* (1998), Bittman (2008)

## The political economy of conflict maintenance

In some cases, the economic rationale of long-running violent conflicts is so apparent that it is possible to think that armed groups are motivated only by profit. Towards the latter years of Northern Ireland's 1969–94 Troubles, pro-British loyalist militants were perhaps better known for their drug dealing and protection rackets than for their actions to defend the Union with Great Britain (Silke 2000). Economic rationales often become more visible once a conflict is established and once markets and entrepreneurs have determined ways in which to exploit the opportunities of war. When established, conflict economies can become self-perpetuating and entrepreneur-combatants may see few incentives to explore an end to the conflict. Economists have developed sophisticated models to show how looting and other forms of economic predation provide a powerful motive for combatants. But such models reveal little of the human character of civil war economies and the trials faced by citizens in time of war. Anthropologists, on the other hand, have succeeded in illustrating the extraordinary lengths to which individuals, families and communities go to in order to survive. These studies show the adaptability of humans in their attempts to 'get by' and the extraordinary complexity of civil war economies (McIlwaine and Moser 2004).

A common misconception is that civil war economies are very much removed from the faraway mainstream economies of the developed world. The shiny shopping malls and online banking systems of the post-industrialised west seem a million miles away from civil war economies in which many economic transactions are illegal, unregulated or conducted under duress. But as anthropologist Carolyn Nordstrom (2008) reveals, combatants and civilians in the midst of civil wars are often closely connected with the globalised international economy. This insight is important as it suggests that western states and financial institutions – and indeed western consumers – are complicit in the perpetuation of civil war economies in the developing world. Nordstrom (2008) argues that all civil wars rely on technologies (arms, communication, money transfer) and networks (trading partners and political supporters) that are to some extent international and transnational. As a result, the shadow economies of the civil war environment must come into contact with the licit international economy: 'illicit profiteering must make use of legal production, transport, and monetary institutions' (Nordstrom 2008: 290). As David Keen (1998: 42) observes, 'even bandits need to sell what they steal'. The globalised 'buy/sell now, ask questions later' free market makes it easier for the licit and illicit economies to interact, and the sheer complexity of international markets (with multiple brokers) means that the paper trail from manufacturer/grower to consumer is easily obscured.

Nordstrom makes the case that rather than being marginal to the world economy, the apparently 'illicit' and 'shadowy' civil war economies are in fact central to it. Warlords and conflict entrepreneurs convert their illegally made profits into legal investments in the formal international economy or demand the same consumer goods that western shoppers aspire to. Vast sums of money of dubious origin lubricate the international financial markets. Thus, drugs barons' money from Afghanistan and Colombia, once suitably laundered, is invested alongside the pension funds of Anglican bishops. One estimate suggests that $1.6 trillion of illicit money moves across international boundaries annually, much of it through apparently legitimate institutions, and much of it out of developing states, thus further weakening their economies (Baker 2005). Just as consumers in war-torn societies demand goods and services from developed economies, consumers in the developed world demand goods from the sites of civil war. The high street shops selling mobile phones (in 2007 there were 71 million handsets for the 45 million adults in the UK (Schofield 2007)) are just one end of a network of economic

**Plate 4  A Porsche showroom in Beirut: people in war zones want the same consumer goods as those in the peaceful countries**

exchange stretching from the coltan mines of the Democratic Republic of Congo (DRC) from where an essential component in phone circuitry is extracted (Moyroud and Katunga 2002). Similarly, despite extensive international regulatory mechanisms, Sierra Leone's 'blood diamonds' manage to reach apparently legitimate retail outlets.

## Corruption

Western analysts, and particularly the western news media, can be shrill in their condemnation of corruption in developing world and civil war contexts. Certainly kleptocracy by ruling cliques and routine skimming by state functionaries can reach staggering proportions. Mohammed Soharto, Ferdinand Marcos and Mobutu Sese Seko are reputed to have embezzled a collective $50 billion during their respective reigns in Indonesia, the Philippines and Zaire (Denny 2004). But the peculiar economic context of societies experiencing civil war means that we need to reassess our understanding of 'corruption' and 'illegal' market activities. Can corruption be said to exist if the formal economy has broken down and people need to rely on informal market mechanisms simply to survive?

The formal economy may be so dysfunctional (and often over-priced) that citizens have no choice but to operate in the informal sector. In cases of state collapse, there may be no legal economy at all. More commonly the state is weak and only able to regulate a fraction of economic activity within its borders. It is estimated that up to 90 per cent of Angola's economy operates via extra-state exchange networks (Nordstrom 2004), while the post-Saddam British-American protectorate in Iraq has not attempted to institute a general taxation system (Chandrasekaran 2007: 138). Afghanistan's drugs industry was valued at $2.7 billion in 2006, or equivalent to over half the size of the legal economy. In 2005, the Afghan government was able to raise only $330 million in tax revenues and was largely sustained by western handouts (Coghlan 2006).

Just as the formal, monetised and regulated economy has become a way of life for most people in the UK and other western states, the informal economy is a socially embedded behavioural and entirely rational norm in many civil war and post-civil-war societies. It makes sense to use non-patented medicines when patented medicines are either unavailable or exorbitantly priced. The formalisation of the medical industry, through the protection of pharmaceutical patents, would not be in the interests of the vast majority of citizens because it would entail rocketing prices. The careless branding of certain economic activities as 'corrupt' or 'illegal' says as much about the western worldview as it does about the activities themselves (Brown *et al.* 2004). This is not to deny that corruption takes place and that it poses a real hazard to development and donor activity. Instead, it is to caution against the unthinking extension of western yardsticks to non-western, war-torn contexts. Box 1.3 illustrates the absurdity of some western norms in war-affected societies. Kolstad *et al.* (2008) stress the importance of distinguishing between different types and scales of corruption. There is a difference between administrative informality and petty corruption found in everyday exchanges in a remote town where state officials feel the need to augment their wages, and large-scale frauds perpetrated by political leaders or senior bureaucrats. Simplistic moral and ethical judgements may not always be sensitive to the context in which corruption takes place. We should also be alert to the potential for international assistance to use and reinforce existing clientelistic and patronage networks. What begins as the rational use of 'local systems of disbursement' can reinvigorate networks that are less than transparent and may even reinforce warlord politics.

---

## Box 1.3

### *A clash of cultures: Taliban-run Afghanistan and the British insurance industry*

A British colleague, who worked for a major aid agency in Afghanistan in the mid-1990s, tells of his luggage being stolen on his arrival at Kabul airport. The luggage contained an expensive camera, so he thought it would be worth claiming on his worldwide travel insurance. He rang his UK-based insurer, who told him that they would post a claim form out to him (the internet was in its infancy) and that he would need to get it stamped by the police in Kabul. He explained that the Taliban's police did not operate according to western models of criminal justice and public safety, and that with no insurance industry operating in war-torn Afghanistan, they would have no knowledge of what the funny foreigner would be asking for. And anyway, the international postal service to Afghanistan was extremely unreliable. It was beyond the comprehension of the British insurer that a society would not have a police force like that in the UK and that they could not assist in the certification of insurance claims. The claim never got off the ground. The key point is that institutions and activities that may seem 'normal' in a western environment do not necessarily have universal application. Effective bureaucracy and regulated markets, accepted components in western states, may be uncommon in non-western contexts.

In some cases, international connections have served to prop up weak states and their corrupt patronage networks. Bayart (2000) notes how many African leaders have become adept at fobbing off international donors with the message they want to hear:

> [D]emocracy, or more precisely the discourse of democracy, is no more than yet another source of economic rents, comparable to earlier discourses such as the denunciation of communism or of imperialism in the time of the Cold War, but better adapted to the spirit of the age. It is, as it were, a form of pidgin language that various native princes use in their communication with Western sovereigns and financiers. Senegal, one of the main recipients of public development aid in sub-Saharan Africa, is a past master in this game of make-believe. It is no exaggeration to say that the export of its institutional image . . . has replaced the export of groundnuts.
>
> (Bayart 2000: 226)

Essentially, the argument runs, international support has allowed corrupt regimes to continue systems of neo-patrimonialism and defer redistributive political and economic reform.

Legitimate monies often reach civil war societies in the form of external donor aid. Once there, these funds risk fuelling the conflict. For decades, bilateral donors have boosted the Sri Lankan education budget, but it can be argued that this frees up money for the Sri Lankan government to use in its war with the Tamil Tigers. In an ethnically divided society, the infusion of external assistance is likely to be jealously scrutinised by all sides to make sure that their group gets 'its share'. The cash injection might lead to renewed conflict (Herring and Esman 2003: 13). For example, controversy has attended the distribution of reconstruction aid in Lebanon following the 2006 Israeli–Hezbollah war. Shia districts, the main victims of the war, have complained that the Sunni-controlled government has withheld reconstruction funds. In a politically fragile state like Lebanon, such arguments can be potentially destabilising (Mac Ginty 2007: 462). External humanitarian and development agencies are often placed in an invidious position in war-torn societies. Do they sit on the sidelines, refusing to give assistance for fear that aid may fall into the 'wrong hands', or do they muck in and hope that their efforts help the genuinely needy despite the risks? An honest acceptance that civil war contexts are unlikely to leave ethical principles unscathed is required. Moreover, in some contexts, the sheer scale of donor assistance can distort the economy. As one observer noted, 'other than the state itself, the aid business is today the single biggest employer in most African states' (van de Walle 2001: 58).

Just as there is a political economy of war, there is a political economy of humanitarianism and development assistance. Perhaps this is most visible in the micro-economies that spring up to service international humanitarian workers in war-affected societies. The cluster of western-style bars, internet cafés and fast food outlets are often identifiable because of the white 4×4s parked outside. But at the macro-economic level, as will be discussed in later chapters, international economic and development interventions are often deliberately aimed at reshaping the war-affected economy to reconnect it with the formal global economy. Many of the liberal economic 'reforms' actually lead to the further immiseration of citizens: state employees are sacked ('rightsizing bureaucracy'), debts run up by previous regimes must be paid ('respecting international financial obligations'), prices rise as exchanges are formalised and monetised ('regulation'), and indigenous businesses cannot compete with cheap imports ('the global free market'). Kiely (2007: 434) notes how 'liberalisation undermines the capacity of developing countries to develop dynamic comparative advantages', yet liberalisation seems to be the main tool in the international toolbox.

The chief points of this section are that as war further distorts economies, people in war-affected societies (combatants and civilians alike) will take extraordinary measures to survive and this may involve activities that western observers may judge 'corrupt' or 'illegal'. But outside observers may be hypocritical in such judgements: civil war economies are hardwired into the very fabric of the formal international economy. Consumer demand in western states and the international economic structures erected by western states influence the choices and constraints faced by people on the ground in civil war societies. While we can paint an abstract picture of the economic impact of civil war (the 'typical' civil war costs $50 billion (Collier 2004)), it is important that we recognise the human experience of civil war and how many people are brutalised and humiliated by civil war economics, whether by being trafficked, being forced to sell family heirlooms or living in an environment in which theft is regarded as a normal survival mechanism (Mac Ginty 2004).

## Natural resources and conflict

As already noted, economists have claimed that an economic dependency on natural resource exports increases the likelihood of the outbreak of civil war. But the mere presence of natural resources does not lead to armed conflict. As Cramer (2006: 117) observes, 'scarcity and violence are a product of social relations rather than inherent in the relative abundance of a particular good, object or resource.' In other words, it is the management of the resources that really matters. Despite being 'blessed' by nature's largesse, a significant number of resource-rich states are chronically poor. Ross (2003: 22) found that twelve of the world's twenty most mineral-dependent economies were classed as 'highly indebted poor countries' and that five had experienced civil war in the 1990–2002 period. So, in the case of mineral extraction, it is the labour practices (voluntary or coerced), distribution of licences (open competition or patronage) and destination of profits (public or private coffers) that will determine whether states face a resource curse or windfall. Patterns of land ownership are particularly important in developing world contexts, as access to land (and the quality of that land) may afford subsistence and thus some measure of autonomy in economic matters (Miall 2007: 125–9).

Crucially, the perception of the management of resources is important. In a number of cases, minority ethnic, nationalist or religious groups have pursued grievances stemming from allegations that the state was plundering 'their' natural resources with few obvious benefits in return. Thus the Acehenese in Indonesia, Muslims in Mindanao (Philippines), Christians in southern Sudan and the Ogoni in the Niger Delta (see Box 1.4) have all engaged in secessionist conflict with the state and have campaigned for their 'fair share' of returns from resource exploitation. Although natural resources play a crucial role in these conflicts, it is incorrect to conceive of them as pure 'resource wars'. Instead, the conflict arises from a complex mix of the presence of resources, the pattern of resource exploitation, the perception of the benefits of that exploitation and identity affiliations. If the stakes are high, identity affiliations can mutate, with groups and individuals attaching increasing weight to the purity of their ethnic group and rediscovering (or inventing) their 'unique' history (Wilmer 2002: ix). In such ways, conflicts become 'ethnicised' and exclusion from the benefits of natural resources may provide a powerful impetus to escalate conflict.

Winston Churchill's observation that 'God put the West's oil under Middle Eastern feet' is a reminder of competitive geo-strategic interests in natural resources that make resource-rich developing world states prone to intervention by powerful states. Quite simply, advanced and developing economies are dependent on oil. Their ways of life, politics and economics would be utterly unsustainable if ready access to oil were not secured. In the main, the market has been successful in procuring oil,

## Box 1.4

### *Oil extraction in Nigeria's Niger Delta*

Nigeria's oil-rich Niger Delta region has experienced significant levels of
conflict, criminal violence and environmental damage for several decades. The
central government has encouraged major oil corporations to exploit the oil
reserves, but residents in the Delta region claim that any benefits bypass local
communities and that pollution has seriously affected quality of life. Armed
criminal gangs regularly steal oil from pipelines and kidnap foreign oil workers
for ransom, while other local groups have been vocal in their condemnation of
the profiteering, corruption and environmental disregard of 'imperial Abuja' or
have encouraged labour unrest. On top of this, there have been clashes between
rival ethnic groups. Oil company attempts to co-opt tribal chiefs through
payments have made chieftaincies extremely lucrative, sparking conflict and
changing community perceptions of chiefs. In response to the oil-related tension
and violence, the Nigerian government has variously declared a state of
emergency and sent in the army, attempted to buy-off local leaders, reassured
foreign oil companies, promised to invest a greater share of oil in the region and
occasionally mounted prosecutions against corrupt officials (including one
against two rear-admirals accused of stealing an oil tanker: Clayton 2005).
The violence has seriously disrupted oil production, but the potential rewards for
the government, local and national political leaders, and overseas oil companies
are simply too great for anyone to contemplate withdrawing from the region
(Bekoe 2005).

Sources: Bekoe (2005), Clayton (2005)

and major western states are not as dependent on oil from conflict-
affected areas as some analysts suggest. The United States was the
world's third largest oil producer in 2006, and most oil-producing Gulf
states are compliant with western economic and geopolitical strategy.
Indeed, the oil profits of most Gulf states are tied up in the New York and
London stock markets, so oil-rich states have no incentive to spark
economic instability by coming together and attempting to use leverage
over oil supply. But as demand for oil in the developing world (especially
India and China) surges, pressure on apparently finite oil resources
increases. Both the market and states can be expected to act in
self-interested ways to ensure continued access to energy. As the cases
of post-Saddam Iraq, Colombia and Nigeria show, consumer demand is
so great that complexes of private companies and state bodies will come
together to create oases of petrochemical calm in the midst of wider
conflict just to ensure that oil continues to flow.

Demand for oil, water, timber, diamonds and other minerals continues to be the source – or at least fuel (literally in some cases) – of violent conflict. As populations become richer, the natural resources of landscape and aesthetic beauty come under increasing pressure from tourism. This is despite a growing awareness of the environmental costs of most forms of tourism. In a number of cases, western 'tourist bubbles' exist alongside local inequality, repression or conflict (Rogers 2000: 2). The resorts of the Maldives have soared in popularity, despite the suppression of political opposition by the ruling regime (Amnesty International 2003). Perhaps the starkest juxtaposition of the western tourism industry with conflict has been the Royal Caribbean Cruise Line's virtual annexation of a piece of Haiti as a stopping-off point for its cruise liners. Branded as 'Fantasy Island' or 'Magic Island', the term 'Haiti' (let alone its recent history of civil war) is not mentioned in the brochures, and passports are not stamped as tourists enter the leisure enclave. Visitors are warned not to venture beyond the resort boundaries (Orenstein 1997). But over those walls in Haiti proper, life expectancy in 2005 was 52 years, and GDP per capita was one-twentieth of the figure for Norway, the top-ranked nation in the Human Development Index (UNDP 2006: 283). Fantasy Island represents one version of the 'no war, no peace' phenomenon, whereby violent conflict is compartmentalised in certain parts of the state, allowing other parts to function as 'normal' (Mac Ginty 2006). In another example of this compartmentalisation of conflict, Shaw and Mbabazi (2007) demonstrate how southern Uganda has been able to become the poster child of African development, while the north of the country has been mired in conflict.

## Concluding discussion

There is growing consensus among policymakers, academics and others that the escalation, maintenance and transformation of conflict are linked to development. The precise nature of these linkages is still debated. In truth, there is no exact science linking conflict to development; the constellation of variables is simply too great given the variations in context and timescales. Despite the apparent sophistication of econometric modelling or the 'seen it all' world-weary cynicism of development practitioners, conflict interventions and development programming contain a good deal of guesswork and finger-crossing. Western donor governments, such as the Department for International Development (DFID) in the UK, show a commitment to conflict-sensitive programming, or development interventions calibrated to have a minimal or positive impact on a conflict situation. But the volatility and lack of regulation in many war-torn or post-conflict societies mean that the precise effect of development inputs is unknown. The bottom line is that development or reconstruction assistance is a resource and political and militant actors will act rationally in attempting to maximise their access to, or benefit from, the resource. Despite good intentions, development inputs may actually fuel conflict. Moreover, and as will be discussed in Chapter 2, many of the factors that influence development in a war-torn society will be exogenous to that society. Just as many citizens may feel powerless in the midst of conflict, they may also feel that development is a process that is *done to* them.

The relationship between security and development is fraught with thorny questions, especially in the post-9/11 world in which the 'security imperative' is easier to justify among many audiences than a 'development imperative'. Development and reconstruction require a certain level of order if they are to be long-term endeavours. At its most benign, this order can take the form of institutionalisation and regulation; in effect a process of 'normalisation' whereby the uncertainty of a violent context is replaced by the certainty of stability. But in a less benign scenario, there can be unacceptable costs associated with 'stabilisation', such as restraining civil liberties or empowering private security contractors. In a number of cases, most notably in Iraq and Afghanistan, those empowered to make the decision on where the balance between order and development must lie are located outside of the country. In effect, a process of development and post-war reconstruction is as disempowering as the war once was. If a holistic view of development is taken, in which development extends far beyond the narrow confines of economic growth, then the process of development involves a good deal of de-development.

## Summary

- Explanations of the causes of violent conflict have focused on issues of 'greed' (economic causes) and 'grievance' (such as identity).
- Most scholars argue that a mixture of greed and grievance factors contribute to violent conflict.
- The factors that cause a violent conflict may differ from the factors that sustain a conflict.

- Resources alone, such as oil, diamonds or water, do not cause conflict. What is important is the nature of the extraction and management of those resources.
- Just as violent conflict can distort an economy, so too can aid and peace-support, with issues of 'corruption' gaining increasing attention in recent years.

## Discussion questions

1 Do you find that the criticisms of the greed thesis of conflict causation are justified?
2 What are the economic factors that can sustain violent conflict once it has started?
3 Can there be corruption if the formal economy has broken down?
4 Should aid agencies halt all assistance to a conflict area if they know that some of their aid will be siphoned off by combatants, or should they take this as a necessary evil of operating in a conflict zone?

## Further reading

There is an enormous literature on conflict causation. A good starting point for the econometric perspective is Collier, P. *et al.* (2003) *Breaking the Conflict Trap: Civil war and development policy*, Washington, DC: World Bank and Oxford University Press and Collier, P. (2007) *The Bottom Billion: Why the poorest countries are failing and what can be done about it*, Oxford: Oxford University Press. Wider studies of conflict that make connections with international dynamics and structures include two books Duffield, M. (2001) *Global Governance and the New Wars: The merging of development and security*, London: Zed Books and Duffield, M. (2007) *Development, Security and Unending War: Governing the world of peoples*, Cambridge: Polity. Work by journalists and anthropologists is particularly good at showing us what it is like to live in conflict areas. See, for example, Nordstrom, C. (2004) *Shadows of War: Violence, power and international profiteering in the twenty-first century*, Berkeley, CA: University of California Press; McIlwaine, C. and Moser, C. (2004) *Encounters with Violence in Latin America: Urban poor perceptions from Colombia and Guatemala*, London: Routledge; and Fisk, R. (2005) *The Great War for Civilization: The conquest of the Middle East*, New York: Knopf.

# Useful websites

The World Bank has many reports on 'Fragile and Conflict-Affected Countries' at www.worldbank.org/conflict. Reports by the UK's Department for International Development can be found at www.dfid.gov.uk/aboutDFID/ organisation/conflicthumanitarianassistance.asp#Conflict%20and%20Poverty, while USAID's material on conflict can be found at www.usaid.gov/our_work/ cross-cutting_programs/conflict/links/index.html. Useful information can also be found via the International Crisis Group at www.crisisgroup.org. On resource exploitation, details of attempts to reduce the trade in blood diamonds can be found at www.kimberleyprocess.com/. Details of the anti-corruption organisation Tiri can be found at www.tiri.com. More critical material on corruption can be found in Kolstad, I., Fritz, V. and O'Neil, T., *Corruption, Anti-corruption Efforts and Aid: Do donors have the right approach?* (www.odi.org.uk/PPPG/politics_ and_governance/publications/GAPWP3.pdf).

# 2 Institutions: hardware and software

## Introduction

The twentieth century is often termed 'the American century' and there is little indication that the twenty-first century will deviate from American dominance. India, China and the European Union (EU) may grow in influence and economic might, but they are unlikely to knock the United States off its perch. The twentieth century, particularly from 1945 onwards, has also been a century of international institutions. Institutions such as the United Nations, NATO, African Union (AU) and EU continue to play a key role in thwarting and facilitating conflict and development in the twenty-first century. Indeed, a select group of international institutions comprise the primary international instruments dedicated to preventing and minimising the impact of war, spearheading post-war reconstruction and promoting development. At the same time, a select group of international institutions are often blamed for underdevelopment and de-development, and by extension contributing to conflict. To complicate matters, the same institutions have been blamed for contributing both to the escalation and transformation of violent conflict.

The chapter sketches the principal international architecture that provides the context for contemporary conflict and development. Just as it is difficult to discuss computing hardware in isolation from software, it is difficult to gain a comprehensive understanding of international political institutions without discussing their operating 'software' or the principles which define their behaviour. Thus the chapter opens by discussing the

'liberal peace', or the overarching philosophy that shapes many
international peace support operations, post-war reconstruction
programmes and development interventions. International institutions are
given shape and purpose by the principles and worldview of their key
members. It is argued here that the liberal peace has a peculiarly western
flavour that reinforces the dominance of existing elites and promotes
highly specialised western ideas, namely versions of liberalism, democracy
and economics. As will be shown, the liberal peace has decidedly illiberal
aspects. A crucial element of the liberal peace is hyper-globalisation which
supports multiple connections through multiple networks so that conflict
and development on various parts of the planet are linked.

The chapter then moves on to discuss 'hardware' or the principal
institutions that comprise the international political system. It begins with
a brief discussion of the key constituent feature of the international
system: the state. The important factor from our point of view is the
political organisation of the state, particularly in terms of its relationships
with its citizens and market, and its ability to resist or adapt to exogenous
pressure. The chapter then reviews the roles and effectiveness of the
primary collective security and development promotion organisations,
before examining the role of the international financial institutions. The
chapter concludes by recommending that we adopt the lens of complex
multilateralism when reviewing the role of international institutions in
relation to conflict and development. In other words, we need to move
away from a view in which we have compartmentalised entities such as
states and international organisations that have formal and well-defined
linkages between them. Instead, conflict and development operate in a
much more complex environment in which multiple transnational and
international actors cooperate and clash. This 'cast list' is much more
extensive than the traditional list of states and international institutions,
and includes globalised multinational companies, NGOs and transnational
social movements. It is important, when reviewing the international
system and the forces at work within it, to resist any temptation towards
US-bashing. Certainly, the United States, and its allies pursue their own
self-interests, but they are rational to do so and to 'work the system' to
their best advantage.

## Software

Without guidance, international institutions such as the United Nations,
the Asian Development Bank or the African Union, are merely empty

vessels. They do not have autonomous lives of their own. Instead, they reflect the positions of their most powerful members and lobbies. Crucially, international organisations are not neutral (despite professions otherwise). International organisations are the product of a political, economic and cultural reality that has been, and is, heavily contested. At the heart of this struggle is the old-fashioned concept of 'power'; a concept that once dominated political science and international relations and now tends to be overlooked. It is not oversimplistic to say that a basic struggle between power holders and power seekers defines the structure and operations of many international organisations. The power holders, who are often rich western states, international organisations, international financial institutions and corporate interests, wish to maintain their stranglehold over economic, political and cultural power over the power seekers. The latter are often developing world and conflict-ridden states and their populations, minority communities, the dispossessed and those of a critical perspective. The 'software' that directs international institutions to act in prescribed ways is often specifically designed to reinforce the position of power holders and thwart attempts by power seekers to achieve a more egalitarian share of resources. The power holders, and particularly the hegemon in the form of the United States, have been remarkably successful in perpetuating their power. Tim Jacoby (2007: 523) notes how the hegemon is skilled at convincing states that its perpetual dominance is in their own interests, maintains enough military power to cow opposition, and guarantees its material superiority through a heavily biased distribution of resources and capital. This section discusses 'software' or the 'global computer program' that helps run the dominant international political system and many of the international organisations within it.

## The liberal peace

Different scholars use different lenses with which to interpret the world. Feminists, for example, might argue that the main software package that drives the international political system is the patriarchy or the male dominance that is infused into many aspects of life (Tickner 2001). Marxists might be tempted to interpret their known universe through an analysis of the means of production and patterns of ownership and consumption (Maclean 1988). This study finds that the liberal peace lens is particularly useful in explaining many of the meta-influences at work in situations of conflict and development. The liberal peace is a highly specialised form of peace and development intervention promoted by leading states, leading international organisations and the international financial institutions in their attempts to shape the international political system and its constituent parts. It is the 'ideology upon which life, culture, society, prosperity and politics are assumed to rest' (Mac Ginty and Richmond 2007a: 493). The liberal peace is capable of constructing a beguiling and attractive rationale for its own promotion. Thus it speaks of 'responsibility', 'development', 'common interests' and above all, intervention (Williams 2007b: 543).

Sometimes called 'liberal interventionism' or 'liberal internationalism', the liberal peace is most visible in societies undergoing western-backed peace support interventions in the aftermath of civil war. But many of the tools of the liberal peace, particularly in disciplining societies, governments and economies, are also at work in developing states that have not experienced recent war. In non-post-war environments, these interventions are often covered by the terms 'good governance' and 'reform' and we find the same commitment to the market as a prerequisite for debt relief and poverty reduction strategy funding (Craig and Porter 2003; Abrahamsen 2004).

**Plate 5  The UN in Jordan: the UN can be considered as an agent of the liberal peace**

The case study approach is perhaps the dominant method in the study of conflict and development. This is often entirely legitimate and allows scholars to explore in depth the lessons of a particular context. One potential failing of the case study methodology is that scholars are so engrossed in their particular case that they are often unable to make comparisons and connections between cases. The liberal peace tool allows us to make comparisons, sometimes across contexts that may not have obvious similarities or connections. It also allows us to make sense of the strategy employed by the leading political and economic actors in the international system. The liberal peace can be seen as a normatively neo-liberal system of compliance that is variously recommended, induced and enforced by leading states, leading international organisations and international financial institutions. Developing world states and states emerging from conflict often have little choice but to accept the liberal peace.

Many aspects of the liberal peace are deeply illiberal. It promotes a highly specialised form of liberalism that is often highly prescriptive and reflective of western norms (Mac Ginty 2006: 33–57). Rajiv Chandrasekaran's (2007: 7) exposé of life inside Baghdad's Green Zone provides a stark illustration of the crass ethnocentrism at the heart of the liberal peace as manifested in Iraq's Coalition Provisional Authority (CPA). He tells of how US administrators lived in a hermetically sealed compound complete with air-freighted fast food, US sports television channels and other home comforts. The security situation meant that many administrators rarely left the compound, while only a very few Iraqis could gain access to their new rulers. Many CPA-staffers were woefully inexperienced college graduates whose sole work experience had been as an intern for a Republican Member of Congress. This was often enough to justify their appointment to tasks such as helping to write the new Iraqi constitution or organising the privatisation of public services. Most US CPA personnel got their first passport to travel to Iraq, and six of the young 'gofers' were 'assigned to manage Iraq's $13 billion budget, even though they had no previous financial management experience' (Chandrasekaran 2007: 104–5).

The liberal peace promotes the individual as the primary unit of society. While such a viewpoint is unproblematic in western societies, it clashes with many developing world and non-western contexts in which the family or clan-group may also have significant importance. By empowering individuals (for example, as consumers or as voters with free choice) the liberal peace introduces a cultural clash (sometimes characterised as traditionalism versus modernism) in many societies (see Box 2.1). The version of liberalism promoted by the liberal peace is perhaps most significant for its adherence to neo-liberal economic principles. Deudney and Ikenberry (1999: 190) observe the political ambitions of the promotion of open economies: 'liberal states have pursued economic openness for political ends, using free trade as an instrument to alter and maintain the preferences and features of other states that are politically and strategically congenial.'

If one searches the liberal peace or the operating philosophy of leading states for 'red lines' or non-negotiable elements then the belief in open markets seems to be one of the few inviolable principles. Other possible red lines wilt under scrutiny. Commitments to democracy, international law, human rights or ideas of common humanity waiver according to circumstances. They are upheld in certain cases but conveniently overlooked in others. Even commitments to the inviolability of state sovereignty are abrogated when actors feel strong enough to do so. In the first few months of 2008, for example, there were startling cases of the overriding of sovereignty: Kosovo's declaration of independence, US missile strikes on Somalia, and Colombia's raid on guerrilla bases in

---

## Box 2.1

### *A clash of cultures?*

One of the authors' postgraduate classes was having a discussion on democratisation in post-war societies. The author asked a female Afghan student if she was looking forward to voting for the first time when she returned to Afghanistan. She said that she was not. 'My father will decide who I should vote for. So this is not a vote for me. It's an extra vote for him.' She continued to say that she wanted access to decent health care, education and other basic social services more than participating in an election. Moreover, she did not see a direct link between participating in an electoral process and the delivery of such services. 'Afghan society is clientelistic.' she explained. 'It's all about who you know and not how you vote. For me, voting isn't a "gift" from the west. At best it's an inconvenience.' Her views were something of a shock to her western classmates – particularly the females who had been brought up to believe that gender equality was both a right and a norm. The chief point is that the staging of elections in post-Taliban Afghanistan was more a priority for western governments anxious to legitimise the rule of their appointed leader than a priority for many Afghans.

Ecuador. This leaves us with a commitment to the free market (thus reinforcing the existing hegemony) as the core of the liberal peace.

If it is the case that a commitment to the market is the key defining point of the international political and economic system operated by leading western states then this says much about the 'culture' and 'civilisation' upon which it is based. It also explains how radical movements, such as anti-globalisation campaigners or even violent fundamentalists in the form of Al-Qaeda, are able to depict 'the west' as an ethical vacuum. Indeed, a number of the martyrdom videos of actual and failed suicide bombers in the United Kingdom mention the baselessness of western popular culture. Perhaps there is merit to Huntington's (1993a) much criticised 'clash of civilisations' thesis, though according to violent fundamentalists, the clash is between an empty mammon-obsessed west and the more sophisticated entities of non-western identity, religion and customs.

The absence of a unifying political framework is perhaps most visible in Belgium, a wealthy first world post-industrial state in which increasing numbers of citizens and political figures are questioning why the state exists at all and are investigating ethnonational alternatives. The key point is that the combination of economic globalisation and a hollow form of liberalism risks producing soulless societies with few centripedal forces. Those with particularist agendas, for example promoting ethnic or religious worldviews, may find western liberalism an easy target.

As noted earlier, the manifestations of the liberal peace are most visible in situations of internationally supported peacebuilding and post-war reconstruction. Here the levers of the liberal peace include: western encouragement (or coercion) to reach a peace deal, direction in writing a new constitution, assistance in establishing and advising political parties, a donors' conference to fund and direct post-war reconstruction, help in holding electoral contests (and sometimes outright interference in the result), programmes of capacity building for the state and civil society, the introduction of 'good governance' targets and the attaching of economic reform conditions to any reconstruction assistance. In effect, the liberal peace has manifested itself in post-peace accord societies as a conveyor belt of western inputs. This has resulted in criticisms that it has been formulaic, using a template style of intervention that is unresponsive to the variations demanded by local circumstances (Mac Ginty 2006: 176) (see Box 2.2).

## Box 2.2

### *The viceroy of Bosnia-Herzegovina*

Following the 1992–5 civil war, the new state of Bosnia-Herzegovina was ruled first by a NATO and then a European Union interim administration. Certainly, the international community provided the stability and security that was required to pave the way for humanitarian and reconstruction interventions. But critics have pointed out that the extent of international intervention by leading states has diminished the ability of Bosnia-Herzegovina to stand on its own feet and determine its own course. This view contends that in their desire to protect the peace and the rights of minorities, the international community has resorted to draconian methods. The International Crisis Group sums up the western liberal peace point of view thus: 'Bosnia remains unready for unguided ownership of its own future – ethnic nationalism remains too strong' (BBC 2008). This view has led to intense intrusion into Bosnia's affairs to the extent that 'expatriates make major decisions . . . key appointments must receive foreign approval, and . . . key reforms are enacted at the decree of international organisations' (Knaus and Martin 2003: 62). The Office of the High Representative, not an elected official from Bosnia-Herzegovina, remains the point of ultimate political authority and has not been afraid to exercise authority in such a way that it has been likened to a 'European Raj'. Until 2005, officials and representatives dismissed by the Office of the High Representative had no legal right of appeal (Zaum 2006: 471). Indeed Chandler (2007: 605) notes that 'sovereignty has in effect been transferred to Brussels.' The liberal peace imposed a very particular type of order on Bosnia-Herzegovina and sparked enormous resentment among many sections of the population who felt disempowered despite the language of 'inclusion', 'empowerment' and 'participation' that accompanied European interventions.

Sources: Knaus and Martin (2003), Zaum (2006), Chandler (2007), BBC (2008)

The liberal peace is not only restricted to international interventions in societies emerging from civil war. Instead, international interventions can be detected in a range of developing world societies. The main means of advance is through economic reform and leverage, and the 'good governance' agenda of bureaucratic reform. Such 'reform' can often sound innocuous, particularly in its promotion of concepts such as accountability, transparency, the regularisation of bureaucracy and empowerment. Yet the cumulative effect of such interventions (often multiple interventions by multiple international organisations, bilateral relationships, INGOs and NGOs) may have profound cultural and social impacts capable of influencing the relationships between states, their citizens and markets.

Fundamentally, liberal peace interventions are capable of altering the locus of power within a state. For example, citizens in a clientelist political system may have been used to transferring their allegiance to the ruling party at municipal level in return for resources (Martz 1996). This was a rational transaction for both the citizen and the local political leader, and such relationships would have been deeply embedded into the socio-political culture. Politicians from the ruling party would be routinely invited to family weddings and in return for this public expression of loyalty, the family may expect a share of patronage such as public sector employment for a son (Hamieh 2007). According to the western mindset, such behaviour may be regarded as 'corrupt' or 'nepotistic' (and indeed, it is often deeply inefficient and patriarchial). 'Good governance' interventions by western states and international organisations in many developing and post-war contexts have attempted to reform political and economic cultures in order to promote transparency and accountability. In order to build the capacity of municipalities, the United Nations Development Programme may place one of its own personnel in the municipality offices to introduce new administrative procedures. This might involve the ending of discriminatory employment practices whereby loyal supporters received sinecures and protected employment according to who they knew rather than what they knew. The municipality may be unable to refuse the deployment of UNDP staff to its offices because of a directive from central government or because the capacity-building scheme comes with financial inducements. Observers from a western liberal perspective may applaud the introduction of meritocracy at the municipality. But they may be blind to the impact that such good governance 'reforms' have on altering power relationships within the target society. The citizen may no longer attach legitimacy to the municipality, a factor that is likely to have consequences for political participation, legitimacy and stability. So rather than 'state-building', capacity-building activities funded by the international community might actually help to undermine the state or make apparent state weakness. Chandler (2006: 478) refers to the process as 'the privileging of governance over government'. The key problem is that while people can vote for governments (and government opponents), they cannot vote for governance.

The impact of such capacity-building interventions are often quite subtle, and sometimes seem incredibly minor, but their cumulative effect can transform the operating culture and orientation of state institutions (Abrahamsen 2000; Larmour 2005). Whereas a verbal promise between the local mayor and the head of household may have been sufficient in the traditional dispensation, good governance reforms may require the filling in of a standardised form. This apparently innocuous change goes to the heart of some core political and cultural relationships involving issues of trust and reciprocity upon which many societies operate. Under this description, liberal peace interventions and good governance reforms often involve many pinprick involvements. It is also clear that many actors are involved in the liberal peace chain, with much delegation (and abrogation of responsibility) along the way. Thus, international organisations and leading states may direct or encourage developing world states to adopt a set of administrative and economic reforms (in return for being able to access credit on international markets). Many of the reforms would be implemented at national level, but others would be passed down the political chain to regional governments and municipalities and eventually to citizens. INGOs and NGOs may be co-opted as implementation agents for the liberal peace and good governance agenda. Although INGOs and NGOs are well aware of the criticisms of good governance and western-backed peacemaking as a form of neocolonialism that exports a peculiarly western worldview, they find it difficult not to become involved in programmes and projects that fall under the 'good governance' rubric. Often good governance and the liberal peace are the only games in town. They attract funding, whereas other programmes based on alternative worldviews do not.

It should not be assumed that everything connected with international intervention, the liberal peace and good governance is harmful. Often, for example in the case of state collapse, it is only international actors who are empowered to organise national processes (such as elections) or have the capacity to provide the security necessary for the introduction of humanitarian or development assistance. Since the end of the Cold War, western-backed interventions have saved and improved lives across war zones and development contexts. Defenders of the liberal peace point out that many underdevelopment and conflict situations would be worse off if there was no international intervention and that we should swallow objections to the imposition of western values and look to the bigger picture of stability and the potential for economic growth (Quinn and Cox 2007: 518). Moreover, we should not conceptualise the liberal peace as a dastardly plot solely perpetrated by the United States. Rather than being coerced into the liberal peace, many states, organisations and enterprises see it as a way to further their own ends. France, for example, protested loudly at the prospect of the 2003 US invasion of Iraq. It did not, however, sever its ties with the United States, impose sanctions or take any real steps to prevent the invasion. In short, France had much to gain from its generally good relations with the United States and its connections with the global economy.

We should be under no illusions that international assistance is neutral. It reflects the worldview of those who fund and direct it. Although the liberal peace and the good governance agenda have standardised elements that are applied to different societies with minimal regard to local circumstances, it is important to note that western interventions and reforms are applied with different levels of enthusiasm in different locations (Richmond 2005a: 217–18). Moreover, we must be careful not to represent developing world and post-conflict states and communities as mute, powerless actors without agency. In fact, there are many cases of communities resisting, modifying and subverting the original intentions of western policymakers (Richmond and Franks 2007; Franks and Richmond 2008). Whether in Bosnia, Sierra Leone or Timor-Leste, local political leaders, bureaucrats and communities have found ways to exploit the resources and intentions of international organisations and states involved in peacebuilding and development activities.

While this book is interested in contemporary conflict and development, the parameters of the modern liberal peace are historical. We have had numerous 'defining moments' in which political leaders make 'never again' pronouncements and boldly set a 'new' course: Versailles, Yalta, and the declaration of a New World Order at the end of the Cold War are just a few examples. Yet many of the apparently 'new' structures, institutions and modes of operation seem to resemble those of the previous era (Williams 1998: 5–18). Alex Callinicos (2005: 596) finds that the key to explaining the 2003 Anglo-American invasion of Iraq lies not only in the contingencies of the Bush White House but also in long-maintained historical projects: 'The ideal of a global order in which free markets and democratic institutions promoted peace and prosperity was eloquently articulated by Woodrow Wilson during the First World War.' These continuities guide us towards examining international structures that can survive the tectonic shifts in the international economy and polity. In order to understand 'structural liberalism' we now turn to the 'hardware' or international institutions that define contemporary conflict and development (Deudney and Ikenberry 1999: 180).

# Hardware

## States

Rather than provide a 'political science 101' conceptualisation of the ideal state, this section will content itself with making three points about the state or the principal unit in the international political system (see Box 2.3). In lieu of an elementary exposition of the concept of the state, readers may wish to consult classics on the subject such as Waltz's (2001) *Man, the State and War* or Migdal's (1988) *Strong Societies, Weak States*. The first point is an obvious one: there are enormous variations in the resources, power, legitimacy and capabilities of states and thus in their conflict and development status. Indeed some states are 'lucky' in that they are in a stable region with dependable neighbours though (as we saw in Chapter 1) states 'fortunate' enough to have natural resources are often cursed with conflict over the distribution of these resources. The massive variance in state capability leads to uneven international institutions, with some states (and corporate bodies and lobby groups) wielding disproportionate influence. In stark terms, while some states and lobby groups can afford to maintain extensive bureaucracies at international organisations, other states cannot (Robbins 2003: 105). Indeed, Japan is

---

### Box 2.3

#### *Pakistan: strong or weak state?*

Ostensibly Pakistan is a strong state. It covers a huge area (over twice the size of Germany), is rich in resources (including natural gas) and is strategically located (it borders China, India, Iran and Afghanistan). It has an enormous army, is a nuclear power and its economy, though underdeveloped, has experienced strong levels of growth in the post-2004 period. Yet the state is chronically weak. It does not control all of its territory (with insurgent groups regularly defeating the national army in the Waziristan region). The bureaucracy is unable to fulfil its stated aims; thus a large proportion of the economy is corrupt and unregulated and – unable to conduct a census – the state can only estimate the population. Democratic institutions are weak, with the result that military coups, states of emergency, mass riots, human rights abuses and political assassinations have become commonplace. Long-running boundary disputes with India, and the Kashmir conflict, have been a drain on state coffers and attentions. So is Pakistan a strong or weak state? The answer, despite its formidable nuclear arsenal, must be that it is weak. The state faces too many alternative sources of power to be able to assert itself.

reported to pay the International Whaling Commission membership fees for some states in return for support on the right to hunt whales (McCurry 2008).

State capacity is a crucial factor in facilitating, developing and constraining conflict. Adrian Leftwich's (1996: 284) concept of the 'developmental state' is useful in illustrating how states need to 'concentrate sufficient power, authority, autonomy, competence and capacity at the centre to shape, pursue and encourage the achievement of explicit developmental objectives'. As Leftwich (1996) points out, states have pursued this capacity to develop in very different ways, with Taiwan and South Korea achieving very high rates of growth under authoritarian political systems. This leads us to the second point, that the type of state matters, particularly in terms of its internal political organisation. Some forms of state organisation may be more conducive than others to promoting development and constraining conflict. Democracy and development may not always be compatible, and it is unlikely that China could achieve such high economic growth rates if it were embarking on a serious programme of political liberalisation. The state is often the central clearing house for societal conflict, providing rules and mechanisms to allow individuals and groups to coexist. But it may also be inept or incapable, or may have little interest in maintaining its conflict-regulating responsibilities. William Reno (1997b) paints a dystopian picture of west African states in the late 1990s, in which ruling elites regarded citizens as an expensive encumbrance and thus made no pretence at offering public services. Instead, they fixed their energies on the extraction of precious minerals, usually in concert with external commercial interests. In some cases, especially societies with identity fissures, the state may privilege some groups and discriminate against others. An enormous literature posits a link between democracy and peaceful relations between states, but the relationship is by no means simple, and this 'democratic peace' literature tends to overlook the locus of most violent conflict: within the state itself (Doyle 1980; Henderson 2002: 2).

A key point to bear in mind is that in many societies the state is the only political and economic prize worth having. To be excluded from the state means to be cut off from virtually all public resources. Indeed, one can see this quite literally in parts of Africa where the road and electricity pylons stop abruptly because a district did not support the ruling elite. Ian Taylor (2005) observes that

> control of the state serves the twin purposes of lubricating patronage networks *and* satisfies the selfish desire of elites to enrich themselves,

in many cases in quite spectacular fashion. That is what lies at the heart
of the profound reluctance by African presidents to hand over power
voluntarily and why many African regimes end messily, often in coups.

(Taylor 2005: 4)

He goes on to note how neopatrimonialism or clientelistic 'big man'
politics is alive and well across the region. This is despite enormous
democratisation and 'good governance' interventions over many years. In
other words, a political culture may be surprisingly resilient regardless of
externally promoted institutional engineering.

The third point to make in relation to the state is to note the international
community's near addiction to statebuilding as the standard response to
civil war or political transition. It seems as though the only tool in the
toolbox is state rebuilding (as manifested through the already mentioned
capacity-building programmes, good governance, public sector reform,
etc.). In development contexts, Kenny (2003) notes:

> The state is either the solution, the only way to combat structural
> weaknesses that hold back growth, or it is the problem, tying down the
> invisible hand; or it is the facilitator, vital for the efficient functioning
> of the free market.
>
> (Kenny 2003: 413)

Either way, the state is a key ally or enemy in international efforts to
promote development or reduce conflict.

## Failed states

Yet in some parts of the world, the state is patently a dysfunctional
political and economic model. It has failed in entire regions. Peter
Schwab (2004) notes:

> West Africa seems to be in a permanent state of either volcanic
> eruption or desperate economic crises. Its terrorized and poverty-
> stricken populations are exhausted by apocalyptic furies that have
> besieged them, while the world at large has become both leery and
> fatigued by having to constantly come to the rescue of African states.
>
> (Schwab 2004: 139)

Albert Einstein defined madness as someone repeating an electrical
process even though it didn't work the first time. So if a light switch did
not work at first, it would be irrational to repeatedly turn it on and off
again. But given that statehood (or pre-statehood in the form of some
interim international administrations such as Kosovo or the Palestinian
territories) is the only internationally recognised form of political

organisation, then the international community is addicted to shoring up and rebuilding states through bilateral support, development and military assistance, and reconstruction programmes. The fear of statelessness (regarded by many as a deviant form of political organisation) is very grave indeed. According to one observer, 'Failed or failing states are often Petri dishes for transnational criminal activity such as money laundering, arms smuggling, drug trafficking, people trafficking, and terrorism' (Wainwright 2003: 486).

While immense international resources are poured into shoring up and reconstructing states, it is worth noting that the international system is selectively tolerant of different types of state. This tolerance often depends on three factors: the ability of a state to resist or subvert western influence (for example, China), the strategic importance or unimportance of the state (for example, oil-rich Iraq or strategically marginal Haiti), and the points of economic and geopolitical confluence between the state and leading states in the international political system. Consider the Gulf region for example: the oil-rich monarchies that hold power in the region can at best be described as authoritarian and controlling, and at worst as despotic and tyrannical. That it is illegal for a female to drive a motor vehicle in Saudi Arabia is commentary enough on the level of political suffrage enjoyed by citizens. Although a limited reform agenda is underway in some Gulf states, it is clear that the geo-strategic concerns of leading western states outweigh the desire to upset regional power-holders (Ehteshami and Wright 2007). The worldviews of the ruling elites in the Gulf region are congruent with western political and economic interests and so their unsavoury political backyard is spared scrutiny and intervention. Gulf states invest their oil wealth in western economic markets, buy prodigious quantities of western arms and are on the 'right side' in the war on terror and the Sunni versus Shiite struggle. In one of the many contradictions that defines the international political system, this western laissez-faire attitude to capable and compliant Gulf states contrasts with 'failed' or 'failing' weak states that are not in a position to resist western intervention. As George Orwell might have put it: some states are more equal than others.

# International organisations

That international organisations exist at all is remarkable. The jealousies attending state sovereignty and national interests, as well as the fallout from international crises, have meant that the international institutions of previous eras often resembled short-lived tactical alliances rather than permanent forums for the regulation of international society. Even more remarkable has been the existence of some international institutions for so many decades (the United Nations, World Bank and International Monetary Fund for over six decades, and the European Union – albeit in a greatly modified form – for almost five decades at the time of writing).

## The United Nations

As the planet's premier collective security organisation, the United Nations is the target of immense criticism. Common chants are that it's too inefficient, bureaucratic, slow, corrupt, under-funded and unwieldy (MacFarlane and Khong 2006; Weiss and Daws 2007). Yet, the organisation is merely the sum of its parts (member states) and is a largely accurate reflection of states' relationships with one another and their attitudes towards pooling sovereignty for the collective good. That it tends to be reactive rather than proactive, is highly selective in its interventions, and is inconsistent in its attitude towards state sovereignty is not the fault of international mandarins working in a vacuum in New York and Geneva. Instead, it is the fault of the national governments who have created and maintained the system. While it is easy to criticise the United Nations, it is also easy to overlook the immense (and often unsung) development, conflict amelioration and humanitarian work it undertakes (Berdal 1996: 106). Often this work is conducted through specialist agencies, has long-term impacts, and makes a qualitative difference to the lives of millions in underdeveloped and war-torn states. Thus UN agencies are responsible for the physical security, legal protection, nourishment, shelter and repatriation of substantial numbers of individuals and communities: a fact that is routinely overlooked by those who use broad-brush criticisms against the organisation.

The United Nations has developed as a result of disjointed incrementalism. Rather than planned strategic growth, UN capabilities have developed reactively in the face of crises, with the end of the Cold War simultaneously lifting an immense constraint on its ability to operate and presenting it with a vastly increased workload. It responded in the 1990s by having ever more ambitious operations in an increased number of theatres. The growth in peacekeeping operations occurred despite the UN Charter not mentioning the term 'peacekeeping'. In the post-Cold War period there has been a trend towards 'outsourcing' or 'subcontracting', with the employment of regional organisations, INGOs and NGOs to carry

**Plate 6  A UN 4×4 vehicle: the UN is the planet's premier collective security organisation**

out peace-support and development activities on behalf of the United Nations (Richmond and Carey 2005). On the positive side of the ledger, the UN's post-1990 operations showed that the organisation was adopting a more sophisticated understanding of conflict, especially with regard to the complexities of the relationship between conflict and development. On the negative side of the ledger, there was discomfort at the more robust aspects of some peacekeeping interventions in which peace 'keeping' became peace 'making' and peace 'enforcing' (Boulden 2001). Such qualms echoed those over the notion of 'humanitarian war' and concerns that humanitarian interventions could prolong and intensify war (Janzekovic 2006; Belloni 2007). There were also accusations of 'mission creep', whereby originally modest UN interventions became victim to ever-broadening mandates. This was especially the case in missions that required extensive nation and statebuilding, activities that are necessarily long-term and expensive (Pugh 1997). The term 'mission creep' came to prominence in relation to an originally modest UN effort in Somalia in the early 1990s. What was originally an attempt to secure supply routes for humanitarian aid convoys led to direct conflict between UN contingents and Somali warlords.

The United Nations has undergone significant reform, and embarked on major initiatives, since the 1990s. Its eight Millennium Development Goals helped inject focus into development interventions undertaken by it and its member states. The 2001 Brahimi Report, although not fully implemented, recognised many of the UN's organisational shortcomings. The 2003–6 High-Level Panel on Threats, Challenge and Change considered the new range of transnational threats faced by states and the utility of UN structures and practices to deal with them (Hannay 2005; Stedman 2007). The 2005 establishment of a Peace Building Commission illustrated that member states were willing to systematically take on board the lessons from its previous and ongoing peace support operations.

The principal problem facing the United Nations is the perennial struggle between state sovereignty and the collective good. On many occasions the two are simply incompatible. Neo-conservative elements in the United States are at least honest when they voice their suspicions about multilateralism or the potential of any national or multilateral power source to rival its hegemonic position (Callinicos 2005: 598). As the 2003 Anglo-American invasion of Iraq and its bloody aftermath showed, leading states are willing to override the UN when it suits, but not above appealing for UN assistance when they find themselves in a mess. Important decisions on restructuring the Security Council to make it more representative have been dodged and it is likely that the pattern of disjointed incrementalism will continue.

Other international organisations, particularly regional security and economic organisations, have shown themselves to be increasingly capable of pursuing conflict-amelioration and development agendas. The African Union has ambitious plans for an expansion of its activities but, thus far, its capacity remains limited (Murithi 2005). Moreover, it has not fulfilled its promise of adopting 'African solutions for African problems'. Its definitions of peacebuilding, for example, seem to be cut and pasted from western sources and overlook indigenous and traditional forms of dispute resolution that might be found closer to home (Mac Ginty 2008). The Economic Community of West African States (ECOWAS) did have some success in re-establishing stability in Liberia (though less success in Sierra Leone) in the 1990s. NATO and the European Union are probably examples of the most capable regional security organisations. In part, this is because decision-making is easier among smaller groups of states and because of the wealth of their members.

The Afghan and Iraq adventures are interesting in that they reveal that the primary motivation among leading states is security. But there has been a realisation among these leading states (often in the wake of tough lessons) that the promotion of development is essential to long-term security. The 'secure, hold and reconstruct' military strategy road-tested in Iraq, and the deployment of Provincial Reconstruction Teams in Afghanistan, are testament to the internalisation of development programming within security. Clearly this securitisation and militarisation of development also raises profound ethical questions about humanitarian motives and practices (Gallis 2007: 14).

## International non-governmental organisations

Although not strictly 'international organisations', INGOs have transformed international responses to conflict and development since the 1970s. Organisations such as the International Committee of the Red Cross and Red Crescent, Doctors Without Borders or Oxfam have been important for at least three reasons. First, they have allowed official development assistance, conflict prevention and peacebuilding activities to have a much further reach than traditional bilateral or international organisation activity. INGOs are often cheaper and more flexible than official modes of aid delivery, particularly in cases where they subcontract to local NGOs (Richmond and Carey 2005). Second, INGOs have prompted more cases of development intervention by leading states and international organisations. This has been particularly the case in their ability to 'bear witness' and engage in advocacy, thus bringing humanitarian emergencies and chronic development and conflict situations to the attention of publics and polities. The third, and most significant, point has been the ability of INGOs to play a role in shaping the development, conflict prevention and development assistance agenda of leading states, leading international organisations and international financial institutions. This influence has been by no means total, nor has the process been one way, yet INGOs have been incredibly important in broadening governmental understanding of conflict and making obvious the multiple connections between conflict and development.

Yet some INGOs have been co-opted into the liberal peace project. Rather than acting as bulwarks against the ambitions of rich western states, some INGOs are the principal transmission agents of the liberal peace through their promotion of the good governance and reform agendas (Richmond 2005b). The privatisation of development and humanitarianism (for example, through tender processes for development contracts) leaves many INGOs with little choice. To stay in business (and to stay relevant and to fund their other advocacy work) they must compete for contracts released by governments and international organisations. Yet all contracts come with conditions, and some of these conditions may constrain the original development and conflict-amelioration objectives of the INGO. As Box 2.4 shows, increasing privatisation in the humanitarian and development sectors has raised many practical and ethical questions.

## Box 2.4

### *Privatising security, humanitarianism and development*

The private sector is often considered to be more efficient and cost-effective than state-run organisations. The rigour of the private sector has been increasingly applied to the provision of security, humanitarian and development interventions in some contexts as donor states and organisations seek to limit costs and devolve responsibilities. Private military contractors (PMCs, or what used to be called 'mercenaries') have been employed in Iraq and Afghanistan to protect embassies and reconstruction projects. Controversy has abounded, especially in relation to the immunity from prosecution enjoyed by some PMCs in some contexts (Baer 2007). For states sensitive to headlines of body-bags coming home, non-state partners (whether charitable or private) are an attractive proposition. A number of scholars and aid practitioners, however, have pointed out that the apparent privatisation and securitisation of humanitarianism and development are leading to foundational changes in how we conceptualise 'charity', 'aid', 'neutrality' and 'humanitarianism' (Duffield 2007; Spearin 2008).

Sources: Baer (2007), Duffield (2007), Spearin (2008)

## International financial institutions

UN and INGO personnel are often highly visible in conflict and development environments through their blue helmets, white 4×4s and prominent banners advertising their projects. Yet one set of highly influential international actors are frequently less visible: the international financial institutions (IFIs). The World Bank (originally the International Bank for Reconstruction and Development) and International Monetary Fund date from the era when Adolf Hitler was still in power. The framers of both organisations were conditioned by their experiences of the 1930s, with the contraction of world trade and state attempts to 'beat' economic depression through tariffs. Although the IMF and World Bank are often discussed in the same breath, and although both share the same aim of facilitating free trade, they are 'not identical twins' (Hanlon 1996: 25). The IMF's chief role is to smooth international trade through short-term balance of payments assistance to states. Its main focus is on macro-economic matters and it regards low inflation (achieved by tight government spending regimes) as the most important weapon in the regularisation of trade and the stabilisation of currencies (Pollard 1997: 79). The World Bank has a broader brief, and is focused on development and longer-term interventions. It aims to encourage states to change the structure of their economies so that growth and trade can operate unhindered. A welter of associated bodies and permanent conferences (the General Agreement on Tariffs and Trade, the World Trade Organisation, G8, the United Nations Conference on Trade and Development and the Uruguay and Doha Rounds of negotiations, etc.) assist in the overall aim of promoting free trade.

As was made clear in the Introduction to this book, the international financial architecture has been heavily criticised as being designed to perpetuate the poverty and the disadvantaged positions of developing world states (Stiglitz and Charlton 2005). Thus, the IMF and World Bank are routinely demonised as being 'the high priests of neo-classical orthodoxy' (Shutt 1998: 160) or progenitors of 'predatory globalisation' (Falk 1999). The reasons for this derision are clear: the international financial architecture has facilitated the post-Second World War growth in the disparity between rich and poor states and the income disparities in developing states (Seligson 2003: 2). Falk (1999: 13) characterises the international economy as structurally racist: it is an 'economic apartheid' that reinforces a rich white world and is comfortable with the impoverishment of the non-white world. Joseph Stiglitz (2003), for many years an economist with the IMF, pursues a similar theme: the IFIs prioritise the interests of global capital above those of global community.

Given our interest in the international financial architecture is in how it facilitates and thwarts conflict and development, three points can be made. The first point is that the IFIs are here to stay. Although many commentators paint them as pantomime villains (with considerable justification), there are no alternative sources of international economic regulation waiting in the wings. The IFIs have undergone considerable change throughout their history and have presided over many economic downturns (for example, the 1973 oil and dollar shocks, the 1994–5 Mexican peso crisis and the 1997–8 Asian financial crisis, the 2007–9 market instability and credit crunch). Yet, for all of this mismanagement and the disjointed incrementalism of their institutional evolution, there is no political appetite among leading states for root and branch reform (Harris 1999; Underhill 2001: 191). Despite the iniquities of the situation, societies emerging from civil war or suffering from underdevelopment simply have to work with the IFIs. States emerging from civil wars are unable to avail themselves of reconstruction loans or to conduct international trade unless they sign up to IFI strictures. These strictures may include honouring the external debts of the previous regime, even if that regime lacked a democratic mandate.

The second point concerns the worrying absence of democracy and transparency in the affairs of the IFIs. There is a certain irony here in that while democracy and democratisation are often pushed on states emerging from conflict as the route to guarantee them stability, these states must also enter into deeply undemocratic relationships with the IFIs. Joseph Hanlon (1996: 24) noted how, in the aftermath of a civil war, Bretton Woods officials in Washington had 'more power in Mozambique than any Mozambican, up to and including President Chissano.' Unelected IFI officials have been present at many civil war peace negotiations: they are difficult guests to refuse in that reconstruction assistance is often routed through them. While the World Bank, IMF and other international agents encourage transparency among recipient states, the World Bank's own lack of transparency was illustrated by the controversy surrounding a massive pay rise awarded to its president's girlfriend in 2005. George Monbiot (2006) castigates the IMF as 'the world's most powerful dictatorship'. Decision-making power in the IMF is based purely on financial clout, with states enjoying voting rights commensurate with their contributions to the Fund. The world's eighty poorest states share 10 per cent of voting rights (Monbiot 2006).

The third point is that IFI strictures can have profound impacts on social harmony in the aftermath of a civil war and the ability of a post-civil-war government to fulfil its social provision pledges. This can have serious consequences, since the post-civil-war political dispensation will require a broad base of stakeholders if the peace accord is to hold. IMF and World Bank mantras of 'small government' can severely restrict the ability of governments to honour the 'peace dividend' pledges that accompanied a peace accord. As Addison (2003: 264) notes, 'Decisions made in the early phase of the war-to-peace transition alter the distribution of productive assets and thereby the benefits of growth to the rich and the poor for years to come.' The 2006 Nepalese peace agreement, for example, contains a highly ambitious list of social pledges that would make a 1970s Scandinavian socialist government proud. The peace accord has had a shaky start, and different ethnic groups (previously overshadowed by the Maoist–government struggle) are voicing grievances at their poor share of public resources. Yet the Nepalese state does not have autonomy over how it disburses the contents of the public coffers. There is an acute danger of civil war recidivism, and even if the government were minded to throw money at the problem, tight regulation from the IFIs would make that impossible. Post-independence Timor Leste finds itself in a similar situation. Mass rioting in 2005 and the 2008 assassination bids on the prime minister and president have largely been due to the failure of the government to address socio-economic aspirations. While the IFIs do not have peacekeepers or storm troopers on the battlefields, they are not entirely removed from the dynamics that encourage conflict and development.

## Concluding discussion

To return to the software and hardware analogy, it would seem that an incredibly sophisticated and deft software prevails in the form of the liberal peace. Through a mixture of subtle and not-so-subtle inducements and compliance mechanisms, states are encouraged to conform to an order that reinforces existing power-holders. Its chief aims are to stabilise dysfunctional war-torn states, to promote liberal economics, and to perpetuate the control of leading states (Duffield 2001: 10). The liberal peace regime allows some wriggle room: it has been softened by the human security perspective, will face increasing challenges from a more internationally active China and – in certain circumstances – can be subverted by states and communities. Moreover, there are signs that the liberal peace is suffering from a crisis of confidence and credibility if not a crisis of actual influence (Cooper 2007: 606). While the dominant software is constantly upgraded, the hardware (in the form of international institutions) is clunky, slow and often fails to work. In a sense, the software has found ways in which it can work without hardware, or certainly without the original hardware. To stretch the analogy and risk entering geek territory, leading states and international financial institutions have modified parts of the hardware through the use of 'add-ons' or specialist devices that allow them to induce the international system and its states to operate in ways that suit them.

The institutional factors that shape contemporary conflict and development are undergoing simultaneous processes of continuity and change. The forces of continuity are to be found in the rigidity of a UN Security Council that reflects the 1945 balance of power and in the inflexibility of state sovereignty as interpreted by some states. But there are many signs of change, all of which impact on the ebb and flow of conflict and development and the ability of international institutions to react. The range of factors deemed capable of causing conflict (or instability) and thwarting economic and human development is deemed to have grown in the post-Cold War era. The transnational nature of many of these threats (for example, legal and illegal labour flows or environmental degradation) means that traditional state-centric institutions are often poorly equipped to deal with them. While many international institutions have been changing to anticipate or react to a new range of threats, it is not at all clear that the current suite of collective security organisations and development organisations is the best equipped to deal with these threats. It is an incontrovertible fact that none of the current international or regional security organisations in existence was explicitly formed to deal with contemporary civil war or underdevelopment. Quite simply, the international political system is stuck with the wrong tools for the job.

Having said that, many international organisations have undergone processes of reform and there are growing interconnections between the traditional international units (such as states and collective security organisations) and more modern units in the form of INGOs and organised global capital. Shaw et al. (2006) refer to this as 'complex multilateralism', whereby numerous multilateral associations come together, often on specific issues and for limited time periods. Thus campaigns to address blood diamonds, child soldiers or landmines will see 'mixed-actor coalitions' of states, international organisations, pressure groups and private sector bodies cooperate on a single issue. Great strides have also been made since the end of the Cold War in increasing the awareness of the linkages between conflict and development. Thus international organisations and bilateral donors routinely engage in 'conflict-sensitive development programming', or realise that a post-civil-war peace depends as much on socio-economic inclusion as it does on more overt security or identity-related issues.

There seems to be no end in sight to the perennial problem of reconciling the national interests of states and the need for states to put aside narrow national interests to deal with pressing collective problems such as global warming or poverty. International organisations are the clearing house for many of these tensions. In some cases, such as agreement on the Millennium Development Goals, states have been able to cooperate on joint aspirations. Logjams in international organisations, however, have tempted some states and interests to act either unilaterally, or multilaterally though not through an international organisation. Some commentators have suggested the need for a 'league of democracies' or an alliance of western democratic states who could act without the encumbrance of an unwieldy international organisation (Kagan 2008). The advantage would be swiftness of action and unity of purpose in the face of a humanitarian or complex political emergency. Critics, however, have pointed out that such a league would amount to a charter for interventionism and would conveniently free western states of the need to persuade non-western states of the merits of their case.

## Summary

- Rather than simply look at international institutions, it is also important to look at the principles and values behind the institutions.
- The concept of 'the liberal peace' has been used to describe the peace and development support interventions by leading states, leading international organisations and international financial institutions in war-affected and developing societies. According to critics, the liberal peace is guilty of western bias and equates to neocolonialism.
- While good governance reforms might seem wholly sensible to western eyes, they can have a profound effect on important relationships in target societies. For example, they might alter how citizens interact with and perceive the state and fellow citizens.
- The international financial institutions wield immense economic and political power, but it is difficult to think of alternatives to them.
- The international political system increasingly operates according to 'complex multilateralism' whereby a constantly shifting mix of states, international organisations, INGOs, NGOs and private sector interests coalesce and recoalesce at different times on different issues.

## Discussion questions

1 If the United Nations collapsed, what would you replace it with? What principles should underpin any new collective security organisation?
2 Is there any way around the tension between the national interests of states and the collective needs of a community of states?
3 Are there any serious alternatives to the state as the basic political unit in the international system?
4 What advantages can private sector firms bring to security, humanitarian and development interventions?

# Further reading

Williams, A. (2006) *Liberalism and War*, London: Routledge covers some of the key ideas behind western intervention since 1918. Douglas, M. (1986) *How Institutions Think*, Syracuse, NY: Syracuse University Press provides a seminal account on the inner workings of large organisations. Insider's guides to the role of the IMF and US capital in the developing world can be found in Stiglitz, J. (2003) *Globalization and its Discontents*, New York: Norton, and Perkins, J. (2004) *Confessions of an Economic Hit Man*, San Francisco, CA: Berret-Koehler. An extremely good survey of some of the problems facing INGOs and NGOs is Yanacopulos, H. and Hanlon, J. (eds) (2005) *Civil War, Civil Peace*, Oxford: James Currey. Revealing insights into western interventions in Iraq and Afghanistan can be found in Stewart, R. (2007) *Occupational Hazards: My time governing in Iraq*, Pan Macmillan; Chandrasekaran, R. (2007) *Imperial Life in the Emerald City: Inside Iraq's Green Zone*, London: Bloomsbury; and Rick, T. (2006) *Fiasco: The American military adventure in Iraq*, London: Penguin. A wonderfully honest (and funny) reminder of how western preconceptions sometimes travel poorly can be found in Barley, N. (1983) *The Innocent Anthropologist: Notes from a mud hut*, London: British Museum Publications.

# Useful websites

Most international organisations, international financial institutions and INGOs have content-rich websites. Major international organisations include the United Nations (www.un.org), the European Union (http://europa.eu/), the African Union (www.Africa-union.org), the Organisation of American States (www.oas. org), the League of Arab States (www.arableagueonline.org), and the South Asian Association for Regional Cooperation (www.saarc-sec.org). Some of these organisations have agencies or sections with a specific remit for conflict and/or development. For example, the European Commission's Humanitarian Aid Office (http://ec.europa.eu/echo) and the UN's Peacebuilding Commission (www.un.org/peace/peacebuilding) or Department of Peacekeeping Operations (www.un.org/Depts/dpko). The World Bank (www.worldbank.org), IMF (www. imf.org), Asian Development Bank (www.adb.org) and European Bank for Reconstruction and Development (www.ebrd.com) are all represented online. The final report of the Princeton Project, which reviews threats and opportunities for the United States in the twenty-first century is available at www.princeton.edu/~ppns/report.html.

# 3 People: participation, civil society and gender

## Introduction

Public participation is widely regarded as the elixir or silver bullet of western democracy. Through participation comes legitimacy and with legitimacy comes a discourse to justify a particular course of action. In recent years, 'public participation', 'local participation' and 'local ownership' have become prominent themes in relation to development and peacebuilding processes. This chapter examines the issue of participation in relation to conflict and development. One of the overall themes of this book is that people are often written out of the major decisions that surround war, peace and development. The chapter will illustrate how this 'writing out' occurs and consider the steps that have been taken to include or 'write people in' to political and economic processes connected with war and peace.

A fundamental point to make in relation to the inclusion or exclusion of people from conflict and development processes is that human beings are engaged in constant processes of social stratification and discrimination, whether consciously or unconsciously. Social identity and social categorisation theories tell us that people are continuously engaged in mental processes that attempt to order their social environment (Tajfel 1978; Turner at al. 1987). Often these processes of social categorisation and identification are totally innocuous. A walk across any university campus involves many such (often unconscious) calculations: 'He's a bore, I should avoid him'; 'Look at that awful football jersey – there's no way I would wear that'; 'She's got coffee – good idea'. But in societies with ethnic, racial, religious or political fissures, these calculations can be more harmful and define who is to be included or excluded from political decision-making and who is to be afforded or denied resources. The attitudes of many Israelis towards Arabs and Palestinians (and vice versa) are so deeply ingrained that they may be termed as 'structural'. Entire societies and cultures operate according to politico-cultural norms of discrimination. Perhaps the most significant of these norms can be found in relation to attitudes towards women. The 1997 United Nations Human Development Report noted starkly that 'no society treats its women as well as its men' (UNDP 1997: 39).

Just as individuals and groups are involved in processes of discrimination that lead to decisions about the inclusion or exclusion of other individuals or groups, it is worth noting that states and international organisations engage in similar discriminatory judgements – often with profound consequences. States often use extreme precision in their use or avoidance of terms such as 'genocide', 'civil war' or 'terrorism'. The label 'genocide', for example, carries particular historical connotations and an expectation that states and international organisations will intervene to prevent it. As a result, states tend to be very careful in their use of the term. The way in which states and elements of the international community frame conflicts (an internal matter, of international significance, terrorism) and actors in conflicts (terrorists, an oppressed minority, a legitimate government) can have the effect of including or excluding certain actors from peace processes and post-conflict development processes.

The chapter will begin with a discussion of participation and ways in which states, societies and organisations encourage and discourage participation in development, peace and conflict processes. It will then discuss one of the key platforms for the widening of participation beyond closed sets of institutions: civil society. In the final section, the chapter will concentrate on the issue of gender and conflict, peace and development.

## Participation

As Chapter 2 revealed, many of the structures and institutions connected with conflict and development are elite-led and non-participatory. In fact, parts of the international financial architecture have been deliberately designed in order to maintain an oligopoly (Glenn 2008). Similarly, many political structures are maintained to limit participation, or channel it in particular directions. Consider British politics: it is dominated by three London-based parties who offer essentially the same menu of policy choices. They are united by much more than divides them and are committed to the same political structures – particularly the perpetuation of the dominance of the traditional political parties. Electors in the United Kingdom are shoehorned or directed along a particular path in expressing their political views. Even the most minor demonstrations require police permission and will be monitored. Against a backdrop of the essentially conservative nature of many political and economic structures, there has been a growing realisation by some international organisations, governments, INGOs and others that popular participation is the key to legitimacy and thus sustainability. Interestingly, this realisation has tended to be projected from the western developed world towards the developing world, and has not been reflected back into developed world polities, many of which also suffer from democratic deficits. Across many development and peacebuilding spheres there has been an increased emphasis on 'local participation', 'ownership' and 'partnership'.

Plate 7 An Israeli tank on display at a Hezbollah museum in Lebanon: only a few states can engage in high-tech war

Before examining participation in development and peacebuilding, it is worth noting that popular participation (voluntary and involuntary) is required in conflict (Conteth-Morgan 2004: 112–13). There is a startling disparity between the war-fighting practised by a handful of western electronically advanced states and that practised by combatants on the rest of the planet. Techno-war as practised by the United States or UK requires relatively few direct protagonists. The actual number of troops deployed on the ground is often quite small due to technology and a division of labour. Even operations in Afghanistan, Iraq or Sierra Leone, in which large numbers of US and UK troops are deployed, benefited from tremendous 'back office' support in the form of communications and coordination bases thousands of miles from the combat theatre (US military operations are directed from Tampa, Florida: Mulligan 2002), while many support functions (for example, catering and logistics) may be conducted by private contractors (Boot 2007). By late 2003, there were more private security contractors in Iraq than British soldiers (Traynor 2003). Indeed, the combination of professional militaries and 'outsourcing' to private firms means that many citizens in the United States and the United Kingdom are insulated from the fact that their state is at war.

This position differs enormously from most other violent conflict environments. In such cases, the impact and costs of conflict are often felt closer to home and more difficult to avoid. One of the defining characteristics of the so-called 'new wars' in the post-Cold War period has been the deliberate targeting of civilian populations through 'ethnic cleansing' or the calculated displacement of civilians to cause refugee flows (Kaldor 2005). While this is not unique to the post-Cold War period, the displacement of populations often leads to serious knock-on effects in terms of humanitarian emergencies. All organised violence involves 'violence specialists' or actors who take on specific roles during conflicts (Tilly 2002: 20–1). Yet many conflicts involve the mass mobilisation of people whether through rallies, the formation of popular movements or recruitment into militant or militant support groups (Horowitz 1985: 443–59). While western armed forces may be defined by their high-tech methodologies, many other military forces (state and non-state) are decidedly informal and low-tech, and rely on large numbers of lightly armed combatants. In some cases, this may involve child soldiers, militias (who farm their land by day, but serve as a 'home guard' by night), 'dollar soldiers' (whose loyalty is bought) or clan groups (as in Afghanistan) (Marriage 2007). The presence of young unemployed or underemployed males ('a disposable population' in neo-Malthusian parlance) may aid this mass involvement in violent conflict. The chief point is that war may be a mass-participation activity.

In addition to actual combatants, mobilisations require political support. Pro- and anti-Syrian forces in Lebanon sought to demonstrate their strength through rallies and counter-rallies in 2006–8. 'Ethnic entrepreneurs' may seek to mobilise large crowds in support of their cause, often using public demonstrations as a way of indicating their popular support and thus their legitimacy (Kaufman 2001: 5–7). Nineteenth-century commentator Charles Mackay sums up the danger of mobilising crowds in his *Extraordinary Popular Delusions and the Madness of Crowds* (1852):

> We find that whole communities suddenly fix their minds on one object, and go mad in its pursuit; that millions of people become simultaneously impressed with one delusion, and run after it, til their attention is caught by some new folly more captivating than the first. We see one nation suddenly seized, from its highest to its lowest members, with a fierce desire for military glory; another as suddenly becoming crazed upon a religious scruple; and neither of them recovering its sense until it has shed rivers of blood and sown a harvest of groans and tears, to be reaped by its posterity.
>
> (Mackay 1995: preface to the 1852 edition, xv)

Political leaders, aided by symbolism and references to an historic past (real or imagined), may be incredibly successful in mobilising large numbers of people (Mac Ginty 2003: 235–44). War and conflict become, in many cases, mass events involving large numbers of people as participants or active supporters. Over fifty thousand people were estimated to have taken part in rioting in Kosovo in March 2004 (United Nations Mission in Kosovo (UNMIK) 2004). Importantly, mass participation war and conflict may contrast sharply with the situation that prevails during peace negotiations and subsequent peacebuilding in which the opportunities for popular participation are severely constrained. Populations that felt involved in a 'people's war' may find peace or peace negotiations a much less inclusive process. Box 3.1 illustrates the secrecy that surrounded the origins of the 'Oslo Process' between Palestinians and Israelis.

The example of peace negotiations in the aftermath of civil war illustrates how many political networks are 'closed systems' that have firm boundaries of inclusion and exclusion. In the case of peace negotiations,

## Box 3.1

### *The Oslo Peace Process: a closed system*

The 1990s 'Oslo Process' between Israel and the Palestine Liberation Organisation (PLO) began as clandestine negotiations in a secluded house owned by the Norwegian Ministry of Foreign Affairs on the outskirts of Oslo (Pruitt *et al.* 1997: 177–82). Staff at the house were told that the occupants were academics working to a strict deadline imposed by an exasperated publisher. At the time of the negotiations, it was illegal for Israeli citizens to meet with members of the PLO. The talks were so secret that many senior members of the PLO and the Israeli government did not know of their existence. The talks were a useful way for each side to test the seriousness of their adversary should more formal and detailed negotiations develop. Problems arose when news of the talks was made public (Wolfsfeld 2003: 92–3). Both the Israeli government and the PLO had invested heavily into demonising the other side, so they now had to prepare their respective constituencies for the prospect that it might be possible to make a deal with their historic enemies. The seriousness of this task was made clear with the 1995 assassination of one of the architects of the Oslo Process, Israeli Prime Minister Yitzhak Rabin, by a right-wing Israeli who thought that the peace process would lead to ruin. Those involved in the early phase of the Oslo Process faced a real conundrum: do they try to make advances away from the glare and turbulence of publicity, or do they open up the process to public scrutiny before it has had a chance to take root in the minds of the negotiators? Ultimately, the Oslo Process was not sustained. Crucial in its demise was the differential perception of gains and losses held by Israelis and Palestinians. 'Each side to the conflict has continued to see the "other" as being the sole recipient of all the benefits, while not offering anything in return' (Hermann and Newman 2000: 110–11). It is, of course, overly simplistic to say that this perceptual differential was due solely to a failure by each side to prepare their constituencies for the give and take of a peace process, but the interface between the public and private aspects of a peacemaking process requires careful management.

Sources: Pruitt *et al.* (1997), Hermann and Newman (2000), Wolfsfeld (2003)

this may be due to understandable security reasons; spoiler groups may be tempted to use violence outside the conference room to influence events inside it (Darby 2001). In practical terms, complex negotiations are often best left to small and dedicated teams who have mastery over their brief. In many cases (for example, peace processes involving Sri Lanka or southern Sudan) the talks have taken place away from the locus of the conflict to allow negotiators to concentrate on wider issues without being blown off course by the immediacy of political violence and the attendant headlines. Problems arise when the existence of talks are made public.

Antagonists often invest considerable energy in demonising their enemies, so to turn around and to admit to having talks with 'the enemy' requires a delicate massaging of the message. Similarly, the contents of the talks and an admission that compromises may have to be made, also requires the preparing of constituencies that are more used to being sold messages of complete victory (Darby and Mac Ginty 2003: 267–8).

Opportunities for public involvement in peace negotiations may be limited to public demonstrations to signify a desire for peace (or at least an end to violence), a referendum on a peace accord or new constitution, or the election of a post-peace accord government (Reilly 2003). Given the circumstances, these opportunities may be valuable (for example, if elections had not been held before or for a very long time), yet they can be best described as one-off events rather than sustained processes that allow for continued and meaningful relationships between citizens and wider political processes. Specialist post-conflict programmes may require or invite the direct participation of particular sectors: for example, members of the security forces may be compelled to take part in a truth and reconciliation process or combatants may be required to disarm and take part in retraining programmes. For many people though, a peace process may be something that occurs elsewhere (in a capital city) or their only connection with it may be through the media or word of mouth. Thus, the peace process might be 'a creature of the international community and their co-opted national elites and [have] limited connection with the bulk of citizens in the war-affected state' (Darby and Mac Ginty 2008: 5). There may be few opportunities to affect what Harold Saunders (1999) calls 'a public peace process', in which the citizenry can have a substantive input and broaden out formal political processes to involve a wider constituency.

A growing interest in participation among international organisations, INGOs and NGOs is partially a recognition of the dominance of closed systems and the failings that accrue from excluding key constituencies. The pro-participation consensus is based on a belief that people can become 'stakeholders' in projects and feel that as a result of their investment they have ownership in a process. The theory continues that such locally 'owned' processes are more legitimate and more likely to succeed because local constituencies will be able to mould them to suit local needs and aspirations. In such circumstances, external assistance and direction will not be as necessary and local actors will be able to sustain the process. International organisations, INGOs and NGOs now routinely pay attention to issues of participation regarding it as 'a fundamental human right', a way of enhancing 'the sustainability of the settlement' and a means for 'managing inclusion' (ACCORD 2003).

There has, however, been criticism that many participatory schemes are superficial and less empowering than their advocates would suggest. Cooke and Kothari (2002) point to the 'tyranny of participation', whereby communities in developing world and post-conflict environments are shoehorned into superficial participation mechanisms that suit the requirements of donors (allowing them to tick a box attesting to 'local participation'), but do not necessarily involve local communities in meaningful and sustainable ways. Similarly, Alternative Dispute Resolution techniques have been criticised for their 'coercive harmony' whereby individuals and groups are encouraged to participate but find themselves pressured to reach an accommodation even if it leaves grievances unaddressed and unbalanced power structures in place (Nader 1997). Rather than being truly inclusive, the criticism made in many development and post-conflict environments is that participation mechanisms are just another part of a suite of essentially western mechanisms that are top–down, and conceived and funded in the west. According to this view, many participation mechanisms are actually part of a process of disempowerment. Different cultural explanations of 'participation' may be in operation. Western notions of participation may prioritise institutional and technocratic mechanisms that enable participation. There is a danger of reducing participation to quantifiable, one-off events such as elections or consultation exercises. In other societies, participation may be interpreted in more people-centric and relationship-orientated ways, in which participation is a process rather than an event (Lederach 1995: 26). It is important, though, not to romanticise non-western and indigenous means of popular involvement in political or economic decision-making since many of these processes are not above reinforcing social order and conservatism.

Certain phases of development and peacebuilding processes may be more open to public participation than others. Necessarily, for example, the security and 'stabilisation' phases in the aftermath of a violent conflict might actively exclude people and concentrate power in the hands of military forces and a limited number of 'institution builders'. 'Institutionalism before Liberalisation' (Paris 2004) or the belief that stability and functioning bureaucracy must be achieved before democratisation has been accepted by most states and international organisations in post-war reconstruction contexts. Yet, at some stage, all development and peacebuilding processes require legitimacy. The ways in which political leaders (international and national) seek to build and maintain legitimacy are crucial. In some societies, guerrilla movements have transformed very quickly into political parties (the morphing of the Kosovo Liberation Army into the Kosovo Democratic Party provides one example). While the transition from protagonist to pragmatist is obviously crucial in any post-civil-war transformation, there is a danger that some political parties are too narrowly based and merely continue the civil war by peaceful means (Gormley-Heenan 2001). The case of Robert Mugabe's Zanu-PF in Zimbabwe provides an example of a party reluctant to leave behind its civil war roots. When under pressure it has repeatedly used the language of liberation and evoked the independence struggle against white rule: a good strategy for mobilising supporters but of little help for Zimbabwe's economic woes. Many post-civil-war societies have struggled to find a political process that sustains public interest and participation. High levels of voter turnout in initial post-civil war elections may be replaced by more modest levels. In Guatemala and El Salvador, for example, voter turnout is low and declining (as low as 30 per cent in Guatemala's 1995 election). Lehoucq and Hall (2004) note that poor social provision means that many potential voters do not see the relevance of the electoral system to their lives.

## Civil society

Civil society can be regarded as both an institution and as an actor and is often regarded as a bulwark against arbitrary control by government. It is defined by the Centre for Civil Society (CCS) in the following way:

> Civil society refers to the arena of uncoerced collective action around shared interests, purposes and values. In theory, its institutional forms are distinct from those of the state, family and market, though in practice, the boundaries between state, civil society, family and market are often complex, blurred and negotiated. Civil society commonly embraces a diversity of spaces, actors and institutional forms, varying in their degree of formality, autonomy and power.
>
> (Centre for Civil Society 2008)

Through the media, trade unions, businesses, professional associations, voluntary and church groups, citizens can become organised, voice their concerns, and engage in activities that may support or challenge a government (Burnell and Calvert 2004). In the western political mind, a free civil society is regarded as a key indicator of political freedom.

**Plate 8  An anti-war protest in Boston: civil society often acts as a bulwark against the state**

American sociologist Robert Putnam (2000), whose classic study *Bowling Alone* captured the decline of community in the United States, listed the ways in which US citizens could become politically involved:

> contacting local and national officials, working for political parties and other political organizations, discussing politics with our neighbors, attending public meetings, joining in election campaigns, wearing buttons, signing petitions, speaking out on talk radio, and many more.
>
> (Putnam 2000: 31)

To this we can add the internet, which has opened up a new forum through which political views can be aired. For many of us, civil society is non-contentious, has regular and structured access to the corridors of power, and adds colour to the dull routine of politics.

In authoritarian, deeply divided or post-war societies, however, civil society can play a more delicate role and may face significant difficulties in organising and expressing itself. The Chinese regime, for example, attempts to control civil society, believing that civic organisations should merely be a reflection of state institutions. Thus it has engaged in campaigns of ethnic and religious suppression against Tibetans and

Uighurs, often branding religious groups as separatists or terrorists (Human Rights Watch (HRW) 2005; Cumming 2008). In Pakistan, some of the most vocal protests against General Musharraf's 2007 imposition of emergency military rule came from professional associations of lawyers (Perlez and Rohde 2007). In Sri Lanka, a number of journalists have 'disappeared' or were assassinated during 2006–8, prompting speculation that government agents are intent on suppressing reporting on a renewed military offensive (International Federation of Journalists 2007; Greenslade 2008) (see Box 3.2). The key point is that civil society is often on the front line in development processes, the prevention of conflict, and peacebuilding and reconciliation in the aftermath of conflict. Civil society actors are often most prominent in 'bearing witness' or publicising injustice. However, many actors in conflict and developing contexts make it their business to sideline civil society actors. For example, most peace negotiations include armed groups (state and non-state) but tend to exclude civil society actors.

Recognising the utility of civil society, international organisations and INGOs often regard it as a key transmission agent for development,

---

## Box 3.2

### *Press freedom*

By August 2008, the NGO Reporters Without Borders reported that 18 journalists had been killed and 132 had been imprisoned so far that year. While all states and organisations will attempt to influence the media so that they are reflected in a flattering light, some states and organisations attempt to control or suppress the media. From 2001 onwards, Cambodia has witnessed a property boom. With most land records destroyed during the Khmer Rouge regime 1975–9, property speculators have sought to buy up huge tracts of land for resource extraction and development purposes (Leitsinger 2005). In many instances, this has involved the forcible removal of peasant farmers. Journalists who have sought to expose the land grabbing, and the proximity of senior politicians to the land grabbers, have been harassed (Southeast Asian Press Alliance (SEAPA) 2006). In July 2008, a journalist who had exposed land grabbing was murdered by unknown assailants (Human Rights Watch 2008). The threats to journalists mirrored a wider state unease with civil society organisations that sought to draw attention to the eviction of small farmers and the resulting social hardship. The police and other officials were reported to have confiscated anti-land petitions (Chamroeun and Shelton 2008).

Sources: Leitsinger (2005), SEAPA (2006), Chamroeun and Shelton (2008), HRW (2008)

conflict prevention and peacebuilding. As a result, immense energy and resources are invested into creating or shoring up civil society. It is here that problems can emerge. Western interveners may have a particular concept of civil society in mind that may not always fit with the political, social and cultural norms of the host society. Western actors may attempt to create civil society in the image of their home civil society, oblivious to the fact that a vibrant civil society exists in the post-war or developing world context. A classic example of this comes in the form of the US response to the looting that followed the 2003 Anglo-American invasion of Iraq (Mac Ginty 2004). According to US military commanders, the problem was that there was no civil society which could control the civilian population and coordinate attempts to repatriate looted goods with their original owners (BBC 2003). The view that Iraq was bereft of civil society was widespread. According to Toby Dodge, 'Before the liberation of Baghdad it was impossible to talk about civil society in Iraq . . . autonomous collective societal structures beyond the control of the Ba'athist state did not survive' (cited in Pirouz and Nautré 2005: 3–4). Yet, notwithstanding the brutalities of the Saddam Hussein regime, there was some sort of civil society in place: mosques, family groups, professional associations, local Red Crescent societies and other networks. Certainly these networks were very far removed from the plural and voluntary forms of civil society found in western liberal democracies. Yet, to assert that there is 'no civil society' may overlook various forms of social capital that may not be immediately visible to western eyes.

In many post-war societies, western interveners have taken upon themselves to create civil society, often in the image of western models (Prusher 2003). Through 'local capacity building' schemes and the direct funding of NGOs, international actors can create a civil society that is recognisable to them, but may not necessarily have deep and effective roots in the host society (Adamson 2002: 200). One may be forced to ask: what is the essential purpose of this new civil society? Its key role is often to provide a recognisable interface with which international organisations and INGOs can engage. The connection between civil society and the host society may be thin, limited to a particular strata of the host country that has been artificially created by international actors. The new civil society may be unsustainable because of its dependence on western funding streams. A western created and inspired civil society, or the 'democracy sector', is often highly visible in post-war societies. It is often urban, metropolitan and English-speaking (Mac Ginty 2006: 52). Indeed, in many cities, it often inhabits the same physical space as the INGO sector that was responsible for spawning it, and fuels the same micro-economy of vehicle hire, western-style coffee shops and bars, and a conference support sector. The key issues with civil society in any context are the extent to which it can be inclusive, voluntary and act as a real counterweight to state institutions. These issues are particularly acute in deeply divided societies in which society may be structured in a way that excludes or discriminates against particular groups. Elaborate structures (for example, human rights commissions) or legal codes (that outlaw discrimination) may be created in the wake of a civil war, but it does not always follow that institutional engineering will bring with it changes in societal behaviour and thought. Donald Horowitz (2005: ix) warns of the 'adverse consequences' of overly prescriptive constitutional designs.

It is worth stressing that the 'creation' of civil society by external agents and consequent problems between the new civil society and the host society are by no means restricted to post-conflict settings. The phenomenon of the artificial civil society, especially the democracy-promotion sector, is common in many non-conflict developing contexts.

Importantly, civil society need not be restricted to one polity or location. Civil societies can be transnational, especially so in a globalised and digitally connected age. Indeed, given that so many conflict and development-related problems are transnational, it makes sense that civil society mirrors this. Moreover, some locations are so unwelcoming to dissenting civil society organisations, that the only meaningful opposition can come from outside the state boundaries in the form of diaspora organisations.

## Gender

Discussion of gender issues in relation to conflict is made difficult by a potential minefield of stereotyping in which women are characterised as life-givers, nurturers and generally pacific, while men are depicted in the warrior mode (Jacoby 2008: 92). Such stereotypes are best avoided. There is also a tendency in some literature and practice to lump women together as 'victims' or an undifferentiated category without agency. Having opened with a caveat, we can then say that development, conflict and peace impact on men and women in different ways, with the burdens and benefits shared unevenly. But we cannot make blanket statements that have universal applicability; clearly circumstances and context matter.

The principal gender distinction between men and women in times of conflict is that men are often (but not always) the main combatants, while women often perform (but not always) ancillary or support roles (Turshen and Twagiramariya 1998; Rehn and Johnson Sirleaf 2002). But as has been pointed out frequently in this book, contemporary civil wars and contexts of political suppression are very far removed from the classical notion of warfare with professional militaries and clear lines of distinction between combatants and non-combatants. This blurring of the demarcation between combatants and non-combatants has implications for how war impacts on men and women. Often entire ethnonational groups are targeted or mobilised, regardless of gender. Within these groups men and women may be affected in different ways (women more prone to sexual violence or men more prone to arrest and torture) but the group may suffer the same overall experience.

Development processes and the ending of wars provide 'transition moments' in which it is possible to make significant societal changes, for example in relation to land reform, public access to power, or the treatment of women. It is not always clear that these opportunities are taken. Certainly in peace negotiations, issues of territory, security and constitutional design are often prioritised before 'secondary' issues such as gender, truth recovery or social inclusion. If, at best, peace processes can be labelled as 'gender blind', then they bring with them the danger that they reinforce the existing patriarchy. It may be the case that external actors, such as foreign governments and INGOs, favour the inclusion of gender reform in peace negotiations or the formulation of a new constitution. Local actors may not agree: either they may not see the issue as urgent or they may see it as undesirable as it confronts dominant cultural norms. Or local civil society may advocate gender reforms that mark a significant advance for the country in question but are not as radical as some western actors would favour. This raises an interesting series of questions: whose definition of gender equality is to be followed? What are the main components of any gender equality programme? Will the promotion of gender equality place women in danger? Such 'clashes of culture', between western norms and indigenous practices, are common in virtually every aspect of development and post-conflict reconstruction. It is important to note that 'western' and 'indigenous' do not comprise discrete categories: they vary enormously and all social organisations and practices are – to some extent – hybrids. But the key struggle between western and indigenous norms persists. It manifests itself in western notions that there are 'proper' forms of social organisation and governance and development programmes aimed at promoting such 'proper' norms and practices. Conflict may arise as different elements in developing and post-conflict societies may attempt to resist, accept or subvert external development interventions and the cultural baggage associated with them.

It is one thing to outlaw gender discrimination, but it is another thing to change the cultural norms and thought processes that support it. As Antonia Potter (2008: 105) notes, 'reality lags far behind rhetoric on women's involvement in peace processes'. Certainly an impressive legal and normative framework has been erected internationally and in many national contexts over the past few decades to protect the rights of women and encourage their full participation in political life. The 1979 Convention on the Elimination of All Forms of Discrimination against Women, the 1995 Beijing Declaration and Platform of Action and the 2000 UN Security Council Resolution 1325 on Women, Peace and Security, all count as international landmark documents for the inclusion of women. These, and other initiatives, are testament to the incredible energy of women's movements that often operate in unwelcoming environments. Crouch (2004) calls women's mobilisation 'a great democratic phenomenon' that has included

> extreme radicals; sober reformist policy-makers; cunning reactionaries taking the movement's messages and reinterpreting them; both elite and popular cultural manifestations of many kinds; the gradual suffusion into the conversation of ordinary people of elements of the language of an initially esoteric movement.
>
> (Crouch 2004: 62)

Yet, as Potter (2008) politely observes,

> it might not be unreasonable to worry that the slow pace of change implies that misogynist or bigoted views continue to hold a certain amount of sway in the most progressive and liberal societies, even if unconsciously . . . A review of the literature and case studies on post-conflict situations, reveals . . . a depressing paucity of examples of implementation.
>
> (Potter 2008: 107)

It is sobering to think of the enormous gender differentials that exist despite the enormous political, economic and social change experienced by many societies since the 1950s and the massive development and peace-support interventions since the end of the Cold War. Janet Hunt (2004b) sums up the situation thus:

> Women are said to be 70 per cent of the world's poor; have only about 10 per cent of all parliamentary seats in most countries; and in developing countries, on average, they earn only 73 per cent of male

earnings. There is not a single developing country in which women
and men enjoy equal rights under the law. In particular, women are
discriminated against in areas such as their right to land and property,
and their right to conduct business independently. The result is that
women are more vulnerable to poverty than men, especially as a result
of widowhood, separation or divorce, and the consequent loss of
access to productive assets.

(Hunt 2004b: 243)

Many development interventions have sought ways in which to include
women in economic growth. Thus women's participation or inclusiveness
is a built-in part of many development projects or programmes (see Box
3.3 on micro-finance). The hope is that multiple small schemes will have
a cumulative impact, not only on the lives of women but also on the
societal and structural factors that dictate women's position in society.

---

## Box 3.3

### *Women's empowerment through micro-finance initiatives*

Many micro-credit or micro-finance initiatives have had a deliberate gender
dimension. Indeed, in 2006 seven out of ten micro-finance clients were believed
to be women (Armendáriz and Broome 2008). Small loans have been targeted at
women in the hope that the resulting small businesses will first help alleviate
poverty for them and their families, and second act as a means of empowerment.
Women have been given loans to establish themselves as small-scale chicken
farmers or to come together as a cooperative to market their handicrafts (Bigsten
2003: 115). Mayoux (2002) notes how

> Microfinance programmes have significant potential for contributing to
> women's economic, social and political empowerment. Access to savings
> and credit can initiate or strengthen a series of interlinked and mutually
> reinforcing 'virtual spirals' of empowerment. Women can use savings and
> credit for economic activity, thus increasing incomes and assets and control
> over income and assets.
>
> (Mayoux 2002: 76)

There has been something of a bandwagon championing micro-credit. The UN
declared 2005 the 'Year of Micro-credit' and the Grameen Bank (a Bangladeshi
initiative that has subsequently spread to twenty-eight countries) was awarded a
Nobel Prize. There is no doubting that micro-credit schemes have economically
empowered some women, and there is evidence that there have been additional
one-off benefits in terms of social capital and public perceptions of women

(Sanyal 2006). Critics, however, argue that not only are the economic benefits of micro-credit schemes often overblown, but also the schemes may not be as liberating as their advocates suggest. For example, it is suggested that if economic empowerment is not linked to other empowerment (for example, greater legal powers for women such as the right to buy and sell land in certain countries) then stand-alone micro-credit schemes will have limited impact (SIDA (Swedish International Development Cooperation Agency) 2006). Others have noted that indebtedness loads women with an additional burden and may bring them into conflict with men in the home. Just as importantly, without structural change to the organisation of the economy (almost impossible given the power of international economic forces), any changes linked with micro-credit schemes or pro-poor growth strategies are likely to be sporadic and dependent on local circumstances.

Sources: Mayoux (2002), Bigsten (2003), Sanyal (2006), SIDA (2006), Armendáriz and Broome (2008)

## Concluding discussion

Many war-torn or deeply divided societies are marked by very strong social capital, but this tends to be 'bonding' rather than 'bridging' social capital. Bonding social capital, as the term suggests, denotes group cohesion and refers to strong social ties and shared beliefs among a single group, such as Tamils in Sri Lanka. Bridging social capital refers to social ties and shared beliefs that encompass multiple groups, for example Sinhalese, Tamils and Muslims in Sri Lanka. Lebanon provides a good example of a society in which bonding social capital predominates. It has many social organisations and has a strong history of volunteerism. Divisions in Lebanese society however, mean that many social and civil society organisations are located in and operate for one community. Thus different groups have their own media outlets, charitable organisations and social spaces. In themselves, these single-identity organisations and venues often provide very useful social functions. But taken in the context of a deeply divided society, they can be regarded as helping to perpetuate division, stereotypes and insecurity (Morrow 2006: 3–8). Civil society in Lebanon, Sri Lanka, Northern Ireland and other deeply divided societies can be exclusive rather than inclusive, and decidedly uncivil. The task of transforming bonding social capital (which can be intuitive, comfortable, inexpensive and good fun) into bridging social capital (which can be awkward, artificial and expensive) can be incredibly difficult. Hectoring from civil society 'do-gooders' and expatriate 'blow ins' is unlikely to work. The most effective means of 'civilising' deeply divided societies tend to be indirect. Rather than peace projects that consciously attempt to 'correct' a dysfunctional society or 'teach' its members to alter their behaviour, the most meaningful changes in attitudes and behaviour often occur as a by-product of other activities. Thus, for example, if citizens from different traditions can mix in pursuit of a common goal (for example, through employment or accessing public goods) then barriers can break down. Most importantly, such intergroup links are likely to be sustainable and not dependent on the continuation of time-limited project funding. It is not always clear that an internationally created civil society is the best vehicle for this 'civilising' mission. Economic development seems to be a far better vehicle, but as other chapters in this book demonstrate, such development needs to be empowering rather than limiting, inclusive rather than exclusive, and contributory to the local economy rather than purely extractive.

A fundamental issue running through this book is culture and the potential of western norms and practices connected to conflict, peacebuilding and development to clash with local, indigenous or traditional norms and practices. We should, of course, be careful not to build a strict dichotomy in which everything from 'the west' (by no means a discrete category) can be described as top–down, legalistic and rational, and everything found *in situ* in developing and post-conflict environments as bottom–up, organic and traditional. There is a very real danger of romanticising the local and the traditional. At heart is the question of the appropriateness of western intervention and the appropriateness of the type of intervention. A case by case approach is best. In some cases, western states and actors are the only ones with the capability to effect change. In other cases, the actions of western states or actors undermine the capability of local states and actors. Many development and peacebuilding contexts are the scene of a cultural conflict between what might be described as variations of western liberalism, and local belief systems and practices of social and political organisation. These conflicts revolve around the extent to which liberalism is adopted, enforced or resisted.

It is worth ending a chapter on participation by restating the agency of local populations. It is tempting to depict local communities as passive actors who receive or consume conflict, peace and development that is made elsewhere. Certainly the international and transnational nature of conflict and development means that there are few hermetically sealed contexts on the planet. All societies are penetrated by external forces to some degree or another, and the sheer scale of development and peace-support interventions is awesome in some contexts. But we should not overlook the local. Keesing (1992: 2) stresses the importance of seeing 'peripheral populations as active agents in shaping and controlling their engagement with the outside world, giving local meaning to alien ideas, institutions and things, in various ways resisting them.' Local communities have indeed power to absorb, renegotiate, subvert and resist external pressure. Clearly, this power will differ from context to context, but one of the most remarkable aspects of globalisation and liberal peace interventions is the extent of local variation. If nothing else, this local variation is a sign of participation in development, conflict and pacific processes.

## Summary

- Different types of conflict, peacebuilding and development have different ways of excluding and including people.
- Peacebuilders and those engaged in development processes often struggle to establish wide levels of popular participation in their projects.
- Civil society is often regarded as an important bulwark against the unrestrained actions of governments or corporations, but there is a danger that western notions of civil society are regarded as best.
- Development and peacebuilding processes consistently sideline women.
- There is a serious clash between western notions of gender rights and notions of gender rights in non-western contexts.
- At the centre of many conflicts and tensions between western and non-western actors is culture: an issue that western observers often overlook.

## Discussion questions

1  How should development projects attempt to gain popular legitimacy and acceptance in the context of a developing country?
2  What avenues of political participation are available to you in your own country?
3  Must civil society be open to all groups, especially in a deeply divided society?
4  Should women in Afghanistan enjoy the same rights as women in America?

# Further reading

Issues of culture (and how we interpret other cultures) are very important to inclusion and exclusion in development and conflict. Good starting points are Chabal, P. and Daloz, J.P. (2006) *Culture Troubles: Politics and the interpretation of meaning*, London: Hurst, and three modern classics: Huntington, S. (1993) The clash of civilizations?, *Foreign Affairs* 72(3); Kaplan, R.D. (1994) The coming anarchy, *Atlantic Monthly*, February; and Said, E. (1979) *Orientalism*, London: Vintage. Anthropology, journalism and personal testimony often give the best perspectives on the impact of conflict on women. See, for example, Drakulic, S. (1994) *Balkan Express: Fragments from the other side of war*, London: Perennial. See also Enloe, C. (2000) *Maneuvers: The international politics of militarizing women's lives*, Berkeley, CA: University of California Press.

# Useful websites

Many international organisations and international non-governmental organisations have information on their websites labelled 'participation' or 'local partners' though it is useful to consider where the power lies in relationships between local and international actors. See, for example, the Asian Development Bank (www.adb.org/Topics/) or ECHO – the European Commission's Humanitarian Aid Office (ec.europa.eu/echo/index_en.htm). The United Nations Development Fund for Women (UNIFEM) website (www.unifem.org) contains very useful information on gender, development and conflict. Other development related organisations, such as the World Bank (www.worldbank.org) or USAID (www.usaid.gov) contain material on the gender dimension of their programmes. You may have to use the search function on these organisation's websites. See also the gender-related information maintained by Human Rights Watch (www.hrw.org/women/conflict.html), the Hunt Alternatives Fund (www.huntalternatives.org), International Alert (www.international-alert.org) and Amnesty International (www.amnesty.org).

# 4 Conflict resolution, transformation, reconciliation and development

## Introduction

Chapters 4, 5 and 6 are essentially about attempts to effect 'transitions' from conflict and war to a kind of 'peace'. To put it in the words of the OECD's (2007) *Handbook on 'Security Sector Reform'*:

> Recent debate within the international community has centred on the challenge of insecurity and conflict as a barrier to political, economic and social development. If states are to create the conditions in which they can escape from a downward spiral where insecurity, criminalisation and under-development are mutually reinforcing, socio-economic and security dimensions must be tackled simultaneously. The traditional concept of security is being redefined to include not only state stability and the security of nations, but also a clear focus on the safety and well-being of their people.
>
> (OECD 2007: Foreword)

The language of the 'failed state' has now become universal and could be said to apply to many of the cases that now obsess developed world governments and intergovernmental organisations (IGOs) alike. By this is often meant what Ghani and Lockhart (2008) refer to as the 'sovereignty gap': as they define it, the gap 'which exists between the *de jure* sovereignty that the international community affords such states and their *de facto* capabilities to serve their populations and act as responsible members of the international community' (Ghani and Lockhart 2008: 3–4).

This chapter on the challenges of conflict resolution and reconciliation, Chapter 5 on 'reconstruction', and Chapter 6 on the role of humanitarian aid in violent conflicts, harbour a common concern, to examine whether the existing mechanisms used by theorists and practitioners of conflict alleviation are of any real utility to solve the problems caused by conflict and the associated development dilemmas. They also ask whether those who plan and study development in general understand the needs of, and constraints on, those who try to manage, settle, resolve or transform conflicts on one hand (the 'institutions' that we have identified), and the people who are the supposed beneficiaries on the other. Or are those who are supposed to be helped by these obviously linked concerns slipping through the gaps between them? Do the military, bureaucratic and other mechanisms of the international community fail to come to grips with the complexities of how to bring about peace through development, to agree on the appropriate mechanisms, and to better attune these mechanisms to local necessities? However, we are fully aware that, as Tony Addison has put it: '[i]f lack of analysis were a real barrier to ending war, we would be much further forward in achieving real peace in poor societies' (Addison 2005: 409). We all need to approach such difficult questions with due humility.

These three chapters collectively will therefore, first, look at the main strategies employed by the international community or individual powers or groups to try and do something about the conflicts and wars of which we have so far described the genesis. This can be by way of gentle or more muscled intervention, often referred to generically as 'peacebuilding', which we will discuss at some length on pages 96–8. Second, they will ask how successful such strategies have or have not been. Third, they will ask why such strategies have failed or succeeded and how we might try other tactics, up to any including the possibility of total non-intervention.

In all these considerations we have to take into account that the overarching categories we use are shorthand for much more complex and integrated issue areas. Reconstruction, the delivery of aid, or other peacebuilding attempts cannot be separated from attempts at conflict resolution or 'reconciliation' after wars. They may take place sequentially, or simultaneously, while the violence continues at varying levels of intensity (see the debate on 'contingency' in Fisher and Keashley 1990). Equally, each of these concepts is a *matrioshka* doll of other concepts – disarmament, demobilisation and reintegration (DDR) of former combatants being one important embedded 'doll' that will be explored in Chapter 5.

This chapter will, first, look at the concepts that can be used for understanding the practices of conflict resolution (or as we prefer, 'transformation'), as most famously epitomised by attempts to bring about peace in the Middle East. That section will encompass a discussion of the differences between bottom–up and top–down approaches to conflict settlement, management and resolution or transformation as they are discussed in the mainstream literature. It will, second, look at other techniques and ideas that have been developed to try and heal communities after wars, and in particular techniques of 'reconciliation' and 'retributive justice' through truth and reconciliation commissions and war crimes tribunals. The overarching philosophical questions that underlie this inquiry and that we will engage with will be: how can we arrive at a shared understanding of the past, and of 'truth', and how can we envisage the 'reintegration' of a society damaged by war, or as Rigby (2001: 12) puts it, the 'envisioning of a common future together'?

## Dealing with conflict: from 'settlement' to 'sustainability'

In the 1990s there were approximately five intrastate conflicts for every one international war, and the overwhelming evidence is that these 'civil' conflicts have had a habit of becoming regional problems, as we can see in the contagion effect in many parts of the world (Long and Brecke 2003: 5). This is evident in West Africa, where Liberia, Sierra Leone and arguably Côte d'Ivoire have been sucked into a regional conflict; Central and East Africa, where Rwanda, Burundi, the Democratic Republic of Congo, Uganda, Zimbabwe and Kenya – among others – have become part of an arc of conflict; the Horn of Africa, with Eritrea, Ethiopia, Somalia, Sudan and Chad forming varying geometries of interstate and intrastate conflict since the end of the Cold War; and in many other parts of the world, as with the archipelago of Indonesia, where East Timor is an integral part of a network of conflicts.

The above, very selective, list of civil conflicts that have erupted since about 1990 gives a clue as to why war has become both much less devastating on one level while simultaneously being seen as more vicious. Arguably, contemporary wars are not nearly as terrible as the Indonesian civil war of 1965, the Biafran war of 1967–70, Cambodia in 1975–9, not to mention the appalling displacements and death tolls of the two world wars and the Chinese, Russian or Spanish revolutions (Kalyvas 2001: 110). The Dutch think-tank PIOOM (Interdisciplinary Research

Programme on Root Causes of Human Rights Violations) reported that the 1990s had one of the lowest number of battle deaths of the twentieth century ('World Conflict and Human Rights Map' by PIOOM, atf_world_conf_map.pdf). One explanation of this seeming contradiction is that the fighting in previous decades was between industrial powers fighting traditional wars, a 'settlement' of conflict through war, though even here the evidence is of civil wars always having been more numerous than interstate wars (Mack 2006: 6–8). The answer maybe lies in changed perceptions of war itself.

During the last twenty years or so of the Cold War, the Powers (and especially the United States and the Soviet Union) slowly realised that the use of force had its limits as a way of creating peaceful outcomes to conflict. In the early post-Cold War era, with the exception of the intervention in Iraq in 1990–1, the levers of 'hard' power were less willingly used by democratically cautious western states that saw no evident national interest at play for them in many 'obscure' conflicts. Powers now aimed to try and bring about internally 'sustainable' ends to wars, ones that did not need continual revisiting. It became more fashionable, and responded well to a post-Cold War desire for a 'peace dividend', to discuss the use of 'soft' power (Nye 2005), and in particular a rise in the idea that conflicts could be talked down in workshops and off the battlefield. Joseph Nye (2005) defined this as follows:

> [Soft power] is the ability to get what you want through attraction rather than coercion or payments. It arises from the attractiveness of a country's culture, political ideals, and policies. When our policies are seen as legitimate in the eyes of others, our soft power is enhanced.
>
> (Nye 2005: Preface)

The peaceful transitions in South Africa, Mozambique, most of Latin America, even Israel/Palestine (with the Oslo accords of 1993) and, most of all, in Eastern Europe, led to a swathe of books touting the benefits of 'Track One' and 'Track Two' problem-solving, mediation and the like (see pp. 99–105 for more discussion on these distinctions). There was, in the words of Samuel Huntington (1993b), a 'third wave of democratization' that seemed to bring a tantalising possibility that war was now 'obsolete'. Huntington soon reversed his own optimism by declaring the *Clash of Civilizations* (Huntington 1996).

A real change began to happen at the end of the 1990s as a result of the terrible events in Former Yugoslavia and Rwanda in 1994–5. In the late 1990s, and even more so after that, there was a resurgence in the use of hard power in 'pre-emptive' mode in Afghanistan and Iraq and a refusal to negotiate with 'insurgents' in the 'war on terror'. Some writers believe that the UN and some major western states have now embarked on a policy of 'international pacification' and 'pre-emptive regime change' (Duffield 2007 is one such example) which leaves no room for the kinder and less muscular forms of conflict resolution.

It might be more accurate to say that a belief in the use of hard power, as opposed to softer versions, as a way of bringing about an end to conflicts in developing (and more 'developed') countries fluctuates in effect in line with optimism or pessimism about the prospects for different tools to end conflicts and the self-confidence of the underlying belief in prospects for a 'liberal peace'. So much ink has been spilled trying to show the differences between conflict 'settlement', 'management' and 'resolution', often referred to as the 'three generations' trying to bring about peace. However, it must be understood that different approaches are often tried simultaneously or in sequence depending on the conflict being dealt with. So any attempt to be prescriptive about the use of such approaches has to be cautious and hedged around with caveats. History has an unfortunate habit of proving wrong any linear explanation of 'what is happening'.

So why attempt to define such terms? The reason is because they are so described in much of the literature on conflict and because they tend to coincide with particular approaches to international politics more generally. But first we need to put these concepts within the broader emerging paradigm of 'peacebuilding'.

## The practice of peacebuilding and conflict transformation

As Jeong has pointed out, '[t]he practice of peacebuilding originally evolved out of an institutional adjustment to peacekeeping and humanitarian intervention responding to internal conflict situations'. It 'involves a wide range of sequential activities, proceeding from cease-fire and refugee resettlement to the establishment of a new government and economic reconstruction' (Jeong 2005: 1). But it has to be said that such neat definitions often hide real epistemological and practical problems.

Sarah Nayani aptly quotes Knight, who suggests that peacebuilding is more 'described than defined' (Knight 2003, cited in Nayani 2006: 32). The very term often comes with or without hyphens and it still does not appear in the *Oxford English Dictionary*. Johan Galtung (1996) describes his version of 'peacebuilding' as 'building structural and cultural peace' possibly as vague as his core idea of 'structural violence'; John Paul Lederach (1997) writes of it encompassing the 'full array of processes, approaches and stages needed to transform conflict toward more sustainable, peaceful relationships' (Galtung 1996; Lederach 1997, both cited in Nayani 2006: 32–3).

Consequently we might say that it has changed in line with historical context, not only in the 'target' areas where conflict is a problem, but also in the institutional reaction to these areas, for the United Nations itself is also subject to a certain amount of definitional imprecision when trying to explain what peacebuilding aims to do. But what is common to all peacebuilding approaches is a realisation that violent conflict (not conflict per se) 'is inflicting immense damage on the societies and economies of the developing world'. Collier and Hoeffler (2004) have been quoted as estimating that a 'typical' developing country civil war inflicts at least US$64.2 billion of economic and social damage (Collier and Hoeffler 2004, quoted in Addison 2005: 406).

Hence, where they are appropriate and there is some sort of peace to keep, in post-Soviet Russia, Former Yugoslavia and many other parts of the previously communist world, economic and political levers have been consciously used by the United Nations and the west to encourage peace-observing behaviours. This is often a key part of what is generally referred to as 'conflict prevention'. The United Nations (UN 1992, 1995, 2000), the Carnegie Commission on Preventing Deadly Conflict (1997) and many other bodies have tried to develop strategies that would identify signs of impending conflict *before* conflict broke out; to *prevent* their spread; to *resolve* the underlying causes and to *heal* the wounds they cause.

Consequently, no matter which political or economic standpoint one takes, there is a consensus they have to be looked at in tandem (Addison 2005). This 'peacebuilding consensus' has been fed by 'humanitarianism' and accelerated by the process of globalisation itself. 'Public and political pressure and awareness' has become tied up with a generalised desire to '[re]construct a liberal peace' around the planet that all can benefit from. The danger is that governments and IGOs often attempt to find a 'one-size-fits-all' model to implement these laudable intentions, often with disastrous results (Richmond 2007: 74).

The core aim of all of the theoretical and policy tendencies embedded in these terminological turns is the pursuit of a 'sustainable' or even a 'stable' peace. This was classically defined by Karl Deutsch as being when there is the 'real assurance that the members of [a] community will not fight each other physically, but will settle their disputes in some other way', which he defined as a 'security community' (Deutsch 1957, quoted in Kacowicz *et al.* 2000: xi). More recently, it has been defined as where '[political] leaders craft political institutions that will sustain the peace and foster democracy in ethnically divided societies after conflicts such as civil wars' (Roeder and Rothchild 2005: 3). Of course this is a tall order, but in terms of what humans crave as a 'normal' state of affairs not one that would strike most people in the 'North' or 'West' as over-demanding. The problem is that what is 'undemanding' for us in the global North would be an extreme luxury for most people in developing countries. At its heart such a definition also begs a number of sub-questions: what is the necessary link between 'democracy' and the 'solutions to ethnically divided societies', and who says what a 'civil war' is?

This illustrates the vital point that underlying much of the debate about conflict resolution and reconstruction, as with many of the other debates described in this book, is the concept of the 'liberal peace'. In Chapter 2 we talked about how traditions of 'liberal internationalism' have ceased to be one among a palette of potential ideological and policy platforms for dealing with the causes, results and aftermath of conflict. These traditions have become transformed into a much more dogmatic belief that the encouragement or imposition of liberal democracy and capitalism will somehow solve all the problems associated with conflict and civil wars in developing countries. As many development specialists are now keen to point out, this 'West is Best' presumes a 'hierarchy of cultures' and all the dangers of determinism inherent in such thinking (Chabal and Daloz 1999, 2006: vii).

One of the purposes of this chapter, as with the previous and subsequent ones is therefore to ask if such a 'one-size-fits-all' approach can live up to its billing as a universal solution to the problems of post-conflict situations in developing countries. Another is to revisit the central premise of this book, that people have tended to be ignored in discussions about conflict and development. The ways in which they are excluded from the discourse of the search for the 'liberal peace' and the reality of its imposition by intergovernmental institutions and western and developing country governments alike seems to us to be a main driver in making sure that 'resolution' efforts often, even usually, fail.

# Conflict 'settlement', 'management' and 'resolution'

There has been a long-standing tradition in international relations and conflict analysis of saying that different practical approaches to dealing with conflict can be seen as existing in parallel with certain 'paradigms' of international relations theory. This was particularly striking in the 1980s and early 1990s in the so-called 'inter-paradigm' debate in international relations. This is not the place to enter into that debate, or the ways in which it has been superseded by a much more subtle conversation about 'critical', even 'postmodern' theorising about the nature of international activity. These thinkers have in particular attacked the ethos of thinking that 'we' can intervene to resolve 'their' conflicts, a way of thinking that has accelerated with the recent actions in Afghanistan, Iraq and the Middle East more generally. We will touch on these issues below. They are nonetheless key ideas, for as Jeong (2008) points out, all of these techniques and theories aim for a 'just outcome that is not only fair to participants but also meets the broader ethical concerns of a given society, and those of humanity' (Jeong 2008: 243). That is a tall order and unsurprisingly there are many who scoff at its impracticality.

However, the terms that were developed then are still used currently and widely so we need to understand how they might apply to particular ways of dealing with conflict by theorists and practitioners alike. It might also be mentioned that this is not a *linear* debate. Conflict analysis has its fashions and obsessions like every other field of human endeavour, and certain theorists and practitioners use the terms we will now explore in ways that defy exact categorisation. There is no clearly and widely accepted *one* approach that all in this field agree on, just an ongoing, indeed circular debate (Ramsbotham *et al.* 2005 give a good overview of this).

We can break this debate down in many ways, but we think it most useful to look at it first in the simple terms of top–down or bottom–up and then at how this might translate into more precise terminology.

## Top–down or bottom–up?

By *top–down* is meant all of those strategies that have been deployed by third party representatives of a state or IGO. This is often referred to as 'Track One' diplomacy. These kinds of action are in most cases undertaken before the conflict or war has come to the stage of a ceasefire. Sometimes this can be supplemented by 'Track Two' action, which is usually conducted by unofficial players, such as NGOs or officials acting in an unofficial capacity and behind the scenes, or even academics acting entirely on their own without any form of support.

Track One has been given huge prominence by the activities of US presidents and their advisers (like Henry Kissinger) in the Arab–Israeli context since the 1970s starting with the Camp David discussions of 1977 (Touval 1982). The main advantages of Track One are the legitimacy such discussions provide; the resources that can be marshalled in support of any agreement (military and economic aid for example, as has been the case of Israel and Egypt since the late 1970s), and the guarantee of media interest in, and usually support for, such efforts. The disadvantages are that the Powers will use such occasions for their own interests and will cajole, bully or otherwise intimidate the parties and not in any way transform their basic unhappy relationship.

By *bottom–up* is meant the introduction of a methodology for the local participants and victims of war or conflict to resolve their own problems using their own methodologies and systems. In many cases, but not all, these have indeed been elaborated locally with minimal outside help. Such actions usually occur after the fighting has ended, though hostilities may still simmer and flare up.

## Conflict settlement

'Settlement' is usually seen within a power-based realist paradigm where force is the arbiter. This can include 'mediation with muscle' as in the context of the United States using its power to broker agreements over the Middle East (as with Kissinger's mediation at Camp David, 1977: cf. Touval 1982).

### Aim

Conflict settlement's aim is Order, and often it does not shrink from a 'realist' use of military force, sometimes on a huge scale, as in the First and Second World Wars or from zero-sum outcomes. Realists take the view that all peace is a lull between wars and that trust between states and nations is a plausible but unlikely scenario (Mearsheimer 2001; Waltz 2001). They also deny that there is any such thing as an 'international society' with clear rules and processes, but if such a thing exists it is due to a temporary balance of power and the dominance of a hegemon for a given historical period. Indeed, it has been pointed out that: 'War appears to be as old as mankind, but peace is a modern invention' (Sir Henry Maine, quoted by Howard 2000: 1).

## Problems

Conflict settlement often does not work in the sense that only the maintenance of force keeps the 'lid' on the problem, but does not address the underlying problems. Indeed it cannot work, as states are always getting ready for the next war. We might also say that hard power is difficult to use when the areas where it has to be applied are those in a state of civil war ('realism' assumes a functioning state system on the whole) and has a regional nature. As the United States has discovered in Afghanistan (2001 to the present) and Iraq (2003 to the present), the most formidable military machine can get very bogged down in an area wracked by an insurgency with no identifiable 'head'. As Iraq also shows, the idea of 'ending' a war by force can often create a bitter illusion. Wars

Plate 9 A Tamil Tiger cemetery in Sri Lanka: third parties have struggled to gain the trust of both sides in mediation efforts

that are finally 'ended' by force alone are in a distinct minority and arguably always have been (Coker 1997). Even the hardest of realists understands that, as Clausewitz commented, in war all is *friktion*, which might be translated as 'it's easy to get into, but unpredictable in the extreme once engaged upon' (see, for example, Gray 2005). The ethical issues for such thinkers and practitioners are clear, and they are largely ignored.

## Conflict management

A slightly less, but still essentially realist, view is taken by conflict 'managers' who believe that it is usually impossible to do anything but try to grease the wheels of a conflict to make it less violent through the judicious use of a combination of hard power, soft power (usually economic sticks and carrots) and peacekeeping forces. Roland Paris (2004) argues that such 'management' approaches can encompass 'liberalization', which he explicitly equates with 'democratization', a dual concept which we have linked to the 'liberal peace' theory and will be explored further in Chapter 5 (Paris 2004: 5). The ethical problem with this is of course that the 'targets' may not want to be so dealt with.

A feature of such approaches is also the use of 'Track One' mediators, usually in the form of 'good offices' or 'mediation' between leaders of insurgent groups, the established 'state' and any other regional players, a time-honoured use of a third party to help oil the wheels of a negotiation between states. Good recent examples in the 2000s include mediation by African heads of state in the Democratic Republic of Congo and in Liberia. In the post-Cold War period mediation has come to also mean 'an extension and continuation of peaceful conflict management' (for a robust defence of this, see Bercovitch 1997: 127 and *passim*; see also Bercovitch 2002; Bercovitch and Rubin 1992).

### Aim

The aim is the minimisation, but not necessarily elimination of, violence; stability insofar as it can be achieved; and 'realist' expectations of the difficulty of getting people to agree on underlying causes, symptoms and solutions to their problems. The recent resurgence in the study of conflict management in the United States has much to do with the feeling that the optimism of the 1990s was misplaced and 'recognizes that the global environs are both conflict-ridden and often bloody, and it harbors no illusions that murderous enmity will suddenly give way to universal comity' (Solomon 2007: xi).

### Problem

Is conflict management too centred on domestic US obsessions (the 'War on Terror' etc.), so we might question as to whether it therefore sings to a tune not appreciated by others? It does nonetheless ask some very important questions about whether democracy is the 'answer' or stability the main aim and also proposes interesting ideas about new forms of sovereignty and other ways of organising societies to make them less war prone (Marten 2007; Ottaway 2007).

## Conflict resolution

Often delivered by Track Two intermediaries, conflict 'resolution' is usually held to mean an attempt to fully (or mainly) resolve the underlying root causes of a conflict by, it is hoped, resolving (or indeed transforming) the relationship of the parties so that they develop an entirely new and peaceful relationship. Institutionally, one of the best examples was the Oslo Process of the early 1990s, which seemed at the time to be capable of addressing the underlying problems in the Israel–Palestine conflict (Corbin 1994), but is in 2008 seen as a false dawn (for case study, see p. 112).

### Aim

Fully airing differences, usually in a closed and confidential environment, with no pre-conceived agenda and a belief that problems and parties to conflict can be 'transformed' so that a future relationship will be better, less conflictual and ultimately stable (for a wider summary see Miall *et al.* 1999: 58). Ideally it will also 'highlight the wider social and political sources of a conflict in seeking to break the perpetuating cycle of oppression and resistance' (Jeong 2008: 244). One of the best summaries of the characteristics and methodologies used can be found on the Berghof Foundation's website, a resource handbook that is constantly being added to and updated (Fischer and Schmelzle n.d., www.berghof-handbook.net/). It is worth quoting their definition at some length:

First, war as an instrument of politics and conflict management can and should be overcome. Second, violence can and should be avoided in structures and relationships at all levels of human interaction. Third, all constructive conflict work must address the root causes that fuel conflict. And fourth, all constructive conflict work must empower those who experience conflict to address its causes without recourse to violence. In short, conflict transformation must provide those who experience violence with appropriate and innovative methods and approaches, and assistance by a third party if necessary. Ultimately, this is about changing individual attitudes and addressing the issue of structural reforms.

## Problems

An often naive belief in human perfectibility; a belief that 'basic human needs' can be identified and rectified (Mitchell 1981; Banks 1984; Burton 1990). One of the problems with analysing this approach has been the secrecy that is inherent in these processes, that has led to few of the case studies being written up for public consumption. This is now being somewhat addressed by, for example, examining 'transfer effects' that look at how Track Two experiences can be of use in Track One discussions and vice versa (Fisher 1997, 2005). Another more intractable problem is that it is seen by some as having been demonstrated to be just another, if more subtle, use of power by the West to coerce the 'Rest'. Maybe, it has been suggested, the insurmountable barrier to successful conflict resolution lies in the impossibility of understanding another culture, which is an 'ontological' barrier to any real possibility of transformation, a difficult charge to refute as conflict resolution teams rarely even understand the language of those they are dealing with, in developing countries in particular (Vayrynen 2001; Avruch 2003; Jabri 2007). Another criticism that could be directed against such 'naivety' is that in some cases it could be argued that success in transformation is possible only because some form of 'settlement' was already going on. The successful transition in Ethiopia and Eritrea in 1993 (states that subsequently resumed their conflict, 1998 to the present) was maybe because the military victory of the Eritrean and Northern Ethiopian insurgencies had brought about a radically new situation.

All of these categories of third party intervention have as a central aim the improvement of communication, whether it be to signal war or threat, or to enhance understanding of the parties' views, needs and wishes. Much of the theory and practice in third party intervention has been influenced by what could be described as the western, legal, rational perspective. It has also been influenced by theories of bargaining and rational choice – some of which have limited application in the real world. And, as several analysts (Fisher and Keashley 1990; Webb *et al.* 1996) have stressed, multiple conflict transformation approaches can be pursued together, or one at a time, or in different orders, depending on the conflict in question. What we tend to see is a hybridity in peacemaking whereby a variety of initiatives – both internationally and locally inspired – are simultaneously deployed.

Hence we, and many others, believe that the more overarching category of 'peacebuilding' is ultimately a more useful description of the process for creating a lasting peace, above settlement, management or resolution. Conflict settlement and management can be likened to holding a lid on a boiling pot, not attempting to turn the heat down, and conflict resolution has its own problems, as itemised above. So 'peacebuilding' is often referred to as a 'third generation' approach to dealing with conflict (Richmond 2006) as we grope towards a successor to both conflict 'settlement' and conflict 'management', again because the underlying attitudes, causes and structures of the conflict need to be properly addressed.

Hence, it is on the ideal end goal of conflict resolution that we will concentrate, that of 'transformation', as we believe that should be the central aim of all approaches to conflict, even if not to the exclusion of the others, which are still the most widely used. Hence it is our preferred term, but we are aware that no term can be satisfactory, given the extreme complexity of many conflicts in developing countries and the limited resources available for dealing with them (see Chapter 1 for more discussion of these distinctions).

## The issues faced: the need for 'mapping' and 'deconstructing' conflicts

Without wishing to totally revisit the debate on 'new wars' that has been described in some detail elsewhere in this book, we nonetheless need to ask if the kinds of conflicts that can be potentially 'transformed' are amenable to the kinds of theory and practical tools that we have at our disposal. It is now, for example, widely believed that we are dealing with conflicts that are not between *unitary* societies (usually states), as was believed to be largely the case between 1939 and about 1990, but now within ethnically or ideologically *divided* societies. A number of theorists have put this down to the resurgence of ethnic violence (Gurr and Harff 1994; Gurr 2000; Kaufman 2001). Certainly, compared to the period before 1990, one of the areas most identified as being truly 'new' in the post-Cold War conflict mix is the huge rise in what is termed 'ethnic violence'. Ted Gurr was one of the first to recognise this phenomenon in the context of conflict studies but of course there was a huge discussion of nationalism and self-determination well before this (for an excellent introduction to this and the links to the ethnicity question, see Oberschall 2007: Chapter 1).

We might nonetheless question this now practically embedded wisdom about the differences between pre-1990 and post-1990 conflicts (Kaldor 2005, 2006). First, as we have already argued, there were many civil wars *before* 1990 (Kalyvas 2001; Berdal 2003). And, very unfortunately, ethnicity has often been assumed since 1990 to be a key component of a conflict situation both for the participants and for outside supposed 'conflict resolvers'. This 'framing' can have disastrous effects, when it arguably is not the determinant factor by any means. Kaufman (2001) wrongly sees ethnicity as the root of most recent conflict in Eastern Europe for example. A classic example of this was in Bosnia (Campbell 1998a, 1998b), but such misjudged preconceptions have been widely and unfortunately repeated. It is far more likely that economic or ideological factors underpin much 'ethnic' conflict (Nordstrom 2004; Pugh and Cooper 2004).

So, although the analysis of all conflict as 'ethnic' is a neat and workable short-hand in many conflicts, it is not sufficient. As Oberschall (2007) puts it '[t]hese theories lack specificity and context'. His preference is for what he terms 'conflict and conciliation dynamics', which essentially seeks to 'map' the conflict by looking at issues, players and their strategies, and implementation (Oberschall 2007: 29). This idea of mapping a conflict has also been used quite widely in conflict resolution and transformation approaches (including those of Mitchell and Webb 1988; Burton 1990; Fisher 1997; Kelman 2005). For all these theorists we might suggest a widespread belief that a first step has to be to 'deconstruct' a conflict before it can be properly understood and analysed, as a precursor to identifying possible solutions to it (see also Chapter 1 for more discussion of this vital theme).

As we stressed in the Introduction, an important input into this school of thinking has been the work of Edward Azar, who believed that 'protracted social conflict' (Azar 1990) needed 'problem solving', not military solutions. Azar's approach was one that accepted much of what has been written by theorists of 'basic human needs' like John Burton (1990). Their aim was to get a wider acceptance that most conflicts were due to 'the prolonged and often violent struggle by communal groups for such basic needs as security, recognition and acceptance, fair access to political institutions and economic participation' (Azar 1990).

If this is true, then unravelling the motives for perpetrators, victims and interveners alike is far more daunting than dealing with mere ethnic violence, bad as that obviously is. It is obvious that the use of violence has multiple motivations, with correspondingly difficult decisions to be made about how to 'map' these motivations. A key, and growing, element of war has been the reported use of sexual violence, with increasing debates about motivations and potential solutions to the use of rape in war (see Enloe 1993; for a more recent, if controversial summary, see Thornhill and Palmer 2000). We might however also point out that sexual violence in war was as much a part of the repertoire before 1990 as after it. Historians such as Anthony Beevor (2002) have catalogued the widespread use of rape by Russian soldiers in Berlin in 1945 and Edward Newman (2004) has also made a similar point, again in criticising the 'new war' thesis.

Azar's (1990) approach allowed for the analysis to be on a variety of levels – 'identity' at the 'communal level' an analysis of the 'deprivation of human needs'; the crucial factor of the 'governance and the state's role' and the need to look at 'international linkages' (Azar, after Ramsbotham *et al.* 2005: 84–8). All of these need a long-term process that is often beyond the means of Track Two teams and beyond the mandate of Track One mediators. We cannot yet be said to be anywhere near resolving this conundrum (but for some understanding of it, see Fisher 2005).

## Strategies of conflict resolution and transformation

So although purists will immediately see flaws in such a narrative, we can therefore, cautiously, describe most attempts by (usually but not always) outside parties at mitigating or 'solving' conflicts through two major series of approaches, top–down (conflict settlement and management) and bottom–up (conflict resolution or transformation). We can also suggest there is now in place an overall idea of 'peacebuilding', defined by Miall *et al.* (1999) as 'the attempt to overcome the structural, relational and cultural contradictions which lie at the root of conflict in order to underpin the processes of peacemaking and peacekeeping' (Miall *et al.* 1999: 56–7). This can be seen in terms of actions by states or IGOs, and as such it is usually used in the 'reconstruction' attempts we will describe in Chapter 5. But the emphasis in the rest of this chapter is on 'peacebuilding from below', which is what the term often means in the context of conflict resolution, transformation, or attempts at reconciliation, all of which often, though not exclusively, are used by changing the attitudes and practices of the society in conflict.

To put that into simple language: how would you, our reader, think it best to deal with (a) two warring factions within a government, or (b) the reintegration of people who had been killing your neighbours or family? Would you advocate a policy of justice (or revenge) for paramilitary forces that may have destroyed your village or killed your relatives, or their 'reintegration' into society (as suggested in Chapter 5), or getting them to undergo a process of much more personal reconciliation?

## Reconciliation: memory, truth telling and forgiveness

One way to bring about a lasting peace is now seen as being through 'reconciliation', either through the mechanism of truth and reconciliation commissions (TRCs), often referred to as 'restorative justice', or through the use of a much older institution, a war crimes tribunal (WCT), often referred to as a form of 'retributive justice'. The first usually assumes a non-retributional and non-jural outcome, the latter assumes the use of some form of sanction, including imprisonment, or even the death sentence, for 'guilty' parties (Rigby 2001). We will discuss them in turn, but first look at what they can be said to have in common in addressing conflicts in developing countries.

Both of these institutional frameworks attempt to work based on the proposition that we need to establish the 'facts' of any conflict, including the hardest of all, those to do with killing, torture and other massive abuses of human rights. This, it is assumed, will somehow help both victims and perpetrators to come to terms with their experiences and actions and help them to understand, possibly forgive, and hopefully 'move on', to a better and more functional relationship. This proposition is drawn from essentially three sources:

- First, from psychological insights that a 'talking cure' (Freud's term) will enable individuals and societies to make a transition from hostility to peace through the establishment of clearly identified memories and contending 'truths' and that this will then lead to a better ability to deal with collective and individual trauma (Jeong 2005: 155; Fierke 2006).

- Second, it bears more than a passing resemblance to ideas in conflict resolution or transformation theory and practice that a 'ventilation' of grievances and an establishment of the history (or histories) of a conflict will help establish a new point of departure for the players and thus a transformation of their relationship discussed above.
- Third, its proponents often link it explicitly to 'liberal peace' arguments that 'transitions to democracy' necessitate an adoption of market reforms, constitution building and the establishment of a rule of law and a consideration of 'what to do about the past'. Justice and accountability will go hand in hand with prospects for a stable peace (Hayner 2002: xi, Chapter 7).

The first attempts at setting up TRCs were in Latin America (Chile, El Salvador and Argentina in particular) to attempt to draw a line under the 'dirty wars' of the Cold War era (Whittaker 1999: Chapter 2 on El Salvador; Hayner 2002). After 1990 the most prominent examples have been in South Africa after the end of Apartheid (see p. 114 for more detail), the Rwandan genocide of 1994 (Prunier 1995; Corey and Joireman 2004; Moghalu 2005; also see pp. 114–16 below) and in Sierra Leone after the Lomé Peace Accords of 1999 (www.trcsierraleone.org/drwebsite/publish/index.shtml). Suggestions have been made for similar commissions in Former Yugoslavia, in Northern Ireland and elsewhere.

One way of assessing the usefulness of such attempts is to analyse the underlying essential elements of such thinking, and especially the ideas of 'memory' and 'truth'.

## Memory, history and 'truth'

An essential element of reconciliation lies in having common, or at least mutually comprehended, memories of what happened in a conflict or war that need to be reconciled. The aim is not only to establish the 'individual truth' of what happened, but also to interrogate what might be called 'collective' truths. This, it is hoped, will then lead to mutually acceptable changes in the versions of the 'truth' that have long dogged the peoples involved in a long-running feud. If, for example, the Irish and the English or the English and the Scottish people persist in 'remembering' their past histories as exclusively ones of mutual persecution, with 'signposts' along the way that encourage a prolonged feeling of mutual grievance, or even hatred, there is little chance of them being able to make lasting peace with one another. It might be reasonably asserted that the popular film *Braveheart* (Mel Gibson, 1995), which portrayed the heroic and largely blameless William Wallace as fighting a guerrilla war against the heartless and brutal English monarchy did little to foster Anglo-Scottish understanding, and even contributed to the much remarked upon resurgence of Scottish nationalism since the 1960s (Webb 1978). Equally folk memories of Cromwell's massacres at Wexford and Drogheda in the 1650s or the Battle of the Boyne, won by William of Orange against the rump of James III's army in 1690, have been constantly evoked in nationalist propaganda by Republicans and Loyalist alike on the island of Ireland to justify horrific atrocities. Even more recently the memories of the First World War of 1914–18 have been used in Ireland to justify Protestant violence against Catholics in the North (Mac Ginty and Williams 2007).

Lest this be thought a too British and Irish set of examples, it should be noted that in Former Yugoslavia, the Croat and Serb leaderships both evoked historical grievances dating back to the fourteenth century in their pursuit of ethnic cleansing and other brutality. History is indeed a dragon that it is dangerous to awaken! But if that is the case, can history be used as a way of reconciling and resolving conflicts?

Jay Winter, in many ways the Anglophone father of memory studies, has written about the 'memory boom' in contemporary historical studies (Winter 2000). There has been a widespread re-memorisation of war in western Europe as part of a process of reconciling the peoples of western Europe, who only a generation back (and for several before that) were regularly engaged in internecine warfare of the most brutal and uncompromising kind (Winter 1995; Evans and Lunn 1997; Mac Ginty and Williams 2007). The First and Second World Wars were not African or Asian affairs after all; they were purely European innovations, even if they had profound effects on the rest of the world. Many of the insurgents or freedom fighters in wars of decolonisation (Algeria, Kenya, Vietnam, arguably Israel, are good examples) learnt how to fight their colonial masters by fighting alongside them in 1914–45. Their resentment at the pronouncement of adherence to 'democracy', and the evident hypocrisy inherent in such claims, fuelled many uprisings (see, for example, Lewis 2007 on Kenya).

**Plate 10  French First World War cemetery: issues of commemoration can have long-lasting sensitivity**

A number of questions arise immediately:

- How can, or should, these historical ghosts be put back to sleep? Is full or partial disclosure or amnesia better (Rigby 2001)?
- Does the existence of both national mythologies and, in some cases, extremely antagonising personal and collective memories matter in potentially fostering future violence?
- What if there are 'contested memories' (no agreement on what happened) (Beneduce 2007)?
- Who has 'ownership' of a historical narrative and could therefore be trusted to write an account of it that would not (inevitably perhaps) be merely a version to suit the 'Victors', or at least a dominant view of events or put their spin on commemorative activities (Mac Ginty and Williams 2007)?

The case of Israel and Palestine is most instructive in this regard (see Box 4.1).

The main issue is the existence of two opposing historical narratives. If we accept the Israeli narrative, which essentially sees Jews having fled the Holocaust in Europe and settling an 'empty' land and developing it where

## Box 4.1

### *History, Israel and Palestine*

The Israeli–Palestinian conflict is steeped in historical controversy. The British role in promising the Jews a homeland in Palestine in 1917 (the 'Balfour Declaration') was compounded by British agent T.E. Lawrence making promises to the Arab rulers of the area that they could have Damascus and Jerusalem as the capitals of a new Arab state and also the French (the Sykes–Picot Agreement of 1915) that they could have Syria and Lebanon. This has led to endless arguments about 'who owns what and by what right' in the Middle East and is a foundational problem in finding a solution. This was compounded by the circumstances of the foundation of Israel in 1947 after which large numbers of native Palestinians were expelled to neighbouring countries where they and their offspring still live and form the core of anti-Israeli feeling. Israel has had to submit to being attacked on several occasions (1948, 1973 and in numerous cross-border incursions) and been forced (in its view) to carry out pre-emptive wars (1956, 1967, plus major incursions into Lebanon in 1982, 1994 and 2006). The whole region is thus affected. In addition to that, as US President Carter put it:

> People know if they are from a war torn country how difficult it is to sit down across the table in the same room with an adversary. Just consider about the Israelis negotiating with the Palestinians. It is likely adversaries will say: 'We cannot negotiate because we despise the other side too much. They have killed our children, they have raped our women, they have devastated our villages'.

Past and present grievances become as real as each other and therefore a solution needs to address such hurts. The Oslo Process of the early 1990s tried to do so by addressing the triple issues of the 'right of return', the status of Jerusalem and the borders of any future Palestinian state. Those are still the key issues today. The history and the present issues will need a global solution.

Sources: Corbin (1994), Jones (1999), Fromkin (2000)

before there had been desert and poverty, to the benefit of not only the Jewish population but also all those within and indeed without Israel's borders, then a picture of a blameless Israel being attacked by fanatical hoodlums makes absolute sense. If we accept the Palestinian mainstream view that they were expelled in large numbers from their homeland by an alien invader backed by the Great Powers in 1947–8, Powers which were themselves motivated more by their guilt about the Holocaust than any genuine sympathy for either Jews or Arabs, then obviously we can sympathise with the Palestinians. As historians have pointed out (notably

Edward Said: see Ruthuen 2003; Bunzl 2008), these 'mirror-images' or incompatible mythologies are the basis of many protracted conflicts.

## 'Ruptured histories'

The idea that history is 'dead' or that we can have an 'end' to it (Fukuyama 1992) could not be less true than it is today. History informs most, if not all, of the enduring deep-rooted violent conflicts that afflict the developing world. Some of them, like those that pit Japan as a former imperial power against South Korea and China, are vital for understanding the future stability of the whole of East Asia (Miyoshi Jager and Mitter 2007).

So what can be done? Should those identified as having responsibility for crimes of war be brought to book and put before a court of law, national or international, as mentioned above and often referred to as 'reformative justice'? Or should the miscreants be seen as victims as much as perpetrators and allowed or encouraged to reinsert themselves into societies that they once sought to destroy? We will now go through the arguments for both of these courses with the use of historical examples. It should be noted that there are significant differences that exist in the theory and practice of how a conflict can be de-escalated and a peacebuilding process given a chance to begin.

Some general issues need to be addressed first. A conflict might be seen on one level as an inability to trust. Miall *et al.* (1999) put it thus:

> [l]egitimacy, acceptance and trust . . . are integral to the functioning of
> any reasonably stable socio-political system, invisible and often taken
> for granted when differences are being settled relatively peacefully,
> but palpably lacking when they are not.
>
> (Miall *et al.* 1999: 206)

They also point out that 'one of the main obstacles to social and psychological healing is the cumulative hurt' (Miall *et al.* 1999: 207). So a spiral of distrust develops in an uncanny echo of the 'security dilemma' in international politics (for an explanation of this, see Booth and Wheeler 2007). Because you believe that the other side has more weapons than you (or is less trustworthy) you arm yourself more (and trust less). The classic example of a global conflict is the arms race of the Cold War, a more current and local one the ever increasing use of more and more sophisticated small arms in pastoralist conflicts in Africa (Riungu n.d.; Mkutu 2008) (see Box 4.2).

## Box 4.2

### *The South African Truth and Reconciliation Commission*

The end of apartheid in South Africa came after an all-white referendum in 1992 and the freeing of Nelson Mandela by the National Party, led by F.W. de Klerk. De Klerk voluntarily handed over power to a new majority administration of the African National Congress (ANC). The ANC has followed a very 'liberal' path since then, holding a number of elections, encouraging foreign multinational companies to set up and develop in South Africa and avoiding all of the worst excesses of neighbouring Zimbabwe by encouraging a process of reconciliation. This has been concentrated in the Truth and Reconciliation Commission (TRC), set up in 1995, which has heard hundreds of testimonies from former perpetrators from the South African defence forces and many more victims and their relatives (for more on this see pp. 115–16). The idea has been suggested by Archbishop Desmond Tutu, that the truth will heal the trauma of the past and that it will help in the 'nation-building' of South Africa. Some have argued that the process, which has never really addressed the problems of reparation for the crimes committed (although there is provision for this in the TRC's statutes) lets off the perpetrators too lightly. The TRC finished its work in 2002. The government is pursuing a policy of gradual and cautious reform of land for example, which it is hoped will help the reconciliation process along.

Sources: Rotberg and Thompson (2000), Hayner (2002), Williams (2006: 191–4)

## Another hard case: Rwanda

The question we have asked above can be summed up as: can or do TRCs help in dealing with the aftermath of deep-rooted violent conflicts? The South African case is a hard one in that unravelling nearly a century of *apartheid* policies may well take generations. But what about an even harder case, that of Rwanda (see Box 4.3)?

What can we learn from such episodes for the future of reconciliation attempts in developing countries? It is evident that in Rwanda, 'even by strict definitions the episode qualifies as "genocide"' (Straus 2007: 123), so the aftermath of such events is that much more difficult to deal with than, but also different from, the long-drawn-out agony of South Africa. In both cases we could argue that these were 'unforgivable' crimes. In South Africa the fight against apartheid came to be seen as the sole prerogative of the African National Congress (ANC). Mahmood

## Box 4.3

### *Rwanda*

By many calculations 500,000–800,000 mainly 'Tutsi' men, women and children were massacred by their 'Hutu' neighbours in 1994, and many women gang-raped, resulting in a huge subsequent dispersal of the population that committed these massacres as the new government, which was also ethnically mainly Tutsi, came to power and demanded retribution. The international community turned a largely blind eye to the massacres, in spite of anguished pleas to the UN by the UN military commander in the country, General Dallaire. The French government (through 'Operation Turquoise') has been accused of harbouring the 'genocidaires'. The massacres were of an ethnic nature but might be argued to have been about other issues as the two groups were practically indistinguishable. They were certainly about elite competition and demonstrated the power of a centrally organised bureaucratic state in organising such events, as Nazi Germany had previously shown. The post-massacre 'Gacaca' courts, set up in 2002, have attempted to get lesser (that is to say not leading) perpetrators to confront the reality of what they have done in exchange for a lesser or even no punishment. The post-genocide era has seen the imposition of another authoritarian state, and massive intervention by the Rwandan army in neighbouring Congo, though with a lot less violence being committed within Rwanda. About 110,000 were incarcerated awaiting trial in 2001. An International Criminal Tribunal for Rwanda has also been set up by the UN but its effectiveness has been less than impressive in terms of the numbers of those bought before it or punished, though important legal precedents have been established, against sexual violence for example.

Sources: Booth (2003), Moghalu (2005), Kayumba and Kimonyo (2006), Straus (2007)

Mamdani has asked the pertinent question as to whether 'if truth has replaced justice in South Africa, has reconciliation turned into an embrace of evil?' He also points out that 'in Rwanda there are a lot of perpetrators and a few people who benefited; in South Africa there are a few perpetrators, but lots of beneficiaries' (Mahmood Mamdani, quoted by Krog 1998: 146–7).

This conundrum has led many to ask whether the reconciliation in either country is more than skin deep. The post-apartheid crime figures in South Africa (where hundreds of white farmers have been killed and the country has one of the highest murder rates of any country on the planet) suggest a society ill at ease with itself. So is reconciliation the 'lesser of two evils?' Mothers who lost their children have a different view of the idea that reconciliation can help us 'turn the page'. One such mother who testified to the TRC, a Mrs Kondile, commented that she could not forgive a South African policeman, Dirk Coetzee, for killing and burning her son: 'It is easy for Mandela and Tutu to forgive . . . they lead vindicated lives. In my life, nothing, not a single thing, has changed since my son was burnt by barbarians . . . nothing. Therefore I cannot forgive' (quoted in Krog 1998: 142). Others have claimed that, in the case of the TRC, even if the whole truth is not found out, a great deal is learnt and the process is therefore 'therapeutic' (Christie 2000: 173–5).

## War crimes tribunals (WCTs)

Some have suggested that a better solution would be to opt for the forensic truth-seeking of a legal retributive tribunal, as was the case with the Nuremberg and Tokyo trials after the Second World War, the records of which are still taken as one quasi-'definitive' account of Nazi and Imperial Japanese war crimes (Sands 2003).

In recent times the International Criminal Tribunal for Former Yugoslavia has drawn a huge amount of media attention and has led to the prosecution of many alleged perpetrators of war crimes in the Balkans, most famously of Former Yugoslav President Slobodan Milosevic and, in 2008, Radovan Karadzic, the Bosnian Serb leader (Williams 2006: 169–74). There is also now a permanent International Criminal Court (ICC) that serves the international community as a whole, formally founded in 1998 and directed against individual misdemeanours, potentially also by peacekeepers (which is why a number of states have not ratified the treaty setting it up). Its website as of July 2008 tells us that 106 countries are full signatories and that

> [t]he ICC is a court of last resort. It will not act if a case is investigated or prosecuted by a national judicial system unless the national proceedings are not genuine, for example if formal proceedings were undertaken solely to shield a person from criminal responsibility. In addition, the ICC only tries those accused of the gravest crimes.
> (www.icc-cpi.int/home.html&l=en, accessed 30 July 2008)

The ICC has been mainly used in the Democratic Republic of Congo, but most famously in the Darfur conflict in Sudan, the first ever sitting head of state, Omar Bashir, has been accused of crimes against humanity.

If TRCs might therefore be seen as a 'soft' option, as in the cases of Rwanda or Sudan for example, might not 'retributive', legally enforceable, and punitive criminal tribunals be a better option to help in the needed processes of healing described above? The use of the war crimes tribunal has of course been explored in the context of developing countries and their conflicts. The International Criminal Tribunal for Rwanda (http://69.94.11.53/) has been in existence since 1994, just after the massacres, and has as its official brief 'to contribute to the process of national reconciliation in Rwanda and to the maintenance of peace in the region.' The criticism of its breathtakingly slow pace and ineffectiveness have led to some commentators thinking it brings the rule of law into disrepute (Moghalu 2005). There is a similar one for Sierra Leone, the Special Court for Sierra Leone, which used the ICC's facilities in The Hague to prosecute Charles Taylor, widely accepted as being a prime mover in the horrors that afflicted much of West Africa (for more on this, see Wierda 2006).

One potential problem for such tribunals' effectiveness in developing-country contexts is that their roots clearly lie in the Nuremberg and Tokyo tribunals after the Second World War when the circumstances of global politics were very different from now and when the justice being meted out was in the context of inter-state war, not in our predominantly 'new war' era. Another is that which can also be levelled against war crimes tribunals in the industrialised world – on occasion the needs of 'justice' and those of 'peace' are in distinct opposition. How can you expect warlords to lay down their weapons if they know they will be subsequently accused of war crimes and probably executed or imprisoned for life? Equally there is some sense in the US criticism of the ICC that it potentially criminalises soldiers doing their best to do the bidding of the UN. Against this it could be argued that all 'proper' armies prosecute their troops for criminal behaviour, as have the Americans in Iraq for example, and that the above ICC stricture about it being a court of last resort answers that criticism. Maybe more seriously, the ICC was not used in the prosecution of those deemed to be war criminals in Iraq – the executions and other punishments inflicted there were by domestic judicial instances, and might be accused of being essentially Victors' Justice (Bass 2000; Williams 2006). We feel there is not yet enough evidence, for or against, to have a judgement on the effectiveness of such tribunals in the context of conflict in the developing world.

To summarise: the aims of TRCs and WCTs are to try:

- to accommodate the vital role of historical memory: each player in the conflict believes that history is on their 'side' and evokes it to justify ever increasing cycles of violence and revenge

• to deflate this spiral by allowing the inverse process of historical truth-telling to take place, whether through a formal system of justice ('retributive' justice – WCTs for example) or a non-judicial process ('reformative' justice, such as TRCs).

It is important to note that the main aim of both TRCs and WCTs is to make an attempt to address the above aims. Hayner quotes Michael Ignatieff's caveat that: 'The past is an argument and the function of truth commissions, like the function of honest historians, is simply to purify the argument, to narrow the range of permissible lies' (Ignatieff in Hayner 2002: 25). This has given rise to frustrations and potential future conflicts.

## Concluding discussion

Anthony Oberschall sums up the substance of the issues dealt with in this chapter in two sentences: 'Collective Myths are the enemy of truth and justice . . . conflict management and peace building are hampered by crisis framing, the victim syndrome and denial' (Oberschall 2007: 2). While we might disagree about the exact wording, this seems to us a fair summary of the problems faced in dealing with the kinds of problems we see in trying to manage or resolve most conflicts in developing countries, also in some in the 'West' like Northern Ireland, other parts of the European Union (the Basque Country most notably) as well as the Former Yugoslavia and the Former Soviet Union. So a first conclusion has to be that the problems of developing countries are not *sui generis*. They can happen anywhere, wherever there are people struggling to find economic, political or cultural identity and meaning. One of the worst obstacles that needs to be overcome if we are to improve what is a dismal track record of dealing with complex deep-rooted conflicts is to assume that they are easy to resolve, but also that we should not try.

Second, we might also ask whether there are lessons to be drawn from looking at *non*-conflict situations, as any thesis has to be falsifiable. Of course this is the basis of liberal peace arguments. Such theorists would say that the effective deployment of democratic institutions is what makes a state succeed in avoiding destructive conflict and enhancing successful development (see, for example, Paris 2004; Kaldor 2005, 2006). Although such considerations are very interesting, we feel we need in this book to concentrate on attempts to address what does *not* work. What seems clear to us is that the official discourse of participation and empowerment through democracy often falls far short of the reality. In most cases the evidence seems to be that such discourse and practice can actually depoliticise and demobilise the poor who are the subjects and objects of much conflict behaviour (Moore 2001; Williams 2007b).

So the short-term effects of such peacebuilding processes can be perverse. Many have accused the South African and Rwandan TRCs as asking the impossible – forgiveness by victims for unforgivable crimes. An area that needs much more research is in the long-term effects of such attempts and what might be done to improve the prospects for success. The phenomenon of 'intergenerational violence' has been noted. Although the evidence is often anecdotal, it would appear that, for example, in areas of Former Yugoslavia where there were not widespread atrocities during the Second World War, there was a lower level of 'revenge' violence in the 1990s. One obvious area that is now being explored is that of the effects of education on succeeding generations. The German example of education changing wider attitudes is often cited (Dierkes 2007). Likewise the negative evidence of such educational attempts not being made in the teaching of history in Japan, Korea and China has also elicited widespread comment (Bleiker 2007; Miyoshi Jager and Mitter 2007; Yoshida 2007). Not many analyses have yet been done on developing country cases however.

Third, we must ask whether an outside party *should* interfere in the warfare or conflict raging within a developing country, of which there are many examples in such a situation. And will their efforts stand any chance of succeeding, and why or why not? As John Darby (2006) has put it: 'The signing of a multiparty peace accord is unlikely to end violence'. We need to look beyond such 'institutional' concepts as conflict settlement and management, discussed in this chapter, and democratisation, disarmament and the reintegration of former combatants, reconstruction and institutional change, which we will discuss at length in Chapter 5, to see how deeper mechanisms can be used to try to coax whole populations and especially elites towards a more gentle and less confrontational way of solving their inevitable societal conflicts.

Peacebuilding, conflict resolution and the transformation of societies and individuals from the state of violent conflict or war is never going to be an easy task. It is difficult in developed countries like Ireland; it is all the more difficult in conditions of underdevelopment, poverty and state collapse. Chapters 5 and 6 will address these vital corollary issues. Can development 'from without' help societies become more economically and politically stable so that peace can have a chance of succeeding?

# Summary

- Theories of how to deal with conflict (settlement, management and 'transformation') are often seen as dependent on the observer's underlying theory of international relations.
- Most, but not all, conflicts in developing countries are civil wars.
- Peacebuilding and conflict 'transformation' approaches can be 'top–down' or 'bottom–up'.
- Protracted social conflict cannot simply be explained by reference to 'ethnic' differences.
- Reconciliation within divided societies can be attempted by internally organised jural or non-jural tribunals, or by international war crimes tribunals.
- We need to understand the historical roots of conflict in order to have any chance of resolving them.

# Discussion questions

1 Is it true to say that 'new wars' have now largely replaced the 'old wars' of the era before 1990?
2 Should peacebuilding be approached in a 'top–down' or 'bottom–up' way?
3 Are commissions such as the South African Truth and Reconciliation Commission a better way to bring about peace than war crimes tribunals?
4 What role do you think the 'history' of a place plays in helping us understand the causes and potential solutions to conflict and war?

# Further reading

The best introduction to conflict management can be found in Bercovitch, J. and Rubin, J.Z. (1992) *Mediation in International Relations: Multiple approaches to conflict management*, London: Macmillan, or Crocker, C.A., Hampson, F.O. and Aall, P. (eds) (2007) *Leashing the Dogs of War: Conflict management in a divided world*, Washington, DC: United States Institute of Peace Press. The best introduction to the logic of conflict resolution is still Azar, E. (1990) *The Management of Protracted Social Conflict: Theory and cases*, Aldershot: Dartmouth. The best recent book by far on the subject matter of much of this chapter is Ramsbotham, O., Woodhouse, T. and Miall, H. (2005) *Contemporary Conflict Resolution: The prevention, management and transformation of deadly conflicts*, 2nd edn, Cambridge: Polity. Recent excellent summaries on peacebuilding can be found in Jeong, H.-W. (2005) *Peacebuilding in Post-Conflict Societies: Strategy and process*, Boulder, CO: Lynne Reinner; Jeong, H.-W. (2008) *Understanding Conflict and Conflict Analysis*, London: Sage; Lederach, J.-P. (1997) *Building Peace: Sustainable reconciliation in divided societies*, Washington, DC: United States Institute of Peace; and Fisher, R. (1996) *Interactive Conflict Resolution*, Syracuse, NY: Syracuse University Press. A good discussion of the causes and potential resolution of conflicts can be found in Oberschall, A. (2007) *Conflict and Peace Building in Divided Societies: Responses to ethnic violence*, London: Routledge. One critical review of conflict resolution approaches can be found in Jabri, V. (2007) *War and the Transformation of Global Politics*, London: Palgrave Macmillan. Two good overviews of reconciliation after wars are Rigby, A. (2001) *Justice and Reconciliation: After the violence*, Boulder, CO: Lynne Reinner, and Whittaker, D.J. (1999) *Conflict and Reconciliation in the Contemporary World*, London: Routledge.

## Useful websites

The best website on conflict resolution/transformation is Fischer, M. and Schmelzle, B. (eds) *The Berghof Handbook for Conflict Transformation* (www.berghof-handbook.net/). Various wesbites related to particular commissions and tribunals mentioned above include South African TRC: www.doj.gov.za/trc/; Rwanda, the official government website: The International Criminal Tribunal for Rwanda (http://69.94.11.53/); and a University of California site which includes a number of related URLs: http://socrates. berkeley.edu/~warcrime/RW-webley.htm; Sierra Leone: (www.trcsierraleone. org/drwebsite/publish/index.shtml). The International Criminal Court can be found at www.icc-cpi.int/home.html&l=en.

# ⑤ Post-conflict reconstruction and development

## Introduction

This chapter will first look at the often-made assumptions about reconstruction, and its allied concepts, state-building and nation-building, and democratisation, as they apply not only to the 'problem' areas, but also to those who would cure them of their problems. It will then look in particular at a number of what might be termed 'generic' reconstruction attempts, starting with those of Germany and Japan (Japan in 1945 was still a 'developing country' and both operations are even now seen as ideal types), as well as Afghanistan and Iraq. It will ask whether the reconstruction remedy can provide what the United States Institute of Peace called a need for *Managing Global Chaos* (Crocker *et al.* 1996), especially in the post-Cold War period.

This period has not been characterised by a linear rise in intrastate wars, though there was an important rise in 1991–2, but by a decline in such conflicts until 2007 (Peace and Conflict Website, University of Uppsala, www.pcr.uu.se). There has been a rise in the number of peace accords, and a decrease in the number of new wars starting (Gleditsch *et al.* 2002; Münkler, 2005; Mack 2006). In practically all of these peace accords there has been some attempt to remove the factors that caused the fighting in the first place and further attempts to provide some sort of 'reconstruction' help in the aftermath. Understanding these processes therefore becomes imperative not only for supporters of intervention to help the cause of peace, but also for their critics.

We will consequently also look at what might be termed the 'semantics' of reconstruction, for it is in the terms of a phenomenon's description that its core values can usually be determined. In turn, the presentation of a term can lead to its being seen as a use of power, positive and negative. To say as much is not to be 'anti-American' or to accuse the Western Powers of 'imperialism', but to identify how these actions can be seen as such, no matter how pure the intentions of the intervening Powers or even how effective their actions in helping the cause of long-term peace (Williams 2006). A casual reader of the literature on how we should go about bringing peace to war-torn societies after, usually, civil wars is presented with a plethora of seemingly contradictory terms. Our aim is to show how the ideal of 'peacebuilding' described in Chapter 4 relates to 'reconstruction' in the 1990s and since, as well as to 'state-building' or 'nation-building'. This will encompass a review of writing on the peacebuilding idea as a whole, but also how it can be said to reflect differing views and policies that have been implemented in particular cases.

## Changing definitions, changing historical contexts

There are many definitions of what we would now loosely call 'reconstruction'. Many of these arose out of historically specific situations. The term has two main semantic roots, in the logic of colonial/imperial administration and in the American Civil War (Foner 1989; Cramer 2006; Williams 2006).

The first of these has maybe had the longest-lasting impact on thinking about the practice in developing countries and the erstwhile European Powers. In the nineteenth century, the idea was used a great deal by great liberal thinkers such as John Stuart Mill to convey the need to 'civilise' the 'natives', as Mill put it under the guidance of 'philosophical legislators' to create a 'Greater Britain' through colonial emigration to what are now developing countries in the Commonwealth (Bell 2007: 50). Unfortunately, the implantation of white farmers, which was often linked into 'punitive expeditions' to clear 'natives' from large areas of Africa, has had the long-term result of causing massive resentment that came out in such conflicts as the Mau Mau in Kenya in the 1950s and in inter-tribal violence as a sequel to colonially imposed 'solutions' to land and other problems (Lewis 2007). Many of the issues now facing countries such as Kenya, Zimbabwe and South Africa were in part caused by the unintended consequences of liberal attempts to create modern political and economic state structures seen by indigenous peoples as being part of a system of institutionalised inequity.

In the aftermath of the Second World War the term became synonymous with the emergence of the first United Nations agency, the United Nations Relief and Rehabilitation Agency (UNRRA) in 1943, and the Marshall Plan during 1946–52, which did much to help resettle refugee and concentration camp populations and rebuild much of the western European and Japanese economies in the largest such enterprise to date (Hogan 1987; Williams 2006). The creation of the international financial architecture (the International Monetary Fund and the World Bank in particular) also did much to establish the context in which German and Japanese reconstruction could take place. Hence macro-level reconstruction (of the international system) enables micro-level reconstruction at the country level (for more on this see Box 5.1).

International governance of territories was also given an IGO imprimatur, as with League of Nations rule over the Free City of Danzig under the provisions of the 1919 Treaty of Versailles from 1919 to 1939, and the Saar from 1922 to 1935. In several ways we could see this form of activity as having had the same effect as with UNRRA in helping improve the normative image of reconstruction efforts in general. The League's administrators undoubtedly did a great deal to protect minority populations, to act to deal with disputes between the territories and other nearby states and to develop constitutional guarantees for the population. This has continued as a successful strategy since the end of the Cold War by the EU, the Organisation for Security and Cooperation in Europe (OSCE) and UN among other IGOs in Cambodia (UN Transitional Authority in Cambodia (UNTAC), 1992–3), Bosnia-Herzegovina (1994 to the present), Kosovo (UNMIK, 1999–2008) and East Timor (UN Transitional Administration in East Timor (UNTAET), 1999–2002) (Caplan 2005: 29, Chapter 1).

These cases have become paradigmatic in thinking about nation-building and reconstruction ever since. To summarise, the reconstruction exemplars of Germany and Japan have to be seen in the context of a 'reconstructed' macro-international system (especially its financial architecture), and a clear and enforced change in not only the political, but also the cultural mindsets of the countries involved. It was made clear to their populations that only certain beliefs and activities were acceptable and others deviant.

## Box 5.1

### *German and Japanese reconstruction, 1945–55*

At the end of the Second World War the victorious Allies (the 'United Nations', led by Britain, China, France, the United States and the Soviet Union) decided to dismember Germany into 'zones', dismantle the political, economic and social organisational structure of the National Socialist State and in effect rebuild the German nation. The same fundamental logic was used for Japan and, to a much lesser extent, Italy. The process was interrupted after 1947 by the onset of the Cold War between the former partners, but the western zones of Germany, Japan and Italy all benefited from a huge ($50 billion) injection of soft loans and direct aid to rebuild the shattered infrastructure of the countries and more widely of western Europe as a whole. This 'Marshall Plan' was largely successful in creating or at least enabling the 'economic miracles' in Germany and Japan in the 1960s. There was little or no obstruction from the previous power hierarchies who had been comprehensively defeated in battle. Reconstruction took place on the following levels: physical infrastructure; institutions; political and cultural; 'de-Nazification' or 'democratisation'; legal; military; and civil and economic. The legal efforts aimed at 'reconciling' the defeated countries to their neighbours both internally and by a form of retributive justice (see pp. 116–17) in war crimes tribunals, some of which were directed by international legal teams.

Sources: Killick (1997); Beschloss (2002), Dobbins *et al.* (2003)

## Reconstruction after the end of the Cold War

There are important differences in the normative background to discussions of efforts at 'reconstruction' in the post-Cold War period. Primary among these is a changed environment for claims to, and discussions about, sovereignty, a subject we broached briefly at the start of Chapter 4. Sovereignty has been termed the 'master noun' of international relations and derives much of its underlying meaning from classical western political thought, and especially from thinkers like Thomas Hobbes and Jean Bodin. This has consequently greatly coloured the global view of what a state is and what rights and duties states owe their citizens and vice versa (Slomp 2008). It might be argued that, as with the debate on democracy, the Western Powers that dominate the global system have come to be seen in developing countries as moving the goalposts whenever developing countries interpret sovereignty in ways deemed unacceptable in western capitals. So, as many writers (e.g. Caplan 2005; Jackson 2007) have pointed out, the 'new interventionism'

**Plate 11 Rebuilding a war-damaged bridge in southern Lebanon: post-war reconstruction includes not only infrastructure but also rebuilding fractured relationships in society**

and its allied concept of a 'responsibility to protect' (R2P) represent both a realist, national interest-based justification for intervention to address UN Charter Chapter VII 'threats to international peace and security' and liberal impulses to protect vulnerable populations in civil wars. Governments and populations in developing countries may be wrong to see R2P as 'imperialism' on occasions, as in Afghanistan, Iraq or Sudan currently, but they nonetheless do often so feel.

As a consequence of these twin impulses, various new epithets have emerged to join with the existing ideas of reconstruction and international administration that predate 1990. Primary among these are 'nation-building' and 'state-building'. The first of these is usually taken to refer to the 'people' of a given area and to an ethos, the second to the building of institutions, though the two have often been semantically confused in recent times. Caplan (2005) distinguishes 'international administration . . . from nation- or state-building (the two terms are frequently used interchangeably) though state-building is very often an integral part of an international administration' (Caplan 2005: 3). We might therefore suggest that the definition of what exactly 'reconstruction' means changes in line with the state of the international system and the obsessions of the actors that are prominent power holders within it, rather than the objective needs of the populations affected by conflict and war.

## Nation-building

The successes of the essentially US-funded initiatives between 1943 and the early1950s gave rise to a belief that the 'nation-building' of Japan and Germany were paradigmatic examples of how it should be done and were much evoked in subsequent reconstruction efforts, notably, and probably most misleadingly, in the aftermath of the 2003 invasion of Iraq. Francis Fukuyama (2006), an advocate of the intervention in Iraq, is surely right when he says that both conservative (for which read mostly Republican) and Democrat (or 'liberal') Americans 'have come to support nation-building efforts at different times – conservatives as part of the "war on terrorism" and liberals for the sake of humanitarian intervention' (Fukuyama 2006: 1). It might also be said that many Americans would defend the parallels of the intervention in Afghanistan and Iraq with that of Germany and Japan and refer to this as 'nation-building' – as in both cases they see it as constructing political institutions, coupled with economic development. In American minds, nation-building reflects 'the specifically American experience of constructing a new political order in a land of new settlement without deeply rooted peoples, cultures and traditions' (Fukuyama 2006: 3). However, this was certainly not the case in Germany, Japan, Afghanistan or Iraq, where there were existing political and other traditions, albeit illiberal ones.

'Nation-building' is explicitly defined by the American think-tank, the Rand Corporation, as 'the use of armed force as part of a broader effort to promote political and economic reforms with the objective of transforming a society emerging from conflict into one at peace with itself and its neighbors' (Dobbins *et al.* 2007: xvii). This explicit espousal of military force sits uneasily with those who wish reconstruction to come from within a society, the basic desire of the liberal, and not to be imposed from without, the basic instinct of the realist. The Rand authors call this distinction 'co-option', where 'the local population are actively involved in all stages of the planning and execution of a nation-building' exercise and 'deconstruction' as was the case in Germany and Japan in 1945 (Dobbins *et al.* 2007: xx).

This easily gives rise to claims that the United States has used a relatively benign expression to hide its essential national interest, or what Jacoby (2007) calls the '*Realpolitik* of [its] hegemonic interest'. He finds it strange indeed that parallels with the Second World War reconstruction efforts have been used uncritically and ahistorically by the United States' administration to justify policies that are muddle-headed and 'focussing on "how", rather than "why"' they should be undertaken (Jacoby 2007: 522). Other writers also question the 'purpose, legitimacy, goals and effectiveness of "nation-building"' and point to its 'mixed' record. Democracy, a prime aim in all such efforts since 1990, has resulted and brought about a semblance of order in some cases (Bosnia, Namibia, Sierra Leone and East Timor are key examples), while in others (like Cambodia) peace, but not democracy, has resulted, and in yet others (Somalia, Afghanistan, Iraq, the Democratic Republic of Congo, Haiti) neither peace nor democracy have resulted (Hampson and Mendeloff 2007).

What is certain is that 'reconstruction' as a term is deeply embedded in the historical consciousness of the great Western Powers, and especially of the United States, and that it will have other resonances in other parts of the world, in particular in the developing countries that are our main focus. For them 'reconstruction' and its successor terms, 'nation-building' and 'state-building', have the tinge of 'imperialism', inevitable given the majority of these states' experience of contact with the west. What seems like a good idea to a victorious power is not necessarily experienced in the same way by a vanquished one. It also has direct consequences for interveners, as happened in Somalia, for example. To use Keen's expression: '[o]ne of the most important roots of violence is a sense of having been *humiliated*' (Keen 2008: 50, his italics).

Nonetheless we now have books emerging with snappy titles like *The Beginner's Guide to Nation-Building*, a kind of do-it-yourself approach to dealing with failed states, also produced by the Rand Corporation (Dobbins *et al.* 2007), with useful graphs and chapters on every conceivable aspect of the task. More seriously, such manuals do tend to show us that although: '[e]ach nation to be rebuilt may be unique . . . the nation-builder has only a limited range of instruments on which to rely'. The 'instruments' are itemised as various kinds of military and administrative personnel, as well as 'experts in political reform and economic development' (Dobbins *et al.* 2007: vii). It is tempting to point out that this process tends to exclude the 'locals' at the expense of outside 'experts', and books like Dobbins *et al.* (2007) do tend to put such an emphasis on the outside agents concerned. But can the locals be ignored? A more liberal school of 'state-building' would tend to disagree.

# State-building

The main reason why reconstruction has been so warped in its conceptualisation and implementation is that it is now usually deployed in what Kaldor (2006) calls 'new wars', and these are nearly always in developing areas of the world. These wars have the characteristics described earlier in the book, where globalisation and state failure have combined to create a caste of freelance economic military entrepreneurs, often claiming ethnic or cultural motivations, but also often having distinctly economic motivations, such as the extraction of commodities for their own enrichment (Pugh and Cooper 2004). This combination of appeals to 'greed' or 'grievance' (Collier 1999) has 'state-disintegrating' consequences, as in the Democratic Republic of Congo, that are difficult to deal with locally given the enormous resources that wars put in the hands of these warlords.

To temper this 'new war' emphasis on the negative economic results of globalisation on many wars, it could also be claimed that economic factors have persuaded some warriors to lay down their arms in return for the economic benefits of peace, as in Ireland and, maybe, in Former Yugoslavia. This could be seen as a consequent explanation of the seeming paradox of the reduction of the number of wars discussed at the beginning of this chapter. The effects of economic interdependence on war and peace are much as they were when first described by Norman Angell (1910) and now by scholars who follow a broadly similar logic (Harff and Gurr 2004). But we would still maintain that the logic of economic gain generally tends to reinforce Pugh and Cooper's (2004) thesis above and Carolyn Nordstrom's findings of the essentially economic nature of the motivations of many who fuel the new wars in the context of globalisation (Nordstrom 2004).

In many ways, the features of, and the solutions to, these processes are analogous to what happened in Europe in the late Middle Ages when state structures grew and eventually led to the emergence of systems of security and law. Other writers have referred to a 'neo-Medievalism' that characterises the wars we are now seeing, defined by Hedley Bull as 'a system of "overlapping authorities and criss-crossing loyalties"' (Bull 1977, quoted by Winn 2004: 1). Indeed one of the differences between many developing states and those established 'developed' ones is that they are precisely often not 'a sovereign entity dominated by a single predominant national culture. An enormously compelling mixture of legitimacy and efficiency'. Instead, much of the developing world more resembles the City States of Renaissance Italy or Europe before 1630 than the settled nations of modern Europe (Berdal 2003; Winn 2004: 2–3).

But, as Herfried Münkler (2005) has pointed out, the difference with the Europe of the Thirty Years War, which devastated huge areas of Europe between 1618 and 1648, or the English Civil War (1642–9) is that:

> the *state-building wars* in Europe or North America . . . took place under almost clinical conditions, with no major influences 'from outside', whereas this has not been the case with the *state-disintegrating wars* in the Third World or the periphery of the First and Second Worlds.
>
> (Münkler 2005: 8, his italics)

We might also add that although the Westphalian system of states was the ideal after 1648 in many parts of Europe, it was not the reality until very recently. There were also far more stable groups of states in Africa than in Europe in 1960, even if many of them have since then not been characterised by economic or political stability.

So, how can *state-building* be brought about? As we have seen, the end of the Cold War has led to a very different set of problems than those which prevailed until 1990. Caplan (2005) has summed it up as follows:

> State-building refers to efforts to reconstruct, or in some cases to establish for the first time, effective and autonomous structures of governance in a state or territory where no such capacity exists or where it has been seriously eroded.
>
> (Caplan 2005: 3)

For the above reasons, and because we think that new thinking on the term 'reconstruction' is required, we use a broader definition than that usually employed. Hence, we believe that:

> [R]econstruction encompasses short-term relief and longer-term development. It extends far beyond physical reconstruction to include the provision of livelihoods, the introduction of new or reformed types of governance, and the repairing of fractured societal relationships. Thus reconstruction is not merely a technocratic exercise of rebuilding shattered infrastructure. Instead, it is an acutely political activity with the potential to effect profound social and cultural change. Post-war reconstruction holds the capacity to remodel the nature of interaction between the citizen and the state, the citizen and public goods, and the citizen and the market.
>
> (Mac Ginty 2007: 458)

This definition in no way detracts from the aims of the Marshall Plan period, but it does put them into some stark contrast with the more recent attempts to emulate the successes of the 1940s which have come unstuck. The next section will explore how the underlying rationale(s) used in such efforts may be said both to hold out hopes of success, and to point to inherent dangers.

## The 'stages' of peacebuilding: towards 'sustainable' peace

Many writers on whatever kind of nation-building, state-building, or peacebuilding we consider see the process of achieving success in somewhat mechanistic terms. So, for example, Roeder and Rothchild (2005) lay down a series of 'stages' that they believe are essential if the international community is to bring 'sustainable' peace to an area. Jeong (2005) sees them as necessarily 'sequential'. The touted solutions usually have to do with the encouragement or imposition of 'democracy' which corresponds with the liberal mantra that 'democracies do not go to war with each other'. Empirically that is true, but the concern is that countries in a state of *transition* to democracy, or even more so in a transition to *statehood* do. In recent times, Eritrea and Ethiopia have fought each other (1998–2000), and both are in transitional processes towards democracy. Developing countries are often in states of transition of some kind and are consequently more violent than those that are not.

Paris (2004) has suggested that given the difficulties of transition to democracy it would be better to concentrate on 'institutions' before changing political practices. The initial problem in the reconstruction of any developing country, he notes, is the lack of basic security. In successful states the monopoly of power is held by the state; in states that have experienced a civil war this is certainly not the case. So 'the first task of peacebuilding is to restore the monopoly as a foundation and precondition for all further institution-building efforts' (Paris 2004: 206–7).

We shall therefore now outline how that initial logic usually unfolds in terms of policy prescriptions and suggest how many writers have seen problems in the implementation of those prescriptions.

## Actors

The primary actors in the processes of reconstruction and state-building since 1990 have been:

- states
- IGOs and IFIs
- NGOs
- the press.

## States

In spite of George W. Bush's famous dictum 'we don't do nation-building' during a presidential candidates' debate in 2000, that is precisely what the United States has been doing in many parts of the world. The European Union has in many ways been an enthusiastic supporter of such efforts, taking a leading role in Former Yugoslavia through the European Agency for Reconstruction (www.ear.eu.int/home/), as well as in Cambodia. The UK has played a determinate role in Sierra Leone with military, civil and other assistance on a large scale, through the innovative Conflict Pools system pioneered by the Foreign and Commonwealth Office, Department for International Development and the Ministry of Defence (Ginifer 2004). So has France in its former colonies, such as Côte d'Ivoire and Chad, often through the African Development Bank (ADB). The EU and other groupings of states, like the Commonwealth, have played an important role in election monitoring.

## IGOs and IFIs

The role of intergovernmental organisations (IGOs) and international financial institutions (IFIs), like the IMF in Russia in the immediate aftermath of the Cold War, has been followed by a subordinate role for that organisation in other places. There has been the establishment of such specialist bodies as the European Bank for Reconstruction and Development (EBRD) and the Organisation for Security and Cooperation in Europe (OSCE).

The role of the World Bank has undoubtedly been the most important in reconstruction efforts, providing technical assistance in a myriad of ways. The way this has been applied has drawn criticism even from within the World Bank itself (Stiglitz 2003) for advocating policies which tended to kill the patient, rather than cure him or her. The World Bank has moved in recent years from the much-criticised Structural Adjustment Policies (SAPs), which often reduced the social safety nets for the poor in developing countries, in favour of Poverty Reduction Strategy Papers (though neither of these are specifically for post-conflict countries). IFIs also act as important coordinators of effort through such mechanisms as 'donor conferences'.

Most such organisations are western inspired and based, if nominally international. There are comparable economic organisations in the developing world, such as the Economic Council for West Africa, and regional development banks (such as the ADB). There are also embryonic political organisations, like the African Union, which is playing an important role in Darfur in Sudan. But the really big financial resources still come from western sources.

### NGOs

On the ground, NGOs have played vital roles both in primary assistance, such as the alleviation of hunger and medical assistance, in war and post-war situations, but also monitoring roles (as with the International Committee of the Red Cross (ICRC) and the Red Crescent). There has long been a tension between the human rights and civilian focus of such groups and the military or security focus of peacekeepers and military personnel more generally in the final stages of a conflict. 'Soft' and 'hard' NGOs and IGOs have on occasion found it difficult to cooperate, as in Iraq before 2003 when there was some friction between human rights NGOs and IGOs engaged in monitoring the (alleged) weapons of mass destruction.

### The press

The press presence is a phenomenon that has drawn much attention since the first Gulf War of 1990–1, and conflicts in Somalia, Rwanda and Bosnia in the early 1990s with the 'CNN' effect, the effect on western public opinion of the presence of media reporters in the midst of disaster areas (Hammond 2007: 12–13), being seen as a major pressuriser of governments to be 'seen to be doing something'. This is part of what might be called the 'framing' of international conflicts, affecting the types of intervention undertaken in significant ways (Hammond 2007). The media are also seen as a major necessity in the creation of civil societies by such bodies as the EU (Loewenberg and Bonde 2007).

## Democratisation

After the 'ceasefire' the job has only just begun, a realisation that first really dawned at the end of the First and Second World Wars. How do you pick up the pieces left by violent conflict? The job of disarming the German armies in those wars' aftermaths was relatively simple as they were disciplined organisations that obeyed orders and could be largely trusted to comply with agreements. The disorganised militias of the current period have a tendency to split into ever smaller factions. There are also 'drivers' that often mean that holding on to their weapons is a rational choice in a way that an army demobilising to return to a normal civilian life of work and family would not contemplate.

The international organisations, especially the United Nations, were arguably a bit slow in realising the importance of disarming insurgent groups in attempts at post-conflict development. Partly this was because in the early 1990s it was not fully appreciated how many wars would now be 'internal'. The first understanding of this came with the 'Agenda for Peace' (UN 1992, 1995), but as late as 1997 organisations like the Carnegie Commission on Preventing Deadly Conflict (1997) put less emphasis on 'conventional' disarmament than they did on that of nuclear, chemical and biological weaponry, so it was not until the UN Brahimi Report of 2000 (www.un.org/peace/reports/peace_operations/) that a clear commitment to conventional disarmament got a real boost and a consequent stressing in policy debates. The United Nations Institute for Disarmament Research (UNIDIR: www.unidir.org/html/en/home.html) has published annual reports on the progress of individual missions by the UN in countries like Cambodia, Sierra Leone and many others. The World Bank has been the leader in demobilisation and reintegration projects but did not get involved in disarmament until about 2003 (Muggah 2005: 243–4).

## Disarmament, demobilisation and reintegration

The resulting policy trio, disarmament, demobilisation and reintegration (often referred to by the acronym DDR), is directed at reducing the most obvious proximate source of violence in a conflict. The main system-level solution that is always touted to help the (re-)integration of former combatants, which Ozerdem (2008) describes as 'becoming civilian', is to create a working democracy. This includes reviewing the civil–military relationship, a feature in many coup-prone countries (as with Fiji or Pakistan), or with countries where dictators have an unhealthy relationship with their armed forces), as for example in Zimbabwe, which is arguably worse in the long run for local and regional prospects for peace and prosperity alike. An important corollary to this is security sector reform (SSR) where the army and police are reformed to make them more reflective of democratic norms and practices, not mere protectors of the elite and their own livelihoods. SSR has been defined as follows: 'Security sector reform aims to develop a secure environment based on development, rule of law, good governance and local ownership of security actors' (GFN-SSR: www.ssrnetwork.net/about/what_is_ss.php).

First, these efforts can collectively be summed up as attempting

> [t]o devise transitional arrangements for the short term. These must
> provide the modicum of political stability necessary to conduct
> elections to a constitutional assembly and the security for delegates
> to assemble, conduct constitutional debates and craft political
> institutions to maintain stability and foster democracy for the longer
> term.
>
> (Roeder and Rothchild 2005: 2)

Second, these efforts also attempt to build arrangements for the longer term, in the form of rewriting constitutions, even devising new parameters for the 'state'. Most prominent among these have been the 'Taif Accord' in Lebanon of 1989 (www.al-bab.com/arab/docs/lebanon/taif.htm) and the Good Friday Agreement in Northern Ireland of 1998 (www.nio.gov.uk/the-agreement).

The importance of, and potential for, DDR and SSR in using the tools of development to try and transform conflicts are therefore huge. Their aims are both on the individual and the collective level. On the individual level the aim is the transformation of rebel movements into peacetime security forces or other economic groups and the demobilisation of huge numbers of young people who have often known nothing but war and killing in their short lives. This individual demobilisation has to provide extensive educational, social and psychological help to young former combatants (Peters 2007). The group from which they come then has to be transformed into a political party that relies on the ballot box, not the gun, for its legitimacy. Jeroen de Zeeuw (2008: 1) is succinct in his assessment of the likely result of this: 'Experiences from people directly involved in the transformation of such movements show that the process is extremely complex and time-consuming and has a high risk of failure'.

Nonetheless it has often been tried. One recent example is instructive. In Sierra Leone the difficulties of transforming the Revolutionary United Front (RUF), the rebel group led by Foday Sankoh, into a 'less violent political organization' failed until the UN peace mission effectively detained 'a large proportion of the movement's more politically articulate elements' (Richards and Vincent 2008: 91). RUF foot soldiers have not, on the whole, been retrained, except within the new regime's armed forces and police. Richards and Vincent (2008) conclude: 'Unless the problems of an expanding and increasingly impoverished youth underclass are addressed, violent instability is likely to return to the forests and diamond districts of rural Sierra Leone' (Richards and Vincent 2008: 100).

On the collective level DDR and SSR aim to provide the basis for a lasting political settlement, through such processes as constitution writing (Caplan 2005: 29), which has occurred in over 200 states since the early 1970s, nearly always internationally brokered by IGOs like the Commonwealth or think tanks like the United States Institute of Peace (Widner 2005). It is a complicated procedural process that often drags on for years during or, sometimes, after the conflict is mainly 'over', and aims 'to develop a sense of inclusion and trust (social capital)' in a process that will hopefully encourage peaceful dialogue not conflict through providing frameworks of cooperation where different sections of the population feel their interests are being acknowledged. This content of representation (after Pitkin 1967) has been found by some researchers to have 'no major effects on post-ratification levels of violence in some parts of the world, such as Europe, but do make a difference in Africa, the Americas and the Pacific together' (Widner 2005: 516). This would seem to indicate that such efforts have some empirical evidence to back up their claims.

As Roeder and Rothchild (2005) admit, the underlying rationale for these actions is a belief that democracy is the essential tool that can calm the fervid spirits of war. But what if the erstwhile combatants have been divided by religious, ethnic or other problems that might lead them democratically to want to *divide from, not unite with,* each other? 'Majoritarian democracy can be a potential source of heightened interethnic conflict' (Roeder and Rothchild 2005: 5). So one solution that has been widely touted is 'power sharing', as was widely tried in the 1990s.

## What is missing from the democracy and DDR analyses?

The following issues will be discussed:

- Having a peace to keep?
- 'Spoiler violence' in post-conflict reconstruction
- The challenge of small arms proliferation
- How can former combatants be 'demobilised and 'reintegrated'?
- The challenge of public health
- The challenge of the presence of outside actors.

### Having a peace to keep?

The main 'official' issues identified in most DDR operations by the UN have been with

> 1) problems associated with the establishment and maintenance of a
> security environment early on, and 2) problems concerned with a lack
> of coordination efforts among the regional and international
> communities, the various groups involved in a peace mission, the
> peace mission itself, and the post-conflict reconstruction effort.
> (UNIDIR 1996–8: 211, quoted by Gamba 2006: 54)

DDR assumes the war is 'over' or at least in its final throes. But is there not (again) an 'artificial distinction between armed conflict and post-conflict'? And are the international organisations putting an excessive emphasis on DDR policies as 'magic bullets' (Muggah 2005)? There are therefore a number of grounds on which the above democracy and DDR orthodoxy can be challenged. Some of them are generic and some (even many) more are based on the empirical observation of case studies.

We can also point to a more complex problem. As we have stressed, the causes and results of wars are intimately linked (Blainey 1988). But what if the DDR process itself actually makes people who are already very upset even more so? Grievances from before a conflict are carried into it and beyond it. Can the bringing of democratic institutions persuade combatants to feel that they can now lay down their weapons and all these hatreds will just evaporate? Keen's analysis that 'greed' and 'grievance' are not sufficient to explain why conflict breaks out, with which we broadly agree, means that a very deep-rooted analysis has to be made about all actors' responsibility for the fighting that has taken or is taking place, not just the militias (Keen 2008). Maybe, as with Sierra Leone, the

Elders provoked violence by their insensitivity over a long period to the demands of youth. Are they to be the new 'Members of Parliament'? How does a democratic process address a perceived lack of 'respect' agenda? How does the DDR process address a cycle of abuse, maybe over many generations? How do they know they will not be further 'betrayed' (Keen 2008: Chapter 3)?

## *'Spoiler violence' in post-conflict reconstruction*

In addition, in the aftermath of a number of civil wars and conflict in developing countries, it has been found that the main occupation of many in the youthful population of the country has ceased to be 'normal', but rather revolves around membership of various militias, groups that often indulge in 'freelance' work on the side. In Afghanistan, for example, former Taliban and other militia, or 'non state' armed forces' members took a long time to demobilise after the Bonn Accords of 2001 (http://ec.europa.eu/external_relations/afghanistan/intro/index.htm#bonn), and often resumed their former activities under cover of nightfall, for example (Giustozzi 2008). This was in spite of there being a new Constitution in 2004 and elections. On a more positive note, although youthful, badly 'demobilised' soldiers can become the thugs of the new 'parties' who intimidate their opponents, they can also form the nucleus at pro-democratic party rallies.

One related obvious area (dealt with elsewhere in this volume) is in the area of 'post-conflict crime' and what is referred to as 'spoiler violence' by disaffected paramilitary groups or even by 'official groups'. Sometimes it is driven by a deliberate attempt to undermine peace accords, sometimes by more venal motivations, but the results are identical. The point is that such violence seems attendant on most, if not all, post-conflict situations. It has been defined as 'violence that deliberately attempts to undermine peacemaking processes and peace accords' (Mac Ginty 2006) and it clearly will have a major impact on attempts at post-conflict reconstruction. However, as John Darby has put it, 'although substantial research attention has been paid to the origin and dynamics of ethnic violence, to the first moves towards negotiations, and to spoiler violence, the threat to post-accord reconstruction is under-researched' (Darby 2006: 6).

Spoiler violence can be generated by unofficial actors (militias, criminal groups, etc.), who feel that the DDR process has failed them, as in Liberia in the 1990s, or by the state itself provoking violence, as in Zimbabwe with the taking of land from white farmers in clear violation of the 1979 Lancaster House Agreement, or the government of Rwanda in 1994 by provoking the genocide. Often this is because a conflict in its final or initial post-conflict stage is still one where groups contesting established governmental power are jockeying for position for both a negotiated outcome and on the 'battlefield' while the state is trying to do the same (Höglund and Zartman 2006). The Taliban was not 'defeated' in 2003 and has been trying to bomb its way back into Afghan political life; it certainly does not consider the war 'over'. Neither do the various parties destabilising Iraq as of 2008, whether they be disaffected ex-soldiers and officials of the Saddam Hussein regime, or 'Al-Qaeda' or other Islamic insurgents. In other words, the parties and those attempting to 'manage' or 'resolve' the conflict do not operate on one sole path, but rather on parallel paths. Conflicts are not resolved in nice neat linear ways, but by a process of trial and error, more like a spiral than anything else (Lederach 1997).

In places like Northern Ireland, where there exists a fully functioning state apparatus of police, army and law courts, many previous paramilitaries have found that crime and spoiler violence is a lucrative occupation, the only one in many cases for which they have any training (Mac Ginty 2006). How much more so is this the case in countries that have no, or little, formal educational structures in place to fit people for more productive employment?

It must also be said that other forms of 'spoiler violence' are deeply ideologically satisfying for groups that feel they have not been given adequate recognition in the process of reintroducing structures of government. In the chaos brought about by the 2003 invasion of Iraq, for example, very little thought was given to what would be done about demobilised members of the Iraqi armed forces (see Box 5.2). It was certainly not considered that foreign insurgents would also join in the aftermath of the 'end' of the war proclaimed in May 2003 by President Bush, again for ideological reasons.

We shall return at the end of this chapter to what this might say about future prospects for such massive 'nation-building 'projects backed by military force and with a clearly defined economic and political agenda.

## Box 5.2

### The problems of reconstruction and DDR in Iraq, 2003–8

The official 'end' of the war in Iraq in May 2003 was followed by a demobilisation of nearly all the Iraqi armed forces and a purging of practically all of the former regime's officials, with an interim Coalition Provisional Authority (CPA) that became an Iraqi government after elections in January 2005. The country has since collapsed into civil war with an estimated 200,000 civilians killed in intra-communal violence, an Al-Qaeda inspired insurgency, the actions of the international interventionary forces and by general criminality. Very little of the many billions of dollars disbursed in reconstruction funds has been used for that purpose, but rather has been lost to corruption or to the sheer cost of security. The CPA spent only a fraction of the $18.6 billion allocated for reconstruction by the US Congress for that purpose for example in 2003–4 alone (Diamond 2006: 176). It has since emerged that all the preparation for the transition by the Future of Iraq Project within the State Department has been essentially ignored and the Pentagon has been allowed to dictate a failed post-war policy, the rule of law flouted by the occupying forces (epitomised by atrocities by US troops in Abu Ghraib prison) and the Shia and Sunni militias alike. The only relatively peaceful area of Iraq since 2003 has been Kurdistan, which was effectively independently governed from the mid-1990s anyway. A 'surge' in US forces in 2007 led to a reduction in violence, but no one predicts a return to normalcy any time yet. Tensions also exist with Iraq's neighbours Iran (accused of aiding Shia violence by the United States), Turkey (which has been attacking Kurdish irredentists in the North) and Saudi Arabia (accused of encouraging extreme Sunni ideology, if not of actually supporting Sunni insurgents). Iraq has become a battleground for regional and global differences, thus complicating the reconstruction efforts immeasurably.

Sources: Ismael and Ismael (2005), Dodge (2006), Allawi (2007), Dobbins *et al.* (2007), Duffield (2007: Chapter 6)

### The challenge of small arms proliferation

Many writers (Duffield 2001; Muggah 2005; Kaldor 2006 are just a few examples) have noted that recent conflicts leave countries awash with small arms. In Ireland, where great efforts have been made to 'put weapons beyond use' this has not made them disappear for ever. Globalisation has ensured that small arms get sucked into conflicts far more easily than was the case in the Cold War, where at least the Superpowers acted as some sort of gatekeepers for violence and where

**Plate 12 No weapons sign at the entrance to a UN facility: disarmament, demobilisation and reintegration are often among the thorniest of post-war problems**

states were propped up, not, as they now are, in a state of collapse. This is not to minimise the horrible effects of superpower actions in many parts of the world, with the obvious after-effects of such actions still very visible in South East Asia, the Horn of Africa and elsewhere – we must be careful not to fall into Cold War nostalgia.

But the evidence of the destabilisation of many people's lives has particularly been evident in Africa where 'traditional violence' has been horribly incremented by the dissemination of huge quantities of small arms, often of former Soviet Bloc and Chinese manufacture. This in turn has destabilised whole societies and had devastating effects on the men, women and children involved, as well as on the stability of the states concerned (Mkutu 2008; Riungu n.d.). So yet again we have the paradox of fewer actual 'wars' but increased insecurity encouraged by the after-effects of 'old wars' that stimulate the lower level of violence that is a feature of the 'new' ones.

In the case of Ireland, Colin McInnes (2000) has identified a number of issues that have to be addressed when decommissioning weapons. They can act as shorthand for other cases (McInnes 2000; Fitz-Gerald and Mason 2005).

1 WHEN to decommission? Before or after the final political agreement? Should this be a prerequisite for negotiation?
2 LINKAGE to other issues? In Ireland, those issues included release of prisoners. Problems included 'inequality' of concessions.
3 HOW to decommission – who provides data on weapons held; phasing of weapon surrender; to whom?
4 WHOSE weapons – those of 'insurgent groups'; 'Government' or 'occupying forces'?
5 WHAT weapons. Small arms, explosives . . . ? N.B. 'the real "weapon" is the skill and experience of those who made them'.

(McInnes 2000: 89)

In general, what we can say is that disarmament is therefore a phase that overlaps demobilisation and reintegration. This is because the signing of a peace agreement often leads to large numbers of young men using their weapons in a freelance way – usually through preying on their own or other communities. In Africa, where there are few if any effective border controls (or indeed clear borders), armed gangs of former combatants regularly cross into areas that have low policing on missions of loot and rapine. This post-accord criminality is thus both a national and an international feature of efforts at DDR (Muggah 2005; Mac Ginty 2006).

## How can former combatants be 'demobilised' and 'reintegrated'?

Solutions have included the absorption of former combatants into existing police and military forces, even if DDR and SSR should clearly, and ideally, lead to far greater reintegration at other levels of society. It should therefore aim to 'help them develop alternative income-generating activities so they can provide for themselves and their families', though de Zeeuw comments that '[i]n many cases, the real socio-economic needs of the rank and file of former rebel organizations . . . are not addressed' (Zeeuw 2008: 12–13). The World Bank and major western governmental agencies like DFID have in particular urged such 'best practice' on IGOs trying to implement such schemes. Surveys of such practice (as with Fitz-Gerald and Mason 2005) are as yet inconclusive with evidence clearly tending to vary according to a number of factors. These can be said to include the following:

- The commitment of donor countries to the process.
- The conditions on the ground. So (we might say) in [country x] and [country y] there are reasons to be optimistic. In [country z] these conditions do not prevail, so [the following conclusions can be drawn]. We clearly have to be careful about overgeneralisation.
- The commitment to, and the ability to supervise 'security sector reform' (SSR).

SSR is a particularly difficult area that has been increasingly studied and implemented in recent years, by both IGOs like the OSCE in Eastern Europe and civilian forces operated in conjunction with the UN more widely. Prominent among such organisations are the Global Facilitation Network (GFN) for Security Sector Reform (http://ssrnetwork.net/) run by the UK Government's DFID (GFN-SSR 2007); the OECD (2007) and UN-INSTRAW (International Research and Training Institute for the Advancement of Women, a UN agency that is particularly interested in the implications of SSR for gender relations).

GFN–SSR (2007) identifies four particular areas that need to be addressed in SSR:

1  Core security actors (police, gendarmerie, civil defence, militias, etc.)
2  Management and oversight bodies
3  Justice and the rule of law
4  Non-statutory security forces ('liberation armies', private security organisations etc.).

It has to be said that in some cases the record of the international community in SSR has been very patchy. The Dayton Agreement of 1995 had important SSR elements in it, though Dayton has been severely criticised for leaving three separate armies in existence (Fitz-Gerald and Mason 2005: 13), a gap that has been addressed in Kosovo by setting up a police training school.

Some of the worst examples in terms of levels of violence can be found in the linked conflicts of Angola and the Democratic Republic of Congo as well as in the Sudan, though there are many other candidates (a good source is the Geneva-based 'Small Arms Survey' organisation: (www.smallarmssurvey.org/index.html). Angola was struggling to emerge from a civil war which dated back to independence from Portugal in 1975 (for a good overview, see Cramer 2006: Chapter 4). The DRC has fallen into total, and heavily armed, chaos since the arrival of huge numbers of Rwandan *genocidaires* after the massacres of 1994 in Eastern Congo, some of whom have been supported by local and international actors with free supplies of cash and arms. The international community's efforts, through the United Nations Angola Verification Missions, UNAVEM I, II and III in the 1990s (www.un.org/depts/DPKO/Missions/unavem1) to disarm the combatants in Angola was a humiliating failure, blamed by some on its inadequate budget and force levels (Gamba 2006: 61), but by others on its fundamental misreading of the nature of the civil war in which it was trying to intervene. Cramer (2006: 143) puts this down to the impossibility of rounding up the huge numbers of guns that have always flooded into Angola from the west since the seventeenth century and 'international linkages, political and economic' which are part of '500 years of violent conflict' (Cramer 2006: 147). In effect, Cramer asserts that the spread of capitalism, through globalisation, is the problem and liberally minded IGOs can do little about this. We might also reiterate the point made earlier, that war is a profitable enterprise and that combatants have to be given very clear reasons why they would want to substitute that earning potential for the economic uncertainties of peace (Nordstrom 2004).

For even if it could be argued that such generalisations ignore the very real benefits that capitalism has bought for many previously poverty-struck developing countries, we also have to admit that the record of capitalism as a force for non-violent beneficial change is hard to show in much of Africa (see Box 5.3 on the DRC), but that is demonstrably not the case in much of Asia, for example. In a globalising world, the boundaries of where such spoiler violence can be found are unpredictable in the extreme. The same could be said of externally generated violence for more venal reasons in the DRC where freelance groups, multinational companies and different 'allied' or 'enemy' governments use the opportunity of the chaos to line their pockets with diamonds, coltan (a vital ingredient in mobile phones: see Pugh and Cooper 2004) and other raw materials. Without a viable state it seems clear that no war ever 'ends'.

---

## Box 5.3

### *Disarmament, demobilisation and reintegration and security sector reform in the Democratic Republic of Congo*

The civil war in the DRC erupted after the genocide in Rwanda in 1994 forced many hundreds of thousands of Hutu extremists and refugees to flee to the DRC from Rwanda. The *genocidaires*, or *Interhamwe*, took their arms with them and set up enclaves from which they embarked on raids into neighbouring countries and preyed on the local populations with the national army being in no state to stop them. Other local militias formed and the area descended into anarchy, not helped by predatory capitalist entrepreneurs making the most of the anarchy to enrich themselves, as did the armies of Rwanda, Angola, Zimbabwe and Uganda, whether invited or not by the government in the capital, which had very little effective control over its eastern provinces. An 'All-Inclusive Accord' was signed between most of these warring parties in 2002 and agreed terms of reference for both SSR and DDR. UN Peacekeepers were deployed to the Eastern (Kivu and adjoining) areas and a semblance of national control re-established. The situation, however, remains very tentative, so although there have been serious attempts at DDR by the UN and other organisations the situation in the East of the country is still chaotic with local warlords regularly challenging the Blue Berets and DRC official forces, often successfully. Over 4 million people are considered to have been direct victims of the fighting and accompanying destruction. Perhaps 3,000 of the at least 20,000 militia in Kivu alone can be said to have been successfully demobilised.

Sources: Pugh and Cooper (2004), Boshoff (2005)

## The challenge of public health

Developing countries generally have a very low ability to provide even basic levels of health care for their citizens, a problem exacerbated by conflict, which drives out both the central government as well as IGO and NGO provision. Therefore a clear potential beneficiary of the bringing of stable government to an area or region, it is hoped, is that it will not only reduce levels of crime and violence but also help in the stabilisation of the institutions of the state, which generally include educational, medical, and other social welfare facilities. The re-establishment of these institutions is often overlooked in writings on reconstruction, but by far the greater proportion of deaths and other suffering come from public health failures. Of the over 4 million victims so far of the civil war in the DRC, '[r]ather than battlefield deaths, most of these fatalities have been the result of disease and malnutrition as the state has failed to provide public health care or maintain sanitation and related infrastructure' (Mac Ginty and Williams 2005: 173). It is certain that in the calculation of 'war-related deaths' we have to take into account those caught in the cross-fire of different groups, as well as the increase in morbidity due to people being displaced by the fighting, the spread of disease and the reduction of spending on health care by governments fighting for survival against insurgent groups (Muggah 2005: 240).

**Plate 13  A UNICEF water tank in southern Lebanon: public health issues often pose a greater danger than direct violence**

In some cases, failures of the health care system in developing countries can be the *cause* of men joining an insurgent group in the first place. One story we were told by a researcher in Sierra Leone was that a young man whose pregnant wife was refused treatment without a bribe at the (supposedly free) local hospital, as a result of which she died, used the first bullets from his new Kalashnikov to shoot up the maternity ward and its head doctor (Ahorsu 2007). It must also be understood that with the widespread use of rape as a weapon of war and the systematic abuse of women in war zones, huge mental and physical health problems are caused that can take decades to heal, if they ever can be (Nordstrom 1999).

## The challenge of the presence of outside actors

The success or failure of the liberal peace has at its heart the dilemma of *who* or *what* is to do the reconstructing. The assumption is that this will be done by the 'international community' working together in the United Nations and other IGOs, or subcontracting the work to NGOs (Richmond and Carey 2005). This is what happened in the cases of Germany and

Japan in the 1940s (Williams 2005) and in those cases the local populations generally accepted the legitimacy of the actions taken. The same cannot necessarily be said of more contemporary examples.

## The UN, IGOs and NGOs

The problem in many contemporary conflicts is that the international community acting though IGOs like the UN are rarely the only players. Their military muscle is generally weak or absent, and like NGOs they are reliant on peacekeeping forces to be able to operate (for the experiences of NGOs in East Timor and Sierra Leone, see Jackson 2005). In some cases, NGOs and the United Nations are reliant on tacit or overt militia (even insurgent) support and are therefore both subject to often intolerable pressures to conform to what can be seen as 'alien' cultural practices by the local populations. Hence in Afghanistan during the period of rule by the Taliban, the UN and NGOs were in effect forced to comply with extreme *Sharia* law principles banning the unveiling, or even touching, of women. Even more seriously, in Iraq NGOs and the UN were forcibly put on notice that their presence would not be tolerated (Monshipouri 2005). In this (albeit extreme) case, the dissuasion was by the expedient of a large bomb which destroyed most of the UN HQ in Baghdad and killed its Representative Sergio Vieira de Mello in 2004.

In less violent cases the presence of 'alternative' reconstruction groupings can directly challenge both the operations and the logic of liberal peace 'official' players. One example can be found in Lebanon where Hezbollah has its own 'reconstruction' arm, Jihad Al-Bina, and the Gulf states sponsor rival groupings, often to counter the ideological leanings of other groups. Such groups can rapidly marginalise the UN and conventional NGOs. The UN cannot, for example, distribute $12,000 in cash per household as Jihad Al-Bina did after the July 2006 war in Lebanon (Mac Ginty 2007: 458).

## Concluding discussion and suggestions

What can be done to improve matters? One depressing conclusion might be to say that all efforts at bringing about better outcomes in reconstruction and its allied strategies of DDR and SSR will always fail because of the necessarily violent nature of civil wars and endogenous state building (Cramer 2006). A liberal peace interpretation might well be to say that there is a need for better institutional responses (for example Paris 2004; Gamba 2006). Chabal and Dalloz would point to an embedded enthnocentricity in such statements, an unwillingness to accept that we need to take cultural and historical context into account in condemning local practices or trying to impose 'a linear, when not a singular, form of modernisation resulting in Westernisation' (Chabal and Daloz 2006: 9). A less extreme critical analytical position might be to say that we need to listen to local populations more (Mac Ginty 2006). A more 'structural' approach would point to the underlying economic problems that assail many developing countries. As we saw with the above discussion of Sierra Leone, DDR and SSR will work only if employment can be found for the vast underclass that is now a feature of so many developing countries. War, to put it bluntly, is profitable; peace is not (Nordstrom 2004).

More widely, it is clear that the misuse of the term 'reconstruction' in the early 2000s may well in the long run serve as the most hubristic of all misuses of a term, simultaneously devaluing a major historical success by misassociation and damaging hopes of any further use of the model in the future, a much greater potential problem as it is a basic ingredient of the policy toolbox of advocates of the 'liberal peace' (Williams 2007b). We assert that the distinction that dates back to the American Civil War between accusations of 'carpetbagging' and the more noble term 'nation-building' used about Germany and Japan in 1945, still has some force in the latest attempts at 'reconstruction' in Afghanistan and Iraq in the 2000s (Williams 2006: 139–45).

We therefore hope to have shown that the political arguments for reconstruction both lie on unstable historical foundations and have been further damaged by historical and recent experience, especially in Afghanistan and Iraq. In addition, economic arguments for intervention of all kinds have also been more fundamentally challenged from two key perspectives. Writers such as Cramer (2006) and Chabal and Daloz (1999, 2006) argue that the current debate on development in general and reconstruction in particular tends to downplay the importance of culture as a variable. This debate is arguably part of a much wider one, which suggests that there is no longer a coherent field of 'development studies' with 'competing schools of theory or paradigms' but that it has become subsumed within other disciplines (as with 'area studies') or hacked to pieces by those ('post-structuralists', 'postmodernists', 'post-Marxists') who have undermined all the 'positivist', for which read 'rational', bases for the study of development (Hoogvelt 1997: xi). One lasting impact of such epistemological uproar has been to make analysts (but not necessarily policymakers and politicians) focus more on what is specific to any reconstruction 'event' and less on what is generic, what might be termed a 'sociological turn'. We need to look at cases and their specificities, as well as to find 'one-size-fits-all' solutions.

It must also be remembered that some strategists such as Edward Luttwak (1999) and Stephen Van Evera (1999) think that the best and surest path to peace in most developing countries is to 'give war a chance', in other words not to interfere in any way or form, but to let the naturally dominant party emerge through war. This might be put differently by asking: *when does a conflict 'end'?* As we have stressed, the concept of bringing about a 'sustainable' peace is at the heart of thinking about the end of a conflict. But, as a growing number of writers have pointed out, the 'ending' of a conflict is in itself a problematic issue, and so too therefore is the concept of 'post-conflict development' and reconstruction. Both these perspectives are joined by one key commonality – the belief that war is the midwife of stable nation states, and it is the lack of such stability in various parts of the world that provides us with most of our problems. So we must look in every case at the underlying rationale for development and what makes for a successful nation in itself as a prelude to seeing what might go wrong with the process of 'state-building' or even 'nation-building'.

The botched 'reconstruction' of Iraq will stand as the key case study that will inform all attempts at nation-building for the foreseeable future. It has been pointed out by Stiglitz (2008) that the cost of the war to the American taxpayer (with the attendant lost opportunity cost for American education, health care and other policy areas) has been, after five years of fighting, over $3 trillion. The cost to Iraqis, in terms of their development and levels of life, has been arguably even worse since the first American intervention in 1991. One calculation has Iraqi per capita income dropping from $2,279 in 1984 to $627 in 1991 and $450 by 1995, and levels like those of Madagascar and Rwanda immediately before the 2003 war (Ismael and Ismael 2005: 613). Toby Dodge has pointed to the 'neo-conservative' belief that the United States would inherit a functioning Iraqi state, while it in fact collapsed with the invasion (Dodge 2006: 188). Charles Tripp goes further and suggests that the Iraqi state had in effect collapsed far earlier than 2003 and the looting of ministries was just the final act. But he also postulates that the Iraqi 'shadow state', organised along local lines of patronage, has since 2003 been able to organise a 'headless' insurgency that has tied Coalition troops down and further degraded the lives of ordinary Iraqis to catastrophic levels. There is, he postulates, no democracy to defend (Tripp, *Le Monde* 2008, quoted in a lecture at St Andrews University, 22 February 2008).

So what might be done to address these dilemmas? One way is to look back in the 'toolbox' and ask what we have used in the past. Should the aim be to allow state-building in the developing world to progress independently of outside interference, if Münkler's point about the need for 'clinical' conditions is to be met? One idea from the Cold War period is that of 'self-reliance', a decoupling from globalisation and a deliberate development of indigenous industry at the expense of manufactured imports, as was suggested in the 'New International Economic Order' of the 1970s in the United Nations Conference on Trade and Development (UNCTAD). But how would self-reliance stop the determined 'new' warlord intent on extracting his Coltan or diamonds from a decrepit African state (Pugh and Cooper 2004)? On the other hand, there is much to be said for Galtung's point that the terms of trade that this exchange implies (southern commodities for manufactured products from the west), means there is 'an enduring acceptance of a long-term inferior position in which it will be difficult to satisfy the basic needs of local people' (Galtung, paraphrased by Jeong 1999: 36).

In Chapter 6 it is hoped to take on these challenges and suggest how peace might conceivably be brought to developing countries by surveying approaches that attempt to examine the root, and especially the economic causes and consequences of conflict to try and resolve deep-rooted processes both locally (from below) and from above through institutional action.

## Summary

- The concept and practice of 'reconstruction' over many years has left it with a problematic image that cannot easily be repaired.
- Concepts and practices like state-building and nation-building give rise to questions about the motivations and practices of those who try and implement them.
- One-size-fits-all approaches to reconstruction are unlikely to lead to optimal peacebuilding outcomes.
- Disarmament, demobilisation and reintegration (DDR) as well as security sector reform (SSR) lie at the heart of most, if not all, attempts at post-conflict reconstruction and are in themselves problematic.

● The international community needs to take more notice of the specific cultural and other needs and constraints of any particular situation before embarking on reconstruction attempts.

## Discussion questions

1 Why has reconstruction had such an uneven reputation for effectiveness in the past decade or so?
2 Should the international community or powerful states attempt to 'reconstruct' economies and polities after wars?
3 What is wrong, or right, with the proposition that democratising a country will bring about a stable peace there?
4 What are the main features of the practices known as DDR and SSR?
5 How might the international community approach the question of reconstruction better in the future?

## Further reading

Some of the best recent discussions of the problems and potential of reconstruction can be found in Barakat, S. (ed.) (2004) *Reconstructing War-Torn Societies: Afghanistan*, London: Palgrave Macmillan, and Barakat, S. (ed.) (2005b) *After the Conflict: Reconstruction and development in the aftermath of conflict*, London: I.B. Tauris. The following is also very useful: Caplan, R. (2005) *International Governance of War-Torn Territories: Rule and reconstruction*, Oxford: Oxford University Press. The best defence of recent reconstruction attempts in Afghanistan and Iraq are Dobbins, J., Jones, S.G., Crane, K. and Cole DeGrasse, B. (2007) *The Beginner's Guide to Nation-Building*, Santa Monica, CA: Rand Corporation and Dobbins, J., McGinn, J.G., *et al.* (2003) *America's Role in Nation-Building: From Germany to Iraq*, Santa Monica, CA: Rand Corporation. The best short single criticism of this is Dodge, T. (2006) Iraq: the contradictions of exogenous state-building in historical perspective, *Third World Quarterly* 27(1): 187–200. The best introductions to DDR and SSR are Gomes Porto, J. with Alden, C. and Parsons, I. (2007) *From Soldiers to Citizens: Demilitarisation of conflict and society*, Aldershot: Ashgate, and Ozerdem, A. (2008) *Becoming Civilian: Disarmament, demobilisation and reintegration*, London: I.B. Tauris, as well as Fitz-Gerald, A.M. and Mason, H. (eds) (2005) *From Conflict to Community: A combatant's return to citizenship*, Shrivenham: Global Facilitation Network for Security Sector Reform.

## Useful websites

Details of current conflicts and wars can be found at Peace and Conflict Website, University of Uppsala, www.pcr.uu.se. Some details of important peace accords can be found at 'Taif Accord' in Lebanon (1989, www.al-bab.com/arab/docs/lebanon/taif.htm) and the Good Friday Agreement in Northern Ireland of 1998 (www.nio.gov.uk/the-agreement). Some key reconstruction agencies can be found at the following sites: European Agency for Reconstruction (www.ear.eu.int/home/); Department for International Development (UK) www.dfid.gov.uk/. On the UN's thinking on DDR, see the Brahimi Report of 2000 (www.un.org/peace/reports/peace_operations/) and the United Nations Institute for Disarmament Research (UNIDIR, www.unidir.org/html/en/home.html). GFN-SSR can be found at www.ssrnetwork.net/.

# 6 Development, aid and violent conflict

## Introduction: how are aid and conflict prevention linked concepts?

Before the end of the Cold War and the (re-)emergence of ideas of conflict management and resolution and reconstruction, which were the subject of Chapters 4 and 5, for a long time it had been believed that 'aid' would help developing countries to overcome their 'development' and 'conflict' problems in the broad senses of these terms. Even today some standard texts on conflict have very little mention of aid in their indexes, good as they may be in other respects. But since the end of the Cold War that omission makes increasingly less sense. The characteristics of the wars that we have identified have now put humanitarian agencies in the front line, not only as distributors of conventional aid, such as foodstuffs, but also as potential participants, along with conventional government agencies and military forces, and paramilitary actors in rebuilding 'failed states' (Ghani and Lockhart 2008). The actors that try to help alleviate the suffering of those increasingly caught up in current wars are collectively the 'humanitarians' in Hoffman and Weiss's (2006) term. 'External assistance' has become vitally important for both governments and IGOs, and it has also become big business for firms who disburse or build infrastructure for the disbursement of aid and other economic help (Boyce and O'Donnell 2007). One important question that all who now study the conflict–development nexus are now asking is whether they can provide any kind of solution to the evident suffering of developing countries' populations, or whether they are indeed part of the problem.

The most obvious victims of wars in developing countries are civilians, but so are also those who attempt to help them. Hoffmann and Weiss point out that not only are 'the victims of war . . . the actors' intended targets', but also '[h]umanitarian organizations have reacted to the new wars but have not adapted' (Hoffmann and Weiss 2006: xvi–xvii). Other writers go further and see the aid agencies as part of both a new pattern of global governance by the North whereby the populations of the South are made to feel their 'exclusion' in new ways and to enforce the ideological precepts of the liberal peace, in effect as agents of a new 'imperialism'. According to this view, underdevelopment has come to be seen as a security threat, not just a humanitarian disgrace, and consequently all those who try to correct this insecurity are in effect complicit in such a logic (Duffield 2001, 2007; Easterly 2006). Equally problematic, these and other observers see aid as actually *fuelling* wars, keeping them going. Carolyn Nordstrom reports a conversation she had in Angola with a local youth during the civil war – 'Peace? Forget it, there's too much money being made here' (Nordstrom 2004: 191) – as one example of such feelings.

We have therefore chosen to extract the idea of 'aid' from our wider discussion of conflict in developing countries, because we believe that, as with issues of gender, health and other 'personal' issues, the problematic of aid's motivations and delivery gives us a powerful series of perspectives on what is right or wrong with current approaches to conflict and development. So aid provides another link to understanding the dynamics of conflict. It is usually seen as being part of a wider attempt to arm societies against negative influences – to develop their economies and in particular to help them pursue liberal democratic peace strategies. Before 1990, it was often a part of Cold War strategy in the war of the two blocs. Since 1990, aid has been seen as using the 'anticipated "peace dividend" to repair the ravages of the superpower competition in many war-torn and conflict-prone societies' (Forman and Patrick 2000: 2) and as an integral part of the liberal peace tool kit (Marriage 2008: 5–6).

## The purpose and history of aid

The *purpose* of aid has been defined, first, as an

> international social contract . . . a broad understanding amongst
> developed countries that, in order for the world to be, or to be seen to
> be, a moderately equitable place, or at least to alleviate some of the

worst suffering, there needs to be some form of international
assistance.

(Hunt 2004a)

Janet Hunt points out that, as well as this laudable aim, '[m]any donors
provide aid not only for humanitarian reasons, but to enhance their own
economic and political interests, through encouraging their own exports,
or shaping the economic policies or political persuasion of recipient
countries' (Hunt 2004a: 67). It could be seen as yet another weapon in the
arsenal of 'economic statecraft', to use the famous phrase coined by
David Baldwin (1985).

So, aid has never been an unproblematic issue. Like all the other concepts
we have used in this book, arguments in favour of and against aid have
tended to be couched in evolving conceptual discussions, often more to
do with the politics and economics of the West than any objective analysis
of what is best for developing countries themselves. They were supposed
to be grateful for whatever they could get.

## Aid in historical perspective

In one of its first formulations as a result of the Marshall Plan (the full
title of which was the European Recovery Program, initiated by the US
Foreign Assistance Act of 1948), 'Marshall Aid' was open to the same
criticisms as those levelled against 'reconstruction' more recently. It was
seen as politically motivated, with strings attached which tied the
recipient into an economic and political system that they did not
necessarily want, and it was often only a sticking plaster on a big wound.
Nonetheless, until the 1970s 'aid' was seen by non-Marxists as a largely
unproblematic extension of the idea of 'charity', helping out those less
fortunate than oneself. As a child, I was told that any food I did not eat
would be sent by parcel to help the 'poor children of Africa'. But in the
1970s that critique got more intellectually acute; it was now asserted that
aid gave rise to 'dependency' and that was as a bad a thing in LDCs as it
was on the streets of London. Peter Bauer revived the idea that trade, not
aid, was the key to development. He saw the positive examples of
countries like Singapore and other newly industrialised countries (NICs)
forging ahead by opening up their economies and the progressive
sclerosis affecting the socialist developing countries and those who still
put their faith in handouts from the rich countries (Bauer 1991). This
view was, and is, unpopular in some quarters – the *Guardian* described

him as 'the shrillest Thatcherite spokesman against development aid for the third world' (Roth 2002).

Both superpowers used the idea of 'aid' in their own ways to buy influence in the newly emerging developing world. The Soviet Union set up 'radial' trade and development agreements (so called as they radiated from the hub of the Soviet Union), of which one of the most notorious was the provision of cultural, industrial and security assistance (including nuclear arms) to Communist Cuba, in return for Cuba providing much of the Soviet Union's needs for sugar, tobacco and a security base in the Caribbean. The United States provided huge amounts of Marshall Aid to western Europe and followed that up with technical assistance, soft loans, etc. as well as military 'advice'. This activity was predicated on the American success in rebuilding its own economy after the Great Depression. It also fell away after the debacle in Vietnam in 1975 and the rise of the new economic orthodoxy of free markets epitomised by President Ronald Reagan and British Prime Minister Margaret Thatcher, as will be explored further below (Ekbladh 2006; Sutton 2006).

## The economics and politics of aid: the case for intervention in developing countries

In the context of a book like this, a first set of questions about the case for intervention has to take into account both the economic and the political. These have tended to be put into separate disciplinary boxes, but such an approach can be seen as one-sided and prone to leading us into many misapprehensions and misconceptions.

## The economic case for intervention

British Labour Party politician, Jack Straw, summed up why there is a widespread belief that poverty and conflict overlap:

> Look at where there are people living in poverty, on less than $3 a day and where there is conflict. The overlap is an exact fit. And look at where people live in prosperity and lack of conflict. Again the fit is exact.
>
> (Straw, BBC Radio 4, 10 February 2007)

Jeffrey Sachs, author of *The End of Poverty* (2005), billed by *Time Magazine*, in both 2004 and 2005, and proclaimed on his own website as 'one of the hundred most influential people' on the planet and 'the world's best known economist' (Sachs n.d.) echoed this in his 2007 BBC Reith Lectures:

> War can . . . erupt as a result of the collapse of an impoverished society, one suffering the scourges of drought, hunger, lack of jobs, and lack of hope. Ending poverty is therefore a basic matter of our own security.
>
> Darfur, Somalia, Afghanistan. These are all, at their core, wars of extreme poverty. So too, quite obviously, were the recent wars of Liberia, Sierra Leone, Haiti, and many others. The U.S. has just established a new military command in Africa, declaring Africa to pose new security threats to the U.S. But even as the U.S. spends more than $600 billion on the military, and even as U.S. counterinsurgency forces spread out across the impoverished stretches of the Sahel, the U.S. will never achieve peace if it continues to spend less than one hundredth of the [U.S.] military budget on Africa's economic development. An army can never pacify a hungry, disease ridden, and impoverished population.
>
> (Sachs 2007)

In much of the writing on development there is an implicit or explicit reference to the economic causes of conflict that have made it necessary, or to the potential healing power of economic action. Initially, all of these explanations ask what is it that makes for, in David Landes' (1998) term, the 'wealth and poverty of nations'? His essential point is incontestable – states and regions are differently endowed with economic assets and resources by virtue of nature's distribution of wealth. Landes points to the now somewhat discredited, but still valid, axiom that 'geography, especially climate, influence[es] human development' (Landes 1998: 3). It has been crudely suggested that hot climates can lead to less ardour in the work place and the 'productivity of labor in tropical countries was reduced accordingly', a form of nineteenth-century environmental determinism that many would find distasteful. Disease, high morbidity, especially among infants, and poor water supplies have added to this obvious burden (Landes 1998: Chapter 1; see also Chapter 1 of this volume for more discussion on the human side of underdevelopment).

Classical economists (of whom Landes is one) give us to believe that states emerge from a natural process of a locally and internationally optimal allocation of resources, including land, capital and labour. Hence 'mature' economies have tended to go through a process of development. What is wrong with this? First, the 'mature' economies' all flourished in war and peace under a strong protective shield during their early development, whereas in contemporary times most of the least developed countries (LDCs) have been urged to compete in international markets without such a benefit. Second (and more importantly), societies do not just get to choose their economic policies in a rational way. Some societies, like Switzerland, have managed to survive and prosper in spite of having virtually no economic advantages – mostly low grade and mountainous land areas, endowed with poor natural resources, afflicted by linguistic and religious difficulties and surrounded by powerful and unfriendly neighbours, all factors that have on occasion engendered serious civil strife. Yet there are others, like Nigeria and Russia, that are endowed with enormous natural resource bases and educated populations that seem to be in a state of perpetual strife. Some slightly 'populist' economists like Jared Diamond point to societies that implode through ecological hubris and even 'passivity' faced with overwhelming challenges. Size is on some occasions a benefit and on others a problem (Diamond 2005).

Of course, globalisation might be said to have exacerbated both the differences and the potential benefits and disadvantages of such initial economic profiles. In the first wave of globalisation in the nineteenth century, this became concretised in an imperial relationship often based on economic exploitation. In its earlier manifestations, in the nineteenth century, globalisation has been identified by historians as being categorised as being 'archaic, proto-modern and post-colonial' (Hopkins 2002).

In the latest wave of globalisation since the Second World War, the economic relationship has arguably not changed much, but has been replaced by a 'centre–periphery' relationship often based on the 'centre' being well endowed with capital and technology and the periphery with a wealth of primary resources and cheap labour. This is not a problem, or indeed a surprise to classical economists, but of course it does create tensions that often come out in apportioning blame for both underdevelopment and the ensuing conflict. Scholars have asked repeatedly whether globalisation therefore leads to the 'convergence or divergence' of societies and economies (Hülsemeyer 2003)?

## Is it all about 'economic readjustment'?

One of the major recent wings of 'liberal peace' theory has been that which talks about 'greed and grievance', a theme taken up at some length in Chapter 1. The debate about whether the pursuit of market reform helps or hinders development in LDCs was shown in that chapter to hinge on whether the market alleviates one of the main causes of conflict, which we identified as being *poverty*. The encouragement of trade plays a significant role in liberal thinking about comparative advantage (Adam Smith 1776), as well as in the idea that trade links encourage peace (Mill, Bright etc.). As Jacoby has succinctly put it: '[l]iving freely is thus trading freely' (Jacoby 2007: 524). So what is, potentially at least, wrong with the assumption that if we get the economics of an LDC emerging from war right, we will then get the politics right too?

To put it in a nutshell, if the recipients (or 'beneficiaries') of market reforms are of the clear opinion that they will not be better off as a result of them, they will tend to lump together their sense of grievance, from whatever source that comes, with the message that their main persecution comes from a capitalist, globalised world system. If they are then told that they must comply with a policy of 'reconstruction' they will then reject the whole package. So, as with the *causes, escalation and maintenance* of conflict (Pugh and Cooper 2004) outlined in Chapter 1, so with the attempts to end it. We will explore the reasoning of why intervention

**Plate 14 Repairing war-damaged housing in Bosnia: who should pay for this, and what role should private enterprise play?**

might end up making conflict worse rather than better with a more in-depth examination of the economic arguments below.

In contrast to the 'Keynesian' interventionist, import-substitution, economic policies pursued by western states and the IGOs alike until about 1980, a policy based on much more unfettered free-market principles prevailed. This is often referred to as 'Reaganomics' (after President Ronald Reagan, 1980–8), and was also espoused by UK Prime Minister Margaret Thatcher (who served between 1979 and 1990). This policy had profound effects not only on domestic economic policies across the west, but also in their impact on the thinking of international institutions like the World Bank and the IMF in the 1980s and in the promotion of export-led growth by LDCs. Forceful economic arguments against direct aid were made by writers like Bauer (1991), who claimed it led to a form of welfare dependency similar to that experienced by benefit-dependent dwellers in western inner-city areas. But the main drivers were political and came from Washington and London. The key effect was to limit the granting of direct aid and to make all loans dependent on political and economic 'conditionality'. The result was a weakening of many developing countries' economies, so that the end of the Cold War and the withdrawal of bilateral Soviet or American aid often led to their total collapse rather than the hoped-for transition to democracy.

## More recent thinking about the links between conflict, development and the need to help struggling developing economies

In 2007, the Reith lecture given by Jeffrey Sachs summed up what might be called the most recent version of the 'classical' view on the links between aid, development and conflict:

> Why does Africa lag? Here is where the scientific evidence on extreme poverty is vital. The overwhelming non-scientific assumption held in our societies is that Africa suffers mainly from the corruption and mismanagement of its leaders. With the viciousness and despotism of Robert Mugabe in Zimbabwe, it's an understandable view. Yet this seemingly self-evident view is wrong as a generalization. Zimbabwe may get the headlines, but there are many countries in Africa, like Tanzania and Mozambique just nearby, that have talented and freely elected governments struggling against poverty. But they too face great obstacles, and their people too continue to suffer from extreme deprivation.
>
> (Sachs 2007)

The logic that this has inspired is that deprivation must be tackled by external intervention. One obvious way has been by various educational programmes to provide all children in developing countries with access to a laptop computer, to NGO activity to spread knowledge about the likely vectors of the AIDs virus and to help the 'sustainable development' that western agencies believe will enable LDCs to grow while respecting the environment. In war-torn societies such intervention has most obviously been by direct international assistance. Writers like Mary B. Anderson believe that in certain circumstances, aid can indeed support peacebuilding activities, but that carelessly applied aid will encourage damaging resource transfers and in effect disempower local people from taking control of their own destinies – summed up as 'do no harm', perhaps a newer version of Bauer's strictures on the dangers of welfare dependency (Anderson 1999). Her ideas have certainly struck a chord with those who believe that local solutions to local problems are more likely to be workable and effective than ones imposed by outsiders. It would also be true to say that the freemarketeers (like Bauer) have largely won the day on aid, in that it is now appreciated that throwing money into economies that are incapable of using it in productive ways is not very sensible. But it is also appreciated that aid that goes into countries that are deemed to have a track record of sound market-oriented policies is able to deliver effective, sustained policy reforms. Of course this illustrates how we can see aid as another support for the overarching ideology of the liberal peace.

It also has been widely decided by western policymakers and IGOs that, as we stated at the beginning of this chapter and earlier in the book, the experiences of the 1990s (especially the abortive intervention in Somalia) and the subsequent events after 9/11 show that development is now a security issue. There was 'a mounting perception and articulation that underdevelopment was dangerous and that – by implication – raising the level of development would increase security in the country and ultimately globally' (Schnabel and Carment 2004, Vol. 2).

Hence much aid in the 1990s and since started to be directed towards DDR programmes with the aim of increasing 'human security', an ideal of seeing development and security as closely interlinked, which is an unexceptional statement but which needs much greater clarity to operationalise. The concept is often explicitly linked to conflict prevention, with the idea that if the population's security needs can be provided for, the rest of their economic and social existence will be ensured. Aid and conflict prevention measures in general should therefore 'focus on long-term, structural challenges to build safe, just and stable societies' (Schnabel and Carment 2004, Vol. 2: 109–31). One criticism that can be levelled against the concept is that it also seems to have an inherent belief that basic 'human needs' can indeed be identified, a claim that we have seen in relation to conflict resolution techniques and proposals in Chapter 4. Other commentators on human security are not sanguine as to its usefulness. Marriage comments that it could be seen as so 'infinitely elastic' a concept as to be 'analytically unhelpful. None the less – or maybe because of this – its popularity in policy-making circles has been more enduring' (Marriage 2008: 4, 6; see also Duffield 2001).

## The organisation of aid

Partly inspired by this new policy paradigm, since the end of the Cold War a 'humanitarian network' has emerged to deal with both the results of conflicts and aid and reconstruction efforts alike. Since the start of the 'War on Terror' in 2001, conflicts in Afghanistan, Iraq and elsewhere also show that the delivery of aid for purely humanitarian reasons has become in effect even more subordinate to geopolitics than it was during the Cold War. One example is President Bush's statement in 2003 'Can we have the first bombs we drop be [ones that contain] food?' (*sic*, Keen 2008: 117). Marriage (2008: 2) comments that 'there is abundant evidence that the motivations of donors are mixed and that aid and other interventions are often tempered with blindness or misunderstanding'. What, for example, has been the net result of the huge amount of aid that has been, and continues to be, pumped into the Palestinian territories for the local population? How can it be effective when the macro-political situation (the failed Oslo Accords, the Intifada, and the brutal simmering war between Israel, Hamas and Hezbollah) means that the aid funds which were intended to bolster the peace process are often of limited effect. Chris Wake paraphrases President Bill Clinton on this case – 'no peace deal can be sustainable if it does not genuinely respond to the needs of everyday people' (Wake 2008: 109).

The actors in the delivery of aid are also those present in the full-blown reconstruction efforts discussed in Chapter 5. Donors and deliverers of aid can be bilateral or multilateral, most usually charitable and sometimes denominational. Humanitarian aid can be delivered by both NGO and IGO organisations as well as, most notably, by the International Committee of the Red Cross, which also aims to provide assistance and protection of civilians through the long-established Geneva Conventions. The UN coordinates its activities through the United Nations Office for the Coordination of Humanitarian Affairs (OCHA: http://ochaonline.un.org/).

Hoffman and Weiss (2006) refer to this as a 'humanitarian network', which encompasses a constellation of national, IGO, NGO and private contractors that surround a 'country in crisis, with its own Government, local NGOs and victims/recipients of aid' (Hoffman and Weiss 2006: 122).

The operation of this network obviously varies from case to case. In some areas there will be a great deal of NGO activity, in others very little, as when there is a very poor security situation. To take a particular case study, that of Sierra Leone, here all the above actors were (and are) present in a conflict which is both regional, in that it affects the whole of West Africa, but also with specific elements due to the nature of the country and area. The (maybe only provisional) ending of the civil war was particularly engineered by the UK's armed forces and the post-war situation by the UK's development agencies and aid disbursers, although the United States has funded and mainly runs the UN Special Court for Sierra Leone, seen as a major part of the post-war reconciliation process (see Chapter 4). NGOs in Sierra Leone and in the proximate attempts being made in Liberia have made great strides in bringing 'human security' to the populations of these two states. No one would dispute the need to get rid of the appalling regimes of Charles Taylor in Liberia and Foday Sankoh in Sierra Leone (Atkinson 2008). But surely it would be prudent to say that the installation of democratic governments in these two places as a result of the expenditure of huge amounts of money by western states has not really addressed the underlying problems of these countries, which are not so much about democracy but about economic and social hardship and inequality.

One sure conclusion that has to be drawn from the present stage of capitalist development is that where there is no viable state structure the vacuum will tend to be filled by external and internal groups, usually armed to the teeth, and by the immense monetary capabilities of transnational corporations, who will do practically anything to ensure access to their raw material needs. The most obvious example of this is the trade in 'blood' or 'conflict diamonds', a subject that has spawned Hollywood films but has yet to produce any obviously effective codes of conduct for the extraction and end use of such products, ones which not only grace the necks and hands of some of the most beautiful women in the West, but also lead to the hacking off of equally beautiful necks and hands of women in Africa (see Box 6.1).

## Box 6.1

### *Blood diamonds and Sierra Leone*

The state of Sierra Leone, well endowed with natural resources, including diamonds, but with a succession of weak and corrupt governments, imploded with the end of the Cold War and the emergence of warlords like Foday Sankoh (and Charles Taylor in nearby Liberia) who used terror to extract and monopolise the exploitation of 'blood' diamonds. The international community recognised that markets in the west made such terror profitable and instigated the 'Kimberley Process' to identify and control such processes. This can be seen as being a useful and 'positive start . . . but only a start'. The key variable has to be seen as the need for a regional, or even global, and not purely national, solution to the dissemination of such materials. The links between the illegal and violent export of such goods has even been explicitly linked into the funding of globally focused groups like Al-Qaeda (Grant and Taylor 2004: 399). Maybe this will be what finally leads to their control, not the suffering of the Sierra Leonean and West African population in general. Sankoh was overthrown, but an uneasy truce is all that can be said to be holding.

Sources: Grant and Taylor (2004), Richards and Vincent (2008)

Below we will consider another, more radical, interpretation, that in fact the international community is responsible for the acceptance of a global and regional political economy that both encourages and supports local warlords in their freelance capitalism. Humanitarian action in that case could be only a slight panacea for a much deeper problem of governance on a global scale.

## The problems of aid dispersal

From the 1960s to the 1990s states and international organisations like the World Food Programme (www.wfp.org/english/), the World Bank and the IMF, became the key distributors of aid, increasingly backed up and after 1990 increasingly supported by NGOs like OXFAM. This distinction between Official Development Assistance (ODA) was intended to go up to 1 per cent of gross national product (GNP) by a UN target established in the 1980s. However, OECD countries' contributions had, by the end of the 1980s, increased to only about 0.36 per cent of GNP, though with the honourable exceptions of states, especially in Scandinavia, that have managed to donate up to 0.7 per cent. These sums were often dependent on economic changes, such as the application of structural adjustment programmes, and political conditionalities, such as crack-downs on corruption and the implementation of election monitoring. Furthermore, in many cases promises of aid were only partially delivered (Forman and Patrick 2000). Marc Williams' comment of 1994 that 'no clear standards exist by which to measure aid effectiveness and to determine under what conditions aid is likely to promote growth' (M. Williams 1994: 22–3) is still true today. In spite of this, it is often believed that aid will alleviate poverty and help to solve the conundrum outlined above by Jeffrey Sachs.

Why is this? First, aid cannot be delivered without security and without corruption. This applies as much to the providers of aid, like the United Nations, as to the receivers. It has been suggested that in effect an 'aid economy' grows up in parallel to a 'war economy', 'where the focus is not so much on benefiting from violence as it is on taking advantage of efforts to relieve suffering' (Hoffman and Weiss 2006: 107). In some conflicts, such as Bosnia and Afghanistan, maybe in most, aid can fall into the hands of warlords who exploit their position on the ground in an insecure environment to extort 'protection money' from aid agencies (Goodhand 2004). Second, in purely economic terms, an obvious unintended result of providing (for example) many tons of free foodstuffs to alleviate a famine situation is to make local production of such foodstuffs uneconomic. Third, aid agencies tend to create distortions in local employment patterns, as they can offer better salaries to drivers and translators as well as a more general workforce than the local economy can. In some cases, like the Palestinian Authority (PA), virtually the whole economy has become dependent on outside assistance for public sector salaries and, in that case, two-thirds of all government expenditures (Boyce and O'Donnell 2007: 200). Here aid is a positive incentive to corruption, which has arguably had unforeseen political results, including the rise of Hamas as an alternative to the PA in one section of Palestine (the Gaza Strip) and the consequent breaking up of that proto-state (see Box 5.2).

Hoffman and Weiss (2006) argue that recent thinking among western governments about the role of the private and public sectors (outlined above as a post-Keynesian consensus) has even led to aid being 'privatised' to some extent, to the point where for-profit organisations have been deployed in an effort to eradicate some of the 'inefficiencies' of the UN and public sector organisations. This has led to some 'murky' deals being struck to deliver security in many developing country conflict zones. They can certainly respond more successfully and quickly, where the UN

## Box 6.2

### External assistance and aid to the Palestinian Authority

Part of the peace process that has been under way since the Oslo Accords of 1993 (see Chapter 4) has involved the emergence of an internationally sponsored Palestinian Authority, that it is hoped will one day emerge as part of a 'two-state' solution for Israel and Palestine. The economic assistance given to the PA has been multifaceted and from many sources, including the UN, the EU and a number of individual governments as well as many NGOs. It has been estimated at $8 billion between 1994 and 2004. In 2005 $3 billion more was promised for the following three years and former UK Prime Minister Tony Blair was appointed in 2007 to improve the financial and economic performance of Palestine. GDP per capita has certainly risen since 1993 under the impact of such aid, but is still low by the standards of the Middle East ($1,493 in 2002). This has since dropped to $934 in 2004 under the impact of a renewed Intifada, and recent figures will be much lower still as the peace process has stalled. The key problem is one of a huge dependency on Israel for both access to export markets and imports, a corollary of huge dislike towards Israel, and massive corruption, an issue exploited by Hamas in its attacks on the PLO leadership in Gaza. The lack of any discernible improvement of the lot of ordinary people has increasingly pushed them, mainly out of desperation, into violent support for Hamas and other uncompromising political groups, which are often backed by outside powers like Syria and Iran. The area is a good example of the 'geopolitics of aid' discussed by Keen (2008) and the need for a regional political and economic approach as discussed by Pugh and Cooper (2004).

Sources: Pugh and Cooper (2004), Boyce and O'Donnell (2007: Chapter 7), Keen (2008)

might have to wait for years in a search for a consensus on a mandate (as is now happening in Darfur for example where the Security Council cannot agree on what form of intervention to authorise), but of course they risk suffering from a lack of legitimacy as they are seen for what they are, profit-making enterprises (Hoffman and Weiss 2006: 152–3).

There is also a clear problem of 'turf wars' developing between IGOs, NGOs and governments. In what David Keen (2008) aptly describes as 'complex emergencies', having so many players on the field is bound to lead to them duplicating each other, competing for scarce resources, in effect themselves becoming part of the system that is a civil war. One solution that has been suggested that maybe helps address this problem harks back to an older model. Rather than country-based policies, we arguably need regional policies, as with the Marshall Plan for Europe, or indeed the UNRRA, the first UN organisation that dispersed aid and helped displaced people on a global scale in the period 1943–6 (see Williams 2006: 113–22). After all, the 'new' wars do not respect national boundaries any more than 'old' ones did, and the economic issues of the regions affected have much in common (as in Western Africa) (Pugh and Cooper 2004: 80 and *passim*).

A final initial point for consideration might also be that it has to be asked if the weakest are not in effect the least protected? Tales of rape and child abuse have surfaced in a number of UN-run or sponsored camps in recent years, as far apart as Bosnia and Sierra Leone. The problem has been recognised as acute by refugee advocacy groups like Refugees International (www.refugeesinternational.org/content/article/detail/ 10276/). In addition 'non-standard' refugees tend to get the least attention from aid disbursement agencies partly because of their lifestyle, but also partly because of their evident poverty and lack of 'clout'. Keen's research in an earlier Sudanese conflict (in 1984–5) led him to believe that pastoralists (who are a very common population group in much of Africa) and rural dwellers generally get the worst deal in terms of distribution and help, as do more generally disfavoured sections of any society. The telling parallel he believes is that of the relief so badly delivered to New Orleans in 2005 (where most people who were neglected were black), or to Thailand and Sri Lanka after the tsunami disaster of 2004 where aid was much better delivered to town dwellers and those living in obviously popular tourist zones (Keen 2008: 121–5).

## The problems of protecting aid workers

Another result of the 'new wars' and also of the 'War on Terror' has been the breakdown of the idea that 'host' governments can or should protect aid workers to anywhere the same extent that used to be considered normal. A new phenomenon has emerged, that of the 'armed humanitarian', who is seen by some hostile locals as delivering not only aid but also a message of alien 'democracy' and western mores. For a conservative Afghan elder, bringing education to the women of his area, as UNICEF has done for example, is not a 'neutral' act; it is one that threatens his legitimacy as a lawmaker, and the very culture of his society. More generally we have seen a blurring of the distinction between civil and military actors, even if we must not forget that such distinctions have always to some extent existed. The most obvious example of this blurring

**Plate 15 Armoured UN vehicles: Aid workers have come under increasing threat as humanitarianism has become securitised**

is the use of private security companies to defend aid workers, and in many cases to replace regular military forces altogether, as in Iraq (Kinsey 2009). In the case of Afghanistan, provisional reconstruction teams (PRTs) have often mixed civilian and other non-military personnel with soldiers (for more on this see www.rusi.org/publication/whitehall/ref:I44C63D079FF53/).

As a result journalists, UN staff and other 'neutrals' have found that they are now, like it or not, seen as legitimate targets by warlords. In Afghanistan and Iraq this has particularly been the case, and the UN briefly withdrew its entire staff, humanitarian and otherwise, after the car bomb that killed over forty UN staff in 2003. They can now effectively operate only from bases inside the security 'green zone' in Baghdad. Médecins sans Frontières withdrew from Afghanistan in 2004 for security reasons. Almost one in five humanitarian staff surveyed in 2005 had been a victim of a 'security incident' (Buchanan and Muggah 2005). Many have been killed or kidnapped. Some have suggested that reducing the dissemination of small arms could help solve the problem (Howard 2008: 44), which seems unlikely given the difficulties that such an enterprise would pose in, say, Afghanistan, where possession of a weapon is seen as a basic sign of social status.

# Aid and 'social subjugation'

In more recent times, the discussion on 'failed states' has enlarged the debate on aid to include a critique of what the underlying motivations of the west are in granting aid to states like Mozambique and Afghanistan. One key writer in this mould has been Mark Duffield, whose view is that the discourses and practices of war and development have in effect become merged. He sees the old fear of insecurity as a feature of interstate conflicts having been replaced by a fear of wars within states; 'the threat of an excluded South fomenting international stability through conflict, criminal activity and terrorism is now part of a new security framework. Within this framework underdevelopment has become dangerous' (Duffield 2001: 2).

Duffield (2001) further asserts that the distribution of aid reinforces the position of the dominant local groups who can effectively veto or allow this distribution. In Sudan, he points out that even before the post-2000 fighting in the west (Darfur) there were 1.8 million displaced persons in the vicinity of the capital Khartoum and a further 2.2 million in a 'transition zone' between the Northern and Southern areas of the country. This was because the war until that date (and from about 1983) was between the Northern, latterly 'Islamicist' government and the Southern Sudan People's Liberation Army (SPLA) 'Christian' or 'animist' movement, until an agreement ended that war. The UN has supposed responsibility for the welfare of these people, a role that it is hard pressed to execute given the huge scale of the problem. The majority of the staff have to be vetted and approved by the government in Khartoum, hardly the most neutral agency (Duffield 2001: 202–5).

A case study that Duffield highlights in this context is of the huge numbers of Southern Sudanese Dinka people who have been displaced as part of the overall process. For him the key to understanding the way these people are exploited is to see them as making up 'an integral and self-supporting labour component of the agrarian and urban economy of Northern Sudan' (Duffield 2001: 209). Hence for Duffield 'aid agency models . . . are effectively blind to these structures of dominance and exploitation' (Duffield 2001: 230). Western governments, he asserts, are blind to ethnic differences and therefore to the agendas in fact being pursued by the Northern government to integrate unwilling peoples into their power structures. The same might be said about the brutality being shown to the peoples of Darfur since 2003 (though this is beyond Duffield's scope) (see Box 5.3). Duffield's blunt conclusion is that '[a]id

---

## Box 6.3

### *Delivering aid in Darfur*

The civil war that erupted in the western province of Sudan known as Darfur in 2003 started with the emergence of the Justice and Equality Movement (JEM), who demanded a similar deal for the area to that achieved (after a long civil war) by the Sudan People's Liberation Army in the south of the country. The war was the latest round in a long-standing dispute based on ethnic differences and, in particular, on the very low level of economic development of the area. The Government of Sudan (GOS) responded by using helicopter gunships and the Janjaweed (mounted Arab horsemen) militia that has killed at least 160,000–200,000 people in the subsequent five years. A plethora of UN agencies led by OCHA (World Food Programme, UNHCR, etc.) has attempted to bring help to the resulting 1.8 million people displaced internally and 200,000 who have fled to Chad. Human Rights Watch estimates that a further 160,000 are being denied aid by the direct actions of the GOS. The EU is also present as the European Community Humanitarian Aid Office (ECHO), as is the United States Agency for International Development (USAID) organisation that puts its aid figures at $757 million for 2003 and $509 million for 2005 alone. UNHCR and the ICRC, as well as organisations like the Norwegian Refugee Council, have reported many eyewitness accounts of GOS atrocities. China has been blamed for flouting UN Security Council resolutions and providing the GOS with military assistance and other support, criticisms in many cases backed by high-profile celebrities like George Clooney and Steven Spielberg. ICRC, among other, aid workers have been killed (as in Sirba on 13 February 2008). The EU and African Union are trying to put a peacekeeping force in place, but the maximum that is allowed by the GOS is 10,000, for an area the size of France. The force lacks sufficient helicopters. Jan Eliason, the UN official trying to coordinate aid and assistance, told the Council in March 2008 that 'the situation was getting out of hand'.

Sources: www.usaid.gov/locations/sub-saharan_africa/sudan/darfur.html, http://ec.europa.eu/echo/field/sudan/darfur/index_en.htm and www.irinnews.org/report.aspx?ReportId=76715

---

policy currently reinforces an ethnically structured system of exploitation', by refusing to see local complexity and thereby supporting illiberal regimes in their policies of exploitation (Duffield 2001: 248–54).

## Concluding discussion: does aid make conflict worse?

Many of the assumptions about peacebuilding take it as axiomatic that the development of each country takes a similar course, much in line with the classical view of development outlined in this and previous chapters. Hence, reconstruction that we looked at in Chapter 5 is to install, or reinstall, proper systems of governance and economic development. Even those who believe that such peacebuilding methods are beneficial are aware of the difficulties involved. Roland Paris warns against believing that 'war-shattered states can be hurriedly rehabilitated' (Paris 2004: ix). We might even worry that aid can actually transform power structures and facilitate the emergence of warlord politics. This has been seen as the unhappy experience in Afghanistan in the 1980s and even since the ousting of the Taliban and the emergence of the UN-backed Karzai government since 2001 (Goodhand 2004).

As we have seen above, others go much further and blame aid disbursement for the evolution of predatory capitalism itself and for the complicity of the international community in its worse excesses. Though Duffield's views are certainly at the extreme end of the spectrum of criticism of current aid policies pursued by western governments, IGOs and NGOs alike, his main critique is of the underlying logic of a 'liberal peace' paradigm that only sees what it wants to see, supposedly governments fairly distributing aid to needy people without fear or ideological favour. This he sees as naive and ultimately self-defeating. In recent work he has also accused IGOs and development agencies more broadly of a crude 're-packaging of these aims over the past half-century' that has done nothing to improve the underlying logic or the delivery of aid on the ground (Duffield 2007: 12). The underlying logic for him has been to provide a 'surplus population created through accumulation by dispossession [that] represents life belonging to capitalism' (Duffield 2007: 12). In this logic, what is happening in Darfur, for example, is in the interests of capitalist development but not of the local population.

The critique bears a certain resemblance to those of other writers like Cramer (2006) and Keen (2008), who perceive a variety of errors that derive from the West seeing the problems of development as being those of the aftermath of wars, rather than as due to the problems of a system of internal exploitation of one group by another in most countries that are examined. In effect, slavery has been replaced by a different form of rapacious global capitalism. No solution will, or can, therefore be found without realising that we need to identify the issues within the political economies of countries like Sudan before there can be any hope of addressing the long-term problems of both development and the conflicts that emerge from this, as the main underlying problems are ones of governance in developing countries. Neither, as both Cramer (2006) and

Keen (2008) make very clear, can we get far in understanding these conflicts without an appreciation of the importance of violence in development. It is, in Keen's words, a difficult issue of walking the 'tight-rope between explaining and excusing' (Keen 2008: 5). Violence was a great part in the development of western politics and economies; it is a part of those now undergoing a process of development. Maybe therefore aid can only ever be a sticking plaster on a necessary process of self-harm?

Furthermore, these writers all see the issues involved in development as part of a much wider nexus of liberal governance that perpetuates the North–South dependencies of the colonial period, except that now the main agents of dominance are not governments but western multinational organisations and IGOs that in effect do their bidding, 'the suppliers, facilitators and cultural sustainers of inhumanity' (Duffield 2007, quoting Slim 1998). The emergence of the New Wars has both facilitated and been facilitated by the borderless nature of post-Cold War capitalism, to create what Duffield calls 'network war' (Duffield 2001: 260) or Keen calls 'abusive war systems' (Keen 2008: 9). Aid is for them therefore an essential part of this 'network' or 'system' and must be reformed along with them if it is to help resolve or abate conflict.

The vital question therefore has to be whether aid is only a palliative for much wider problems created by a post-Cold War capitalism that now finds itself unimpeded by Great Power interests and is helped by the slow but sure disintegration of local state structures into a system of local clientelisms that do not respect the borders of national loyalties, but only the allure of money. The 'new' wars have created a new entrepreneurial class that serves powerful outside capitalist interests (for example in the extraction of diamonds in West Africa) and is unimpeded by local state authority. In such a situation aid distribution and the organisation of refugee assistance just adds more grist to local warlord interests. It might help assuage the consciences of western governments and their populations who want to 'do something' to help the starving peoples of the South, but in effect it does the opposite. The botched intervention in Somalia in the early 1990s may be said to be a paradigmatic example of that problem.

May we therefore go back to the question that is asked from opposite perspective by the conservative views of Edward Luttwak and his urging to 'give war a chance' (Luttwak 1999), and the much more radical views of Cramer and Duffield, or the more moderate views of Keen, Hoffman and Weiss? Is aid making the conflicts of Africa and elsewhere worse?

Would it not maybe be better not to distribute aid at all? Is the problem not the one it has always been – outside interference?

Conversely to follow such advice absolutely would be a counsel of despair, as countless more people would die as a result. In spite of their shortcomings, the international community has defined 'Millennium Development Goals'. The Group of Eight (G8) rich countries have made fulsome pledges to reduce poverty. Maybe most important of all, there is a growing awareness among ordinary people in the west that the problems of the developing countries are their problems too and they are willing to support political decisions to help their less fortunate sisters and brothers. More controversially, new donors are emerging, and especially in the Middle East and China, who now hold many dollar surpluses as a result of globalised trade patterns and other factors. But that is for another book to explore. We have to hope that the debate outlined in this chapter will throw up some better ideas for the aid debaters of the future.

## Summary

- Aid – its delivery and logic – has become a key element in understanding contemporary conflicts, and their potential transformation, in the developing world.
- The discussion of aid elicits very different reactions from analysts of development, often depending on the cases they have studied, but also as a result of their intellectual and policy approach.
- Aid is not 'neutral', either in its political logic or distribution.
- The period since the end of the Cold War has seen aid becoming 'securitised'.
- The delivery of aid often requires making difficult moral and political compromises.

## Discussion questions

1 Can a consideration of the motives for and the delivery of aid help us in an understanding of the dynamics of contemporary conflicts and wars in the developing world?
2 What moral and practical problems are there in the delivery of aid?
3 Does aid help in peacebuilding?
4 Why have aid workers now often become targets in developing country conflicts?
5 Should we 'give war a chance'?

# Further reading

Boyce, J.K. and O'Donnell, M. (2007) *Peace and the Public Purse: Economic policies for postwar statebuilding*, Boulder, CO: Lynne Reinner. For a general critique of aid see Duffield, M. (2001) *Global Governance and the New Wars: The merging of development and security*, London: Zed Books; Duffield, M. (2007) *Development, Security and Unending War: Governing the world of peoples*, Cambridge: Polity; Keen, D. (2008) *Complex Emergencies*, Cambridge: Polity; Easterly, W. (2006) *The White Man's Burden: Why the West's efforts to aid the rest have done so much ill and so little good*, London: Penguin.

For a critique of why the international community has gone wrong in its economic and aid policies towards Africa in particular, see Chabal, P. and Daloz, J.-P. (1999) *Africa Works: Disorder as a political instrument*, Oxford: James Currey; Chabal, P. and Daloz, J.-P. (2006) *Culture Troubles: Politics and the interpretation of meaning*, London: Hurst; Cramer, C. (2006) *Civil War is Not a Stupid Thing: Accounting for violence in developing countries*, London: Hurst; Calderisi, R. (2006) *The Trouble with Africa: Why foreign aid isn't working*, London: Macmillan.

# Useful websites

A good summary of the current disasters and responses to them can be found at: 'Relief Web': www.reliefweb.int/rw/rwb.nsf/doc114?OpenForm. Human security is best discussed at www.humansecuritybrief.info. The United Nations Office for the Coordination of Humanitarian Affairs (OCHA) can be found at http://ochaonline.un.org/. The World Food Programme is at www.wfp.org/english/. Some useful websites on the crises in Darfur in Sudan: www.usaid.gov/locations/sub-saharan_africa/sudan/darfur.html, http://ec.europa.eu/echo/field/sudan/darfur/index_en.htm, www.irinnews.org/report.aspx?ReportId=76715.

# ⬤ Conclusion

This book and the reflections on conflict and development contained
therein are intended to give those who are relatively new to the fields of
both conflict and development a better idea about the debates that we
consider to be the most important in understanding the relationship
between them. We are also aware that we cannot and will not have
satisfied all those who read it, as the debates we have summarised are
neither the only conceivable ones we could have considered nor by any
means those that some would have chosen to emphasise. We are also
aware that there are many different approaches that we could have taken,
from purely relating what the international development organisations
have been doing in conflict zones in an uncritical manner, through to a
hard-line 'critical' approach that would take as its point of departure the
premise that all western governments and international organizations are
primarily concerned with continuing their former imperialist ventures in a
postcolonial environment. To be sure, we have to state quite honestly that
we rather veer towards the latter position than towards the former, a
tendency that is shown by our privileging of certain discourses rather than
others. But we would also admit that without IGOs there can be no
delivery of better policies, without western governments there cannot on
the whole be resources and organisational abilities made available to
deliver those policies, and without some form of self-interest being
manifest there will be no incentive to think about what these policies
might be. Globalisation has indeed produced the curious antipathies,
synergies and disjunctures in thinking and action about development
noted here by Mark Duffield, David Keen and many others. We all need to
understand what those relationships are if we are to improve our game in
both the analysis of conflict and the processes of development.

So the approach we have taken in this book has been one premised on the
idea that there are serious problems with the way that the twin issues of

development and the conflict which is so often attendant on that long and painful process are thought about. We fully accept that there has been a huge amount of good will and effort put in over many decades by development economists, workers in international organisations, and even politicians, at every level of the global system to try and ameliorate the conditions of underdevelopment and war in which so many of the people on this planet exist. But we have to admit to some dismay that the main results of all this thinking and action have not been of huge benefit in many cases to those who are its main targets. Neither do we exempt our own profession of conflict analysis from these worries. Those who study conflict have, until quite recently, tended to ignore the problems of development. They have also tended to be stuck in the study of very small-scale examples and to take a 'tourist' interest in what is often abject horror and suffering. Very few analysts of conflict are, for example, prepared to spend more than a few months studying a conflict, visiting the area and developing a thorough understanding of its dynamisms over many years. Understanding requires empathy, and empathy requires a lot of contact with the real world of conflict. So if this book has a primary purpose, it is to get a wider debate going between these different constituencies so that the delivery of aid, the arrangements of post-war conflict situations and thinking about related issues might be improved upon in future.

A Conclusion should not be the place to revisit in detail the conclusions at the end of each chapter, but rather to draw out some of the overarching concerns that could be useful in directing future research and action. What might be some of these overarching concerns?

The first is that we are very adamant in our feeling that we need to appraise more rigorously the pitfalls and huge advantages presented by a use of historical examples in the study of conflict and development. On the positive side, we believe that without establishing clear genealogies of how and why certain terms are privileged in the theoretical and policy discourse, we will never understand why these terms are seen in such different ways by their imposers and recipients. But we also believe that this has to take into account how *local* understandings of historical discourses play out in a conflict (Chabal and Daloz 2006) not just our *western* readings of them. The obvious example that we have talked about at some length is that of 'reconstruction' (Chapter 4). The war in Iraq (2003 to the present day) shows us that the term can easily be linked into both the histories of the Iraqi people and also into that of those doing the 'reconstructing'. This can in turn evoke positive or negative historical connotations in both principal parties of the relationship. The alternative models that can be then generated can either exacerbate an existing conflict within a country or help it come to some kind of successful conclusion. There is already some suggestion that the people of the Middle East are now conceiving and practising more indigenous forms of 'reconstruction' through grassroots organisations, such as Hamas or Hezbollah, which have local credibility, but which evoke hostile reactions from many governments and IGOs. But if the IGOs' and governments' activities give the impression of 'colonialism' to the recipients, can they work? Equally in trying to 'resolve' a conflict or 'mapping' it, there is no use in the outside world imposing its interpretation of how history should be interpreted. Again in line with Chabal and Daloz (2006), we believe the 'interpretation of meaning' has to be local.

On a negative note, we have also tried to show where an understanding of history can actually exacerbate a conflict. In many areas of the world unscrupulous elites have stressed 'their' version of history to denigrate or even to incite their enemies to a hatred they did not previously feel. In the Middle East, for example, we can see that historical misunderstandings have become an embedded part of the discourse of conflict on all sides.

**Plate 16  Ruined tower blocks in Beirut: Hezbollah are organising local reconstruction efforts**

But there is certainly a need for more investigation of how this might apply in many African countries, where the historical and anthropological literature needs to be far better understood by those who study conflicts in those areas. We are far from understanding how history 'plays' in many conflicts in developing countries, either as a force for peacebuilding or as one for peace-destroying. One thing is clear, however: the conflicts or humanitarian emergencies that we might read about in our newspapers did not begin with the last incident. Instead, we need to transcend the tendency towards ahistoricism and realise that current conflicts are often merely the latest instalment in a complex history of conflict, identity changes, population flows, border redrawings and other long-term social, economic and cultural dynamics.

The next major concluding thought is that we are driven to believe that bottom–up activities for peacebuilding are more likely to have long-term effects than top–down approaches. The dangers of giving people the impression that they are having something passed down to them, rather than doing something for themselves, is bound to lead to a sense of disempowerment and alienation. If this is then reinforced by the feeling among a local population that the incoming ideas and power are not really

Plate 17 Stop sign in Jordan: care must be taken in the transfer of western ideas and practices to non-western contexts

there 'for them', then the development or peace that is hoped for will not do much to help solve the conflict in question. The presence of peacekeepers is, for example, often seen as necessary, but cannot be of much use to help a process of peace and development if those peacekeepers distort the local economy, suck out the best labour power, and generally lord it over the local population without contributing much to their security or well-being. The key point is that an appropriate balance between indigenous and external norms and capabilities needs to be struck. Of course, this is easier said than done and the nature of the balance will differ from context to context. But a good starting point for potential interveners is to move beyond a position of assuming that they have all of the answers. Instead, rather than viewing local populations as victims, recipients, dependants or troublemakers, it is important that they are viewed as change-agents with substantial capabilities.

Third, we would not be the only, but we would like to be the latest, couple of thinkers to doubt the all-embracing truth of the 'liberal peace' thesis. It may well be true, even empirically, that 'democracies do not go to war with one another'. But the point is surely that in the case of all developing countries struggling with, or attempting to emerge from, conflict the basic principle does not pertain. Democracies in Europe took many hundreds of years to hone their conflict-resolution skills, ones that still desert them quite regularly even so. The countries of Africa and elsewhere have not in many cases ever achieved full 'state-ness', never mind democracy. Maybe they cannot do so without a long-drawn-out process of violence, as some claim from a variety of standpoints. But even if they can, surely they should be allowed to do so without undue outside interference.

As a corollary to this point we believe that many of the examples we have explored here show that the uncritical use of neo-liberal economic policies has done much to exacerbate the bad odour in which many 'good' western principles are held in the developing world. Democracy is per se a system that most aspire to, but the relentless way in which the World Bank and other organisations have insisted on 'conditionality', 'big bang' changes and structural adjustment has done much to damage the view of those at the local level. This has been observed of course by World Bank officials themselves, with Stiglitz the most prominent among them. Others, like Amartya Sen, have noted that poverty is the greatest enemy of democratic change and have lambasted the IGOs for their narrow emphasis on empowering the elite in developing countries.

Conflict theory may have something to say here in a general way to the development economists and governance experts. Conflict resolution theorists (as was stressed in the Introduction), long derided as 'cranks' for advocating the empowerment of the grassroots of societies, are now seen as having seen the coming of elements of a 'post-state' world (through globalisation) well before the realist/statists did. What once was considered equally crankish in the area of the environment or even in the study of unconventional warfare, is now seen as pretty mainstream. Where only states were taken as the units of analysis in both conflict and strategic analysis, as well as in economics, sub-state actors, structures and individuals are now routinely evoked in suggesting both why problems occur and how to deal with them. IGOs will have to adopt this understanding to a far greater extent if they are to deal with today's and tomorrow's problems in the developing world. We may even have to break open that ultimate realist shibboleth of 'sovereignty' and contemplate reparcelling the states of Africa and elsewhere, or, alternatively, look to much more regional power sharing and identity-based policies. Kikuyu, Hutu, Tutsi or Xhosa people across Africa have to feel they can be given their recognition and dignity without only being referred to as 'Kenyan', 'Rwandan' or 'South African'. This is in much the same way as we have let the local populations of their respective areas sort out their identities in Ireland, Former Yugoslavia or the Former Soviet Union without losing all of the benefits that those 'unitary' bodies once provided. How we keep what is best about old structures, while allowing the emergence of new ones, is not a problem in the developing countries alone.

Fourth, we should be aware that the context in which development and conflict occurs is changing rapidly. This change stems from many sources: an increasing global population and the consequent pressure on resources; the changing nature of power relations as China, India, Russia, Brazil and others stake their claim to be regional and world players; the declining importance of sovereignty in a globalising world; the ever-present and growing dissatisfaction with the United Nations and other multilateral institutions; the growing significance of China, and some Gulf and Arab states as key players in development and humanitarian interventions. The key point is that many of the lenses that we have used to analyse conflict and development over the past decades will need to be radically reassessed to take account of the changing nature of conflict and development processes. What we think we know now, may not necessarily be fit for analytical or practical purposes in the future.

Last, but not least, we hope we have demonstrated that the problems of conflict and development are problems that affect all of us, wherever we live, and that there is a unity of the human spirit and of human suffering that makes us all morally responsible for each other's welfare. This is also true when we are attempting to impose democracy promotion and state building in conflict or non-conflict situations. We have endeavoured throughout this book to see development as both top–down, the work of institutions (Chapter 2), and as one that affects ordinary people (Chapter 3 and elsewhere). That does not mean that we should be prescriptive about the moral universe others live in, but it does mean that we have to take responsibility for the negative effects of our actions in the west when we think about the impact they will have in developing countries. We need a new ethic of development as we need a new ethic of international relations. That will have to be for the authors of another book in this series to think about.

# References

Abrahamsen, R. (2000) *Disciplining Democracy: Development discourse and good governance in Africa*. London: Zed Books.

Abrahamsen, R. (2004) Poverty reduction or adjustment by another name? *Review of African Political Economy* 31(99): 184–7.

ACCORD (2003) Owning the process: public participation in peacemaking – principles to guide policy and practice. Presentation by Conciliation Resources ACCORD Programme at an International Peace Academy Conference, New York, 12 February 2003: www.c-r.org.our-work/accord/public-participation/owning-process.php (accessed 18 March 2008).

Adamson, F. (2002) International democracy assistance in Uzbekistan and Kyrgyztan. In Mendelson, S. and Glenn, J. (eds) *The Power and Limits of NGOs: A critical look at building democracy in eastern Europe and Eurasia*. New York: Columbia University Press, pp. 177–206.

Addison, T. (2003) Communities, private sectors, and states. In Addison, T. (ed.) *From Conflict to Recovery in Africa*. Oxford: Oxford University Press, pp. 263–87.

Addison, T. (2005) Conflict and peace building: interactions between politics and economics. In Addison, T. (ed.) Special issue of *Round Table: Commonwealth Journal of International Studies* 94(381): 405–11.

Ahorsu, E.K. (2007) The political economy of post Cold War conflicts in Sub Sahara Africa: the natural resources factor. The case of the 1991 Sierra Leone civil war. PhD thesis, University of Kent.

Aird, S. (2001) China's Three Gorges: the impact of dam construction on emerging human rights. *Human Rights Brief* 8(2): 24–8.

Allawi, A. (2007) *The Occupation of Iraq: Winning the war, losing the peace*. New Haven, CT: Yale University Press.

Amnesty International (2003) Republic of Maldives: Repression of peaceful political opposition, 30 July: http://web.amnesty.org/library/Index/ENGASA 290022003 (accessed 23 July 2008).

Amnesty International (2008) *State of the World's Human Rights: Amnesty International Report 2008*. London: Amnesty International: http://thereport.amnesty.org (accessed 1 August 2008).

Anderson, M.B. (1999) *Do No Harm: How aid can support peace – or war*. Boulder, CO: Lynne Reinner.

Angell, N. (1910) *The Great Illusion: A study of the relation of military power to national advantage*. London: William Heinemann.

Appleby, R.S. (2000) *The Ambivalence of the Sacred: Religion, violence and reconciliation*. Lanham, MD: Rowman & Littlefield.

Armendáriz, B. and Broome, N. (2008) *Gender Empowerment in Microfinance*. Cambridge, MA: Harvard University Press.

Asian Development Bank (ADB) (2007) *Key Indicators 2007: Inequality in Asia*. Manila: ADB.

Atkinson, P. (2008) Liberal interventionism in Liberia: towards a tentatively just approach? *Conflict, Security and Development* 8(1): 15–45.

Avruch, K. (2003) Context and pretext in conflict resolution. *Journal of Dispute Resolution* 2: 353–65.

Axelrod, R. (1990) *The Evolution of Cooperation*. London: Penguin.

Azar, E. (1990) *The Management of Protracted Social Conflict: Theory and cases*. Aldershot: Dartmouth.

Baer, D. (2007) The immorality of Blackwater. *Guardian*, 6 October.

Baker, R. (2005) *Capitalism's Achilles Heel: Dirty money and how to renew the free market system*. New York: John Wiley.

Baker, S. (2006) *Sustainable Development*. London: Routledge.

Baldwin, D. (1985) *Economic Statecraft*. Princeton, NJ: Princeton University Press.

Ballentine, K. and Nitzschke, H. (2003) *Beyond Greed and Grievance: Policy lessons from studies in the political economy of armed conflict*. New York: IPA Policy Report.

Banks, M. (ed.) (1984) *Conflict in World Society: A new perspective on international relations*. Brighton: Wheatsheaf.

Bannon, I. and Collier, P. (2003) Natural resources and conflict: what can we do. In Bannon, I. and Collier, P. (eds) *Natural Resources and Violent Conflict*. Washington, DC: World Bank, pp. 1–16.

Barakat, S. (ed.) (2004) *Reconstructing War-Torn Societies: Afghanistan*. London: Palgrave Macmillan.

Barakat, S. (ed.) (2005a) Special issue: Reconstructing Post-Saddam Iraq: A quixotic beginning to the 'Global Democratic Revolution'. *Third World Quarterly* 26(4–5).

Barakat, S. (ed.) (2005b) *After the Conflict: Reconstruction and development in the aftermath of conflict*. London: I.B. Tauris.

Bass, G.J. (2000) *Stay the Hand of Vengeance: The politics of war crimes tribunals*. Princeton, NJ: Princeton University Press.

Bauer, P. (1991) *The Development Frontier: Essays in applied economics*. Brighton: Harvester Wheatsheaf.

Bauer, P. (1998) The disregard of reality. In Dorn, J., Hanke, S. and Walters, A. (eds) *The Revolution in Development Economics*. Washington, DC: Cato Institute, pp. 25–39.

Bayart, J.F. (2000) Africa in the World: A history of extraversion. *African Affairs* 99: 217–67.

BBC (2003) Baghdad protests over looting. BBC News Online, 12 April: http://news.bbc.co.uk/1/hi/world/middle_east/2941733.stm (accessed 19 March 2008).

BBC (2008) Country Profile: Bosnia-Hercegovina. *BBC News Online*, 1 January: http://news.bbc.co.uk/1/hi/world/europe/country_profiles/1066886/stm (accessed 23 November 2008).

Beevor, A. (2002) *Berlin: The downfall, 1945*. London: Penguin.

Bekoe, D. (2005) Strategies for peace in the Niger Delta. United States Institute of Peace Briefing, December: www.usip.org/pubs/usipeace_briefings/2005/1219_nigerdelta.html (accessed 1 June 2008).

Bell, D. (2007) *The Idea of Greater Britain: Empire and the future of world order, 1860–1900*. Princeton, NJ: Princeton University Press.

Belloni, R. (2007) The trouble with humanitarianism. *Review of International Studies* 33: 451–71.

Beneduce, R. (2007) Contested memories: peace-building and community rehabilitation after violence and mass crimes – a medico-anthropological approach. In Pouligny, B., Chesterman, S. and Schnabel, A. (eds) *After Mass Crime: Rebuilding states and communities*. Tokyo: United Nations Press, pp. 41–68.

Bercovitch, J. (1997) Mediation in international conflict: an overview. In Zartman, I.W. and Rasmussen, J.L. (eds) *Peacemaking in International Conflict: Methods and techniques*. Washington, DC: United States Institute of Peace Press, pp. 125–53.

Bercovitch, J. (ed.) (2002) *Studies in International Mediation: Essays in honor of Jeffrey Z. Rubin*. London: Palgrave Macmillan.

Bercovitch, J. and Rubin, J.Z. (1992) *Mediation in International Relations: Multiple approaches to conflict management*. London: Macmillan.

Berdal, M. (1996) The United Nations in international relations. *Review of International Studies* 22(1): 95–106.

Berdal, M. (2003) How 'new' are 'new wars'? Global economic change and the study of civil war. *Global Governance* 9(4): 477–502.

Beschloss, M. (2002) *The Conquerors: Roosevelt, Truman and the destruction of Hitler's Germany, 1941–1945*. New York: Simon & Schuster.

Bigsten, A. (2003) Selecting priorities for poverty reduction and human development in Ethiopia. In Addison, T. (ed.) *From Conflict to Recovery in Africa*. Oxford: Oxford University Press, pp. 106–22.

Bittman, M. (2008) Rethinking the meat-guzzler. *New York Times*, 27 January.

Blainey, G. (1988) *The Causes of War*, 3rd edn. New York: Free Press.

Blanchflower, K. (2008) Another poor year for overseas aid. *Guardian*, 5 April.

Bleiker, R. (2007) On the use and abuse of Korea's past: an inquiry into history teaching and reconciliation. In Cole, E.A. (ed.) *Teaching the Violent Past: History, education and reconciliation*. Lanham, MD: Rowman & Littlefield.

Bloomfield, D., Barnes, T. and Huyse, L. (eds) *Reconciliation after Violent Conflict: A handbook*. Stockholm: IDEA.

Boot, M. (2007) In defence of Blackwater. *The Press* (Christchurch), 10 October.

Booth, C. (2003) Prospects and issues for the International Criminal Court: lessons from Yugoslavia and Rwanda. In Sands, P. (ed.) *From Nuremberg to the Hague: The future of international criminal justice*. Cambridge: Cambridge University Press, pp. 1–29.

Booth, K. and Wheeler, N. (2007) *The Security Dilemma: Fear, cooperation, and trust in world politics*. London: Palgrave Macmillan.

Boshoff, H. (2005) Demobilisation, disarmament and reintegration in the Democratic Republic of Congo: pretext for a successful transition. In Fitz-Gerald, A.M. and Mason, H. (eds) *From Conflict to Community: A combatant's return to citizenship*. Shrivenham: Global Facilitation Network for Security Sector Reform, pp. 25–46.

Boulden, J. (2001) *Peace Enforcement: The United Nations experience in Congo, Somalia, and Bosnia*. Westport, CT: Praeger.

Boulding, K. (1990) Future directions in conflict and peace research. In Burton, J. and Dukes, F. (eds) *Conflict: Readings in management and resolution*. London: Macmillan, pp. 35–47.

Boutros-Ghali, B. (1992) *An Agenda for Peace: Preventive diplomacy, peacemaking and peace-building*. New York: United Nations.

Boyce, J.K. and O'Donnell, M. (2007) *Peace and the Public Purse: Economic policies for postwar statebuilding*. Boulder, CO: Lynne Reinner.

Brown, E., Cloke, J. and Sohail, M. (2004) Key myths about corruption. Briefing paper for a workshop on corruption and development presented at the Development Studies Association Annual Conference, Westminster, London, 6 November.

Brown, M.E. (1997) The causes of ethnic conflict: an overview. In Brown, M.E., Coté, O.R., Lynne-Jones, S.M. and Miller, S.E. (eds) *Nationalism and Ethnic Conflict*. Cambridge, MA: MIT Press, pp. 3–25.

Brubaker, R. and Laitin, D.D. (1998) Ethnic and nationalist violence. *Annual Review of Sociology* 24: 423–54.

Buchanan, C. and Muggah, R. (2005) *No Relief: Surveying the effects of gun violence on humanitarian and development personnel*. Centre for Humanitarian Dialogue and Small Arms Survey, UNDP: www.undp.org/bcpr/smallarms/index.htm.

Bull, H. (1977) *The Anarchical Society*. New York: Columbia University Press.

Bunzl, J. (2008) Mirror images: perception and interest in the Israel/Palestine conflict. *Palestine–Israel Journal* 12(2–3): 8–14.

Burnell, P. and Calvert, P. (eds) (2004) *Civil Society in Democratisation*. London: Frank Cass.

Burton, J. (1990) *Conflict Resolution and Prevention*. New York: St Martin's Press.

Bush, G.W. (2007) US takes new steps for peace, prosperity, President says. Statement from United States Embassy, London: http://london.usembassy.gov/bush730.html (accessed 7 August 2008).

Cairns, E. (1996) *Children and Political Violence*. Oxford: Blackwell.

Calderisi, R. (2006) *The Trouble with Africa: Why foreign aid isn't working*. London: Macmillan.

Callinicos, A. (2005) Iraq: fulcrum of world politics. *Third World Quarterly* 26(4–5): 593–608.

Campbell, D. (1998a) *National Deconstruction: Violence, identity and justice in Bosnia*. Minneapolis, MN: University of Minnesota Press.

Campbell, D. (1998b) *Writing Security: United States foreign policy and the politics of identity*. Manchester: University of Minnesota Press and Manchester University Press.

Caplan, R. (2005) *International Governance of War-Torn Territories: Rule and reconstruction*. Oxford: Oxford University Press.

Carnegie Commission on Preventing Deadly Conflict (1997) *Preventing Deadly Conflict*. New York: Carnegie Corporation of New York.

Carter, J. (2006) *Palestine: Peace not apartheid*. New York: Simon & Schuster.

Centre for Civil Society (CCS) (2008) *What is Civil Society?* CCS website: http://www.lse.ac.uk/collections/CCS/what_is_civil_society.htm (accessed 15 August 2008).

Chabal, P. and Daloz, J.P. (1999) *Africa Works: Disorder as political instrument*. Oxford: James Currey.

Chabal, P. and Daloz, J.P. (2006) *Culture Troubles: Politics and the interpretation of meaning*. London: Hurst and Company.

Chamroeun, C. and Shelton, T. (2008) Anger builds over land grab crisis. *Phnom Penh Post*, 11 August.

Chandler, D. (2000) *Bosnia: Faking democracy after Dayton*. London: Pluto.

Chandler, D. (2006) Back to the future? The limits of neo-Wilsonian ideals of exporting democracy. *Review of International Studies* 32(3): 475–94.

Chandler, D. (2007) EU Statebuilding: Securing the liberal peace through EU enlargement. *Global Society* 21(4): 593–607.

Chandrasekaran, R. (2007) *Imperial Life in the Emerald City: Inside Baghdad's Green Zone*. London: Bloomsbury.

Christie, K. (2000) *The South African Truth Commission*. London: Macmillan.

Chua, A. (2004) *World on Fire: How exporting free market democracy breeds ethnic hatred and global instability*. New York: Anchor.

Clapham, C. (1987) Revolutionary socialist development in Ethiopia. *African Affairs* 86(343): 151–65.

Clayton, J. (2005) Nigerian admirals pay the price for stealing captured oil tanker. *Times Online*, 8 January: http://www.timesonline.co.uk/tol/news/world/article409606.ece (accessed 13 June 2008).

Cody, E. (2006) In face of rural unrest, China rolls out reforms. *Washington Post*, 28 January.

Coghlan, T. (2006) Two British soldiers killed as Afghan poppy crop booms. *The Independent*, 3 July.

Coker, C. (1997) How wars end. *Millennium: Journal of International Studies* 26(3): 615–29.

Collier, P. (1999) *Doing Well out of War*. Washington, DC: World Bank.

Collier, P. (2000a) Doing well out of war: an economic perspective. In Berdal, M. and Malone, D. (ed.) *Greed and Grievance: Economic agendas in civil wars*. Boulder, CO: Lynne Rienner, pp. 91–111.

Collier, P. (2000b) *Economic Causes of Civil Conflict and their Implications for Policy*. Washington, DC: World Bank.

Collier, P. (2004) Development and security. Twelfth Bradford Development Lecture, University of Bradford, 11 November.

Collier, P. (2007) *The Bottom Billion: Why the poorest countries are failing and what can be done about it*. Oxford: Oxford University Press.

Collier, P. and Hoeffler, A. (2002) *Greed and Grievance in Civil Wars*, Working Paper Series. Oxford: Centre for the Study of African Economies.

Collier, P. and Hoeffler, A. (2004) Greed and grievance in civil war. *Oxford Economic Papers* 56(4): 563–95.

Collier, P., Elliot, V.L., Hegre, H., Hoeffler, A., Reynal-Querol, M. and Sambanis, N. (2003) *Breaking the Conflict Trap: Civil war and development policy*. Washington, DC: World Bank and Oxford University Press.

Connor, W. (1994) *Ethnonationalism: The quest for understanding*. Princeton, NJ: Princeton University Press.

Conteh-Morgan, E. (2004) *Collective Political Violence: An introduction to the theories and cases of violent conflicts*. New York: Routledge.

Cooke, W. and Kothari, U. (eds) (2002) *Participation: The new tyranny?* London: Zed Books.

Cooper, N. (2007) On the crisis of the liberal peace. *Conflict, Security and Democracy* 7(4): 605–16.

Corbin, J. (1994) *Gaza First: The secret channel to peace between Israel and the PLO*. London: Bloomsbury.

Corey, A. and Joireman, S.F. (2004) Retributive justice: the Gacaca courts in Rwanda. *African Affairs* 103: 73–89.

Craig, D. and Porter, P. (2003) Poverty reduction strategy papers: a new convergence. *World Development* 31(1): 53–69.

Cramer, C. (2002) Homo Economicus goes to war: methodological individualism, rational choice and the political economy of war. *World Development* 30(11): 1845–64.

Cramer, C. (2006) *Civil War is Not a Stupid Thing*: *Accounting for violence in developing countries*. London: Hurst.

Creasy, E. (1876) *The Fifteen Decisive Battles of the World: From Marathon to Waterloo*. London: Bentley.

Crocker, C.A., Hampson, F.O. and Aall, P. (1996) *Managing Global Chaos: Sources of and responses to international conflict*. Washington, DC: United States Institute of Peace Press.

Crocker, C.A., Hampson, F.O. and Aall, P. (1999) *Herding Cats: Multiparty mediation in a complex world*. Washington, DC: United States Institute of Peace Press.

Crocker, C.A., Hampson, F.O. and Aall, P. (eds) (2007) *Leashing the Dogs of War: Conflict management in a divided world*. Washington, DC: United States Institute of Peace Press.

Crouch, C. (2004) *Post-Democracy*. Cambridge: Polity.

Cumming, C. (2008) Quiet death in Xingjiang. *Guardian*, 5 April.

Curle, A. (1971) *Making Peace*. London: Tavistock.

Darby, J. (2001) *The Effects of Violence on Peace Processes*. Washington. DC: United States Institute of Peace Press.

Darby, J. (ed.) (2006) *Violence and Reconstruction*. Notre Dame, IN: University of Notre Dame Press.

Darby, J. and Mac Ginty, R. (eds) (2000) *The Management of Peace Processes.* London: Macmillan.

Darby, J. and Mac Ginty, R. (2003) Conclusion: peace processes, present and future. In Darby, J. and Mac Ginty, R. (eds) *Contemporary Peacemaking: Conflict, violence and peace processes.* Basingstoke: Palgrave, pp. 256–74.

Darby, J. and Mac Ginty, R. (2008) Introduction: What peace? What process? In Darby, J. and Mac Ginty, R. (eds) *Contemporary Peacemaking: Conflict, peace processes and post-war reconstruction*, 2nd edn. Basingstoke: Palgrave, pp. 1–9.

Deininger, K., Castagnini, R. and González, M. (2004) Comparing land reform and land markets in Colombia. *World Bank Policy Research Working Paper 3258*, April. New York: World Bank.

Denny, C. (2004) Suharto, Marcos and Mobutu head corruption table with $50bn scams. *Guardian*, 26 March.

Deudney, D. and Ikenberry, G.J. (1999) The nature and sources of liberal international order. *Review of International Studies* 25(2): 179–96.

Deutsch, K.W. with others (1957) *Political Community and the North Atlantic Area.* Princeton, NJ: Princeton University Press.

Deutsch, M. (1973) *The Resolution of Conflict: Constructive and destructive conflict.* New Haven, CT: Yale University Press.

Diamond, J. (2005) *Collapse: How Societies Choose to Fail or Succeed.* New York: Viking.

Diamond, L. (2006) What went wrong and right in Iraq. In Fukuyama, F. (ed.) *Nation-building: Beyond Afghanistan and Iraq.* Baltimore, MD: Johns Hopkins University Press.

Dierkes, J. (2007) The trajectory of reconciliation through history education in postunification Germany. In Cole, E.A. (ed.) *Teaching the Violent Past: History, education and reconciliation.* Lanham, MD: Rowman & Littlefield.

Dobbins, J., McGinn J.G., Crane, K., Jones, S.G., Lal, R., Rathnell, A., Swanger, R. and Timilsina, A. (2003) *America's Role in Nation-Building: From Germany to Iraq.* Santa Monica, CA: Rand Corporation.

Dobbins, J., Jones, S.G., Crane, K. and Cole DeGrasse, B. (2007) *The Beginner's Guide to Nation-Building.* Santa Monica, CA: Rand Corporation.

Dodge, T. (2006) Iraq: the contradictions of exogenous state-building in historical perspective. *Third World Quarterly* 27(1): 187–200.

Dorff, R.H. (2005) Failed states after 9/11: what did we know and what have we learned? *International Studies Perspectives* 6: 20–34.

Dorn, J. (1998) Competing visions of development policy. In Dorn, J., Hanke, S. and Walters, A. (eds) *The Revolution in Development Economics.* Washington, DC: Cato Institute, pp. 1–21.

Doyle, M. (1980) Liberalism and world politics. *American Political Science Review* 80(4): 1151–1169.

Duffield, M. (2001) *Global Governance and the New Wars: The merging of development and security.* London: Zed Books.

Duffield, M. (2007) *Development, Security and Unending War: Governing the world of peoples.* Cambridge: Polity.

Easterly, W. (2006) *The White Man's Burden: Why the West's efforts to aid the rest have done so much ill and so little good.* London: Penguin.

Ehteshami A. and Wright, S. (2007) Political change in the Arab oil monarchies: from liberalization to enfranchisement. *International Affairs* 83(5): 913–32.

Ekbladh, D. (2006) From consensus to crisis: the postwar career of nation-building in U.S. foreign relations. In Fukuyama, F. (ed.) *Nation-Building: Beyond Afghanistan and Iraq.* Baltimore, MD: Johns Hopkins University Press, pp. 19–41.

Enloe, C. (1993) *The Morning After: Sexual politics at the end of the Cold War.* Berkeley, CA: University of California Press.

Enloe, C. (2000) *Maneuvers: The international politics of militarizing women's lives.* Berkeley, CA: University of California Press.

Evans, M. and Lunn, K. (eds) (1997) *War and Memory in the Twentieth Century.* Oxford: Berg.

Evera, S. van (1999) *Causes of War: Power and the roots of conflict.* Ithaca, NY: Cornell University Press.

Falk, R. (1999) *Predatory Globalization: A critique.* Cambridge: Cambridge University Press.

Fearon, J.D. (1995) Rationalist explanations for war. *International Organization* 49(3): 379–414.

Fierke, K.M. (2006) Bewitched by the past: social memory, trauma and international relations. In Bell, D. (ed.) *Memory, Trauma and World Politics: Reflections on the relationship between past and present.* Basingstoke: Palgrave Macmillan.

Fischer, M., Gießmann, H.T. and Schmelzle, B. (eds) (n.d.) *Berghof Handbook for Conflict Transformation*: http://www.berghof-handbook.net/ (accessed 23 November 2008).

Fisher, R. (ed.) (1997) *Interactive Conflict Resolution.* Syracuse, NY: Syracuse University Press.

Fisher, R. (ed.) (2005) *Paving the Way: contributions of interactive conflict resolution to peacemaking.* Lanham, MD: Lexington.

Fisher, R. and Ury, W. (1991) *Getting to Yes: Negotiating agreement without giving in.* London: Penguin.

Fisk, R. (2005) *The Great War for Civilization: The conquest of the Middle East.* New York: Knopf.

Fitz-Gerald, A.M. and Mason, H. (eds) (2005) *From Conflict to Community: A combatant's return to citizenship.* Shrivenham: Global Facilitation Network for Security Sector Reform.

Fleischer, M. (1998) Cattle raiding and its correlates: the cultural-ecological consequences of market-oriented cattle raiding among the Kuria of Tanzania. *Human Ecology* 26(2): 547–72.

Foner, E. (1989) *Reconstruction: America's unfinished revolution, 1863–1877.* New York: HarperCollins.

Forman, S. and Patrick, S. (eds) (2000) *Good Intentions: Pledges of aid for postconflict recovery.* Boulder, CO: Lynne Reinner.

Frank, A.G. (1967) *Capitalism and Underdevelopment in Latin America.* New York: Monthly Review Press.

Franks, J. and Richmond, O. (2008) Coopting liberal peace-building: untying the Gordian knot in Kosovo. *Cooperation and Conflict* 43: 81–103.

Fromkin, D. (2000) *A Peace to End All Peace: The fall of the Ottoman Empire and the creation of the modern Middle East.* London: Phoenix.

Fukuyama, F. (1989) The end of history? *The National Interest* 16: 3–18.

Fukuyama, F. (1992) *The End of History and the Last Man.* New York: Free Press.

Fukuyama, F. (2004) The imperative of state-building. *Journal of Democracy* 15(2): 17–31.

Fukuyama, F. (ed.) (2005) *State-Building: Governance and world order in the twenty-first century.* London: Profile.

Fukuyama, F. (ed.) (2006) *Nation-Building: Beyond Afghanistan and Iraq.* Baltimore, MD: Johns Hopkins University Press.

Galbraith, J.K. (1964) *Economic Development.* Cambridge, MA: Harvard University Press.

Gallis, P. (2007) NATO in Afghanistan: a test of the transatlantic alliance. *Connections* 6(3): 10–32.

Galtung, J. (1996) *Peace by Peaceful Means: Peace and conflict, development and civilization.* London: Sage.

Gamba, V. (2006) Post-agreement demobilization, disarmament and reconstruction: toward a new approach. In Darby, J. (ed.) *Violence and Reconstruction.* Notre Dame, IN: University of Notre Dame Press, pp. 53–75.

GFN-SSR (2007) A *Beginner's Guide to Security Sector Reform.* Birmingham: GFN-SSR.

Ghani, A. and Lockhart, C. (2008) *Fixing Failed States: A framework for rebuilding a fractured world.* Oxford: Oxford University Press.

Ginifer, J. with input from Oliver, K. (2004) *Evaluation of the Conflict Prevention Pools: Country/Regional Case Study 3, Sierra Leone.* Bradford: Bradford University, Channel Research Ltd, PARC and Associated Consultants.

Giustozzi, A. (2008) Afghanistan: political parties or militia fronts. In de Zeeuw, J. (ed.) *Transforming Rebel Movements after Civil War.* Boulder, CO: Lynne Reinner, pp. 179–204.

Gleditsch, N.P., Lindgren, G., Mouhleb, N., Smit, S. and De Soysa, I. (eds) (2000) *Making Peace Pay: A bibliography on disarmament and conversion.* New War/Peace Bibliography Series. London: Regina.

Gleditsch, N.P., Wallensteen, P., Eriksson, M., Sollenburg, M. and Strand, H. (2002) Armed conflict 1946–2001: a new dataset. *Journal of Peace Research* 39(5): 615–37.

Glenn, J. (2008) Global governance and the democratic deficit: stifling the voice of the South. *Third World Quarterly* 29(2): 217–38.

Gomes Porto, J. with Alden, C. and Parsons, I. (2007) *From Soldiers to Citizens: Demilitarisation of Conflict and Society.* Aldershot: Ashgate.

Goodhand, J. (2004) Aiding violence or building peace? The role of international aid in Afghanistan. In Barakat, S. (ed.) *Reconstructing War-Torn Societies: Afghanistan*. London: Palgrave Macmillan, pp. 37–59.

Gormley-Heenan, C. (2001) *From Protagonist to Pragmatist: Political leadership in societies in transition*. Report published by INCORE, University of Ulster and United Nations University.

Grant, J.A. and Taylor, I. (2004) Global governance and conflict diamonds: the Kimberley process and the quest for clean gems. *Round Table: Commonwealth Journal of International Affairs* 93(375): 385–401.

Gray, C. (2005) *Another Bloody Century: Future warfare*. London: Weidenfeld & Nicolson.

Greenslade, R. (2008) Sri Lankan journalists need protection. *Guardian*, 7 February.

Groom, A.J.R. (1988) Paradigms in conflict: the strategist, the conflict researcher and the peace researcher. *Review of International Studies* 14: 97–115.

Guáqueta, A. (2007) The way back in: reintegrating illegal armed groups in Colombia then and now. *Conflict, Security and Development* 7(3): 417–56.

Guardian (2007) What we've learned. *Guardian*, 15 September.

Gurr, T. (1970) *Why Men Rebel*. Princeton, NJ: Princeton University Press.

Gurr, T. (2000) *Peoples versus States: Minorities at risk in the new century*. Washington, DC: United States Institute of Peace Press.

Gurr, T. and Harff, B. (1994) *Ethnic Conflict in World Politics*. Boulder, CO: Westview.

Hamieh, C. (2007) Intra-party competition in a divided society: Amal versus Hezbollah in Lebanon, 1998–2003. Unpublished PhD thesis, University of York.

Hammond, P. (2007) *Framing Post-Cold War Conflicts: The media and international intervention*. Manchester: Manchester University Press.

Hampson, F.O. and Mendeloff, D. (2007) Intervention and the nation-building debate. In Crocker, C.A., Hampson, F.O. and Aall, P. (eds) *Leashing the Dogs of War: Conflict management in a divided world*. Washington, DC: United States Institute of Peace Press, pp. 679–700.

Hanlon, J. (1996) *Peace without Profit: How the IMF blocks rebuilding in Mozambique*. Dublin: Irish Mozambique Solidarity and the International African Institute in association with James Currey and Heinemann.

Hannay, D. (2005) Reforming the United Nations: the use of force to safeguard international security and human rights. A member's perspective from the Secretary-General's High Level Panel on Threats, Challenges and Change. *Conflict, Security and Development* 5(1): 109–17.

Harbom, L. and Wallensteen, P. (2007) Patterns of major armed conflicts, 1997–2006. *SIPRI Yearbook 2007*. Stockholm: Stockholm International Peace Research Institute (SIPRI).

Harding, T. (2008) A year in Helmand: 4m bullets fired by British. *Daily Telegraph*, 13 January.

Harff, B. and Gurr, T. (2004) *Ethnic Conflict in World Politics*, 2nd edn. Boulder, CO: Westview.

Harmer, A. and Cotterrell, L. (2005) *Diversity in Donorship: The changing landscape of official humanitarian aid*, Report 20. London: Humanitarian Policy Network.

Harris, L. (1999) Will the real IMF please stand up? In Michie, J. and Grieve Smith, J. (eds) *Global Instability: The political economy of world economic governance*. London: Routledge, pp. 198–211.

Harriss, J. (2005a) Great promise, hubris and recovery: a participant's history of development studies. In Kothari, U. (ed.) *A Radical History of Development Studies: Individuals, institutions and ideologies*. London: Zed Books, pp. 17–46.

Harriss, J. (2005b) Do political regimes matter? Poverty reduction and regime differences across India. In Houtzager, P. and Moore, M. (eds) *Changing Paths: International development and the new politics of inclusion*. Ann Arbor, MI: University of Michigan Press, pp. 204–32.

Harvey, D. (2005) *A Brief History of Neoliberalism*. Oxford: Oxford University Press.

Hayner, P. (2002) *Unspeakable Truths: Facing the challenge of truth commissions*. New York: Routledge.

Henderson, E.A. (2002) *Democracy and War: The end of an illusion?* Boulder, CO: Lynne Rienner.

Henderson, E.A. and Singer, D.J. (2002) 'New wars' and rumors of 'new wars'. *International Interactions* 28(2): 165–90.

Hendrickson, D., Armon, J. and Mearns, R. (1998) The changing nature of conflict and famine vulnerability: the case of livestock raiding in Turkana District, Kenya. *Disasters* 22(3): 185–99.

Hermann, T. and Newman, D. (2000) A path strewn with thorns: along the difficult road of Israeli-Palestinian peacemaking. In Darby, J. and Mac Ginty, R. (eds) *The Management of Peace Processes*. London: Macmillan, pp. 107–53.

Herring, R. and Esman, M. (2003) Projects and policies, politics and ethnicities. In Esman, M. and Herring, R. (eds) *Carrots, Sticks and Ethnic Conflict: Rethinking development assistance*. Ann Arbor, MI: University of Michigan Press, pp. 1–25.

Hoffman, P.J. and Weiss, T.G. (2006) *Sword and Salve: Confronting new wars and humanitarian crises*. Lanham, MD: Rowman & Littlefield.

Hogan, M. (1987) *The Marshall Plan: America, Britain and the reconstruction of Western Europe, 1947–1952*. Cambridge: Cambridge University Press.

Höglund, K. and Zartman, I.W. (2006) Violence by the state: official spoilers and their allies. In Darby, J. (ed.) *Violence and Reconstruction*. Notre Dame, IN: University of Notre Dame Press, pp. 11–31.

Homer-Dixon, T. (1994) Environmental scarcities and violent conflict: evidence from cases. *International Security* 19(1): 5–40.

Hoogvelt, A. (1997) *Globalization and the Post-Colonial World*. London: Macmillan.

Hopkins, A.G. (2002) *Globalization in World History*. London: Pimlico.

Horowitz, D. (1985) *Ethnic Groups in Conflict*. Berkeley, CA: University of California Press.

Horowitz, D. (2005) Foreword. In O'Flynn, I. and Russell, D. (eds) *Power Sharing: New challenges for divided societies*. London: Pluto, pp. vii–ix.

Howard, A. (2008) Small arms vs humanitarian aid: opportunities for action: www.aidandtrade.org/review-2007-2008 (accessed 18 July 2008).

Howard, M. (2000) *The Invention of Peace: Reflections on war and international order*. New Haven, CT: Yale University Press.

Hülsemeyer, A. (ed.) (2003) *Globalization in the Twenty-first Century: Convergence or divergence?* London: Palgrave.

Human Rights Watch (HRW) (2005) China: religious repression of Uighur Muslims. HRW statement, 12 April: http://www.hrw.org/english/docs/2005/04/11/china10447.htm (accessed 19 March 2008).

Human Rights Watch (2008) Cambodia: murder of journalist jolts election run up. HRW Statement, 16 July: http://hrw.org/english/docs/2008/07/16/cambod19364.htm (accessed 14 August 2008).

Hunt, J. (2004a) Aid and development. In Kingsbury, D., Remenyi, J., McKay, J. and Hunt, J., *Key Issues in Development*. Basingstoke: Palgrave-Macmillan, pp. 67–90.

Hunt, J. (2004b) Gender and development. In Kingsbury, D., Remenyi, J., McKay, J. and Hunt, J., *Key Issues in Development*. Basingstoke: Palgrave-Macmillan, pp. 242–65.

Huntington, S. (1993a) The clash of civilizations? *Foreign Affairs* 72(3): 22–49.

Huntington, S. (1993b) *The Third Wave: Democratization in the late twentieth century*. Norman, OK: University of Oklahoma Press.

Huntington, S. (1996) *The Clash of Civilizations and the Remaking of World Order*. New York: Simon & Schuster.

Huntington, S. (1998) *The Clash of Civilizations and the Remaking of World Order*. London: Touchstone.

Ignatieff, M. (1996) *Index on Censorship* 'Articles of Faith', May: www.oneworld.org/index_oc/issue596/ignatieff.html.

International Development Committee (2006) *Conflict and Development: Peacebuilding and post-conflict reconstruction*. Sixth Report of the Session 2005–06, Vol. 1. London: The Stationery Office.

International Federation of Journalists (IFJ) (2007) Government comments 'disturbing', and journalist still missing in Sri Lanka. IFJ press release, 27 February: http://www.ifj-asia.org/page/srilanka070227.html (accessed 19 March 2008).

Ismael, T.Y. and Ismael, J.S. (2005) Whither Iraq? Beyond Saddam, sanctions and occupation. *Third World Quarterly* 26(4–5): 609–29.

Jabri, V. (1990) *Mediating Conflict: Decision-making and western intervention in Namibia*. Manchester: Manchester University Press.

Jabri, V. (2007) *War and the Transformation of Global Politics*. London: Palgrave Macmillan.

Jackson, M.G. (2005) A necessary collaboration: NGOs, peacekeepers and credible military force. The case of Sierra Leone and East Timor. In Richmond, O. and Carey, H. (eds) *Subcontracting Peace: The challenges of NGO peacebuilding*. Aldershot: Ashgate.

Jackson, R. (2007) *Sovereignty: The evolution of an idea*. Cambridge: Polity.

Jacoby, T. (2007) Hegemony, modernisation and post-war reconstruction. *Global Society: Journal of Interdisciplinary International Relations* 21(4): 521–37.

Jacoby, T. (2008) *Understanding Conflict and Violence: Theoretical and interdisciplinary approaches*. London: Routledge.

Janzekovic, J. (2006) *The Use of Force in Humanitarian Intervention: Morality and practicalities*. Aldershot: Ashgate.

Jeong, H.W. (1999) *The New Agenda for Peace Research*. Aldershot: Ashgate.

Jeong, H.W. (2005) *Peacebuilding in Post-Conflict Societies: Strategy and process*. Boulder, CO: Lynne Reinner.

Jeong, H.W. (2008) *Understanding Conflict and Conflict Analysis*. London: Sage.

Jones, D. (1999) *Cosmopolitan Mediation? Conflict resolution and the Oslo Accords*. Manchester: Manchester University Press.

Kacowicz, A.M., Bar-Simon-Tov, Y., Elgström, O. and Jerneck, M. (eds) (2000) *Stable Peace among Nations*. Lanham, MD: Rowman & Littlefield.

Kagan, R. (2008) The case for a league of democracies. *Financial Times*, 14 May.

Kaldor, M. (2005) Old wars, cold wars, new wars, and the war on terror. *International Politics* 42(4): 491–8.

Kaldor, M. (2006) *New and Old Wars: Organized violence in a global era*, 2nd edn. Cambridge: Polity.

Kalyvas, S. (2001) 'New' and 'old' civil wars: a valid distinction? *World Politics* 54(1): 99–108.

Kandeh, J. (2005) The criminalization of the RUF insurgency in Sierra Leone. In Arnson, C. and Zartman, I.W. (eds) *Rethinking the Economics of War: The intersections of need, greed and creed*. Baltimore, MD: Johns Hopkins University Press, pp. 84–106.

Kaplan, R. (1994) The coming anarchy. *Atlantic Monthly*, February.

Kaufman, S.J. (2001) *Modern Hatreds: The symbolic politics of ethnic war*. Ithaca, NY: Cornell University Press.

Kayumba, C. and Kimonyo, J.-P. (2006) The failure of media assistance in post-genocide Rwanda. In de Zeeuw, J. and Kumar, K. (eds) *Promoting Democracy in Post-Conflict Societies: Views and lessons from Africa, Asia and Central America*. Boulder, CO: Lynne Rienner, pp. 211–36.

Keashley, L. and Fisher, R. (1990) Towards a contingency approach to third-party intervention in regional conflict: a Cyprus illustration. *International Journal* 45(2): 425–53.

Keen, D. (1998) *The Economic Functions of Violence in Civil War*, Adelphi Paper 320. London: International Institute of Strategic Studies.

Keen, D. (2008) *Complex Emergencies*. Cambridge: Polity.

Keesing, R. (1992) *Custom and Confrontation: The Kwaio struggle for cultural autonomy*. Chicago, IL: University of Chicago Press.

Kelman, H.C. (2005) Interactive problem solving in the Israeli–Palestinian case: past contributions and present challenges. In Fisher, R. (ed.) *Pausing the Way: Contributions of interactive conflict resolution to peacemaking*. Lanham, MD: Lexington, pp. 41–63.

Kenny, C. (2003) Why aren't countries rich? Weak states and bad neighbourhoods. In Seligson, M. and Passé-Smith, J. (eds) *Development and Under-development: The political economy of global inequality*, 3rd edn. Boulder, CO: Lynne Rienner, pp. 413–25.

Keynes, J.M. (1920) *The Economic Consequences of Peace*. London: Macmillan.

Kiely, R. (2007) Poverty reduction through liberalisation? Neo-liberalism and the myth of global convergence. *Review of International Studies* 33: 415–34.

Killick, J. (1997) *The United States and European Reconstruction, 1945–1960*. Edinburgh: Edinburgh University Press.

Kinsey, C. (2009) *Private Security and the Reconstruction of Iraq*. London: Routledge.

Klein, N. (2005) Allure of the blank state. *Guardian*, 18 April.

Klein, N. (2007) *The Shock Doctrine: The rise of disaster capitalism*. London: Penguin.

Knaus, G. and Martin, F. (2003) Lessons from Bosnia and Herzegovina: travails of the European Raj. *Journal of Democracy* 14(3): 60–74.

Knight, W.A. (2003) Evaluating recent trends in peacebuilding research. *International Relations of the Asia-Pacific* 3(2): 241–64.

Kolstad, I., Fritz, V. and O'Neil, T. (2008) *Corruption, Anti-corruption Efforts and Aid: Do donors have the right approach?* Dublin: Advisory Board for Irish Aid: http://www.odi.org.uk/PPPG/politics_and_governance/publications/GAPWP3.pdf (accessed 18 June 2008).

Kothari, U. (2005) A radical history of development studies: Individuals, institutions and ideologies. In Kothari, U. (ed.) *A Radical History of Development Studies: Individuals, institutions and ideologies*. London: Zed Books, pp. 1–13.

Krause, V. and Suzuki, S. (2005) Trade openness, economic development and civil war in the post-colonial world, 1950–1992. *Conflict, Security and Development* 5(1): 23–43.

Krog, A. (1998) *Country of my Skull: Guilt, sorrow, and the limits of forgiveness in the new South Africa*. Johannesburg: Random House.

Lal, D. (1998) The transformation of developing economies: from plan to market. In Dorn, J., Hanke, S. and Walters, A. (eds) *The Revolution in Development Economics*. Washington, DC: Cato Institute, pp. 55–74.

Landes, D. (1998) *The Wealth and Poverty of Nations: Why some are so rich and some are so poor*. London: Abacus.

Larmour, P. (2005) *Foreign Flowers: Institutional transfer and good governance in the Pacific Islands*. Honolulu, HI: University of Hawai'i Press.

Lederach, J.P. (1995) *Preparing for Peace: Conflict transformation across cultures*. Syracuse, NY: Syracuse University Press.

Lederach, J.P. (1997) *Building Peace: Sustainable reconciliation in divided societies*. Washington, DC: United States Institute of Peace Press.

Leftwich, A. (1996) Two cheers for democracy? Democracy and the developmental state. In A. Leftwich (ed.) *Democracy and Development*. Cambridge: Polity, pp. 279–95.

Lehoucq, F. and Wall, D. (2004) Explaining voter turnout rates in new democracies: Guatemala. *Electoral Studies* 23(3): 485–500.

Leitsinger, M. (2005) Cambodia land grab threatens peace, stability. *Los Angeles Times*, 20 March.

Lewis, J. (2007) Nasty, brutish and in shorts? British colonial rule, violence and the historians of Mau Mau. *Round Table: Commonwealth Journal of International Affairs* 96(389): 201–23.

Leys, C. (1996) *The Rise and Fall of Development Theory*. Oxford: James Currey.

Lobell, S.E. and Mauceri, P. (2004) *Ethnic Conflict and International Politics: Explaining diffusion and escalation*. London: Palgrave.

Loewenberg, S. and Bonde, B.N. (eds) (2007) *Media in Conflict Prevention and Peacebuilding Strategies*. Bonn: DW Media Services.

Long, W.J. and Brecke, P. (2003) *War and Reconciliation: Reason and emotion in conflict resolution*. Cambridge, MA: MIT Press.

Lund, M. and Mehler, A. (1999) *Peacebuilding and Conflict Prevention in Developing Countries*. Ebenhausen, Germany: Conflict Prevention Network, Stiftung Wissenschaft und Politik.

Luttwak, E. (1999) Give war a chance. *Foreign Affairs* 78(4): 36–44.

McCurry, J. (2008) Japan accused of vote buying ahead of whaling meeting. *Guardian*, 6 March.

MacFarlane, N. and Khong, K.F. (2006) *Human Security and the United Nations: A critical history*. Bloomington, IN: Indiana University Press.

Mac Ginty, R. (2003) The role of symbols in peacemaking. In Darby, J. and Mac Ginty, R. (eds) *Contemporary Peacemaking: Conflict, violence and peace processes*. Basingstoke: Palgrave, pp. 235–44.

Mac Ginty, R. (2004) Looting in the context of violent conflict: a conceptualization and typology. *Third World Quarterly* 25(5): 857–70.

Mac Ginty, R. (2006) *No War, No Peace: The rejuvenation of stalled peace processes and peace accords*. London: Palgrave.

Mac Ginty, R. (2007) Reconstructing post-war Lebanon: a challenge to the liberal peace. *Conflict, Security and Development* 7(3): 457–82.

Mac Ginty, R. (2008) Indigenous peacemaking versus the liberal peace. *Cooperation and Conflict* 43: 139–63.

Mac Ginty, R. and Richmond O. (2007a) Myth or reality: opposing views on the liberal peace and post-war reconstruction. *Global Society* 21(4): 491–7.

Mac Ginty, R. and Richmond, O. (2007b) The Liberal Peace and Post-war Reconstruction. Special issue of *Global Society: Journal of Interdisciplinary International Relations* 21(4).

Mac Ginty, R. and Williams, A. (2005) Editorial: The Commonwealth and the inheritance of armed conflict. *Round Table: Commonwealth Journal of International Affairs* 94(379): 173–5.

Mac Ginty, R. and Williams, A. (eds) (2007) Commemoration and Remembrance in the Commonwealth. Special issues of *Round Table: Commonwealth Journal of International Affairs* 96(393).

McIlwaine, C. and Moser, C. (2004) *Encounters with Violence in Latin America: Urban poor perceptions from Colombia and Guatemala*. London: Routledge.

McInnes, C. (2000) A farewell to arms? Decommissioning and the peace process. In Cox, M., Guelke, A. and Stephens, F. (eds) *A Farewell to Arms? From 'long war' to long peace in Northern Ireland*. Manchester: Manchester University Press, pp. 78–92.

Mack, A. (2006) *Human Security Brief 2006*. Vancouver: Human Security Center, University of British Columbia: www.humansecuritybrief.info (13 March 2008).

Mackay, C. (1995) *Extraordinary Popular Delusions and the Madness of Crowds*. Ware, Hertfordshire: Wordsworth Reference.

Maclean, J. (1988) Marxism and international relations: a strange case of mutual neglect. *Millennium* 17(2): 295–320.

Mandelbaum, M. (2002) *The Ideas that Conquered the World: Peace, democracy and free markets in the twenty-first century*. New York: PublicAffairs.

Marcos (1994) Transcript of interview with Subcomandante Marcos. La Jornada: http://flag.blackened.net (accessed 15 September 2007).

Marriage, Z. (2007) Flip-flop rebel, dollar soldier: demobilisation in the Democratic Republic of Congo. *Conflict, Security and Development* 7(2): 281–309.

Marriage, Z. (2008) Ambiguous agreements: aid in negotiating processes. *Conflict Security and Development* 8(1): 1–13.

Marten, K. (2007) Is stability the answer? In Crocker, C.A., Hampson, F.O. and Aall, P. (eds) *Leashing the Dogs of War: Conflict management in a divided world*. Washington, DC: United States Institute of Peace Press, pp. 619–36.

Martz, J. (1996) *The Politics of Clientelism*. New Brunswick, NJ: Transaction.

Mathiason, N. (2005) Consultants pocket $20bn of global aid. *Observer*, 29 May.

Mayoux, L. (2002) Microfinance and women's empowerment: rethinking best practice. *Development Bulletin* 57: 76–81.

Mearsheimer, J.J. (2001) *The Tragedy of Great Power Politics*. New York: Norton.

Mearsheimer, J.J. and Walt, S. (2007) *The Israel Lobby and US Foreign Policy*. New York: Farrar, Straus & Giroux.

Meier, G.M. and Rauch, J.E. (2000) *Leading Issues in Economic Development*. New York: Oxford University Press.

Miall, H. (2007) *Emergent Conflict and Peaceful Change*. Basingstoke: Palgrave Macmillan.

Miall, H., Ramsbotham, O. and Woodhouse, T. (1999) *Contemporary Conflict Resolution*: *The prevention, management and transformation of deadly conflicts*. Cambridge: Polity.

Migdal, J. (1988) *Strong Societies, Weak States: State–society relations and state capabilities in the Third World*. Princeton, NJ: Princeton University Press.

Mitchell, C. (1981) *The Structure of International Conflict*. London: Macmillan.

Mitchell, C. (1994) Conflict research. In Groom, A.J.R. and Light, M. (eds) *Contemporary International Relations: A guide to theory*. London: Pinter, pp. 128–141.

Mitchell, C. and Webb, K. (eds) (1988) *New Approaches to International Mediation*. New York: Greenwood.

Miyoshi Jager, S. and Mitter, R. (2007) *Ruptured Histories: War, memory and the Post-Cold War in Asia*. Cambridge, MA: Harvard University Press.

Mkutu, K. (2008) Disarmament in Karamoja, Northern Uganda: is this a solution for localised violent inter and intra-communal conflict? *Round Table: Commonwealth Journal of International Affairs* 97(394): 99–120.

Moghalu, K. (2005) *Rwanda's Genocide: The politics of global justice*. London: Palgrave.

Monbiot, G. (2006) Don't be fooled by this reform: the IMF is still the world's viceroy. *Guardian*, 5 September.

Monshipouri, M. (2005) The NGOs' dilemmas in the post-war Iraq: from stabilisation to nation-building. In Richmond, O. and Carey, H. (eds) *Subcontracting Peace: The challenges of NGO peacebuilding*. Aldershot: Ashgate.

Moore, M. (2001) Empowerment at last? *Journal of International Development* 13(3): 321–9.

Moore, M. (2005) Arguing the politics of inclusion. In Houtzager, P. and Moore, M. (eds) *Changing Paths: International development and the new politics of inclusion*. Ann Arbor, MI: University of Michigan Press, pp. 260–84.

Morrow, D. (2006) The new common sense? Implementing policy for sharing over separation. In Northern Ireland Community Relations Council (CRC), *Sharing Over Separation: Actions towards a shared future*. Belfast: CRC.

Moyroud, C. and Katunga, J. (2002) Coltan exploration in Eastern Democratic Republic of the Congo (DRC). In Lind, J. and Sturman K. (eds) *Scarcity and Surfeit: The ecology of Africa's conflicts*. Pretoria: Institute of Security Studies, pp. 159–85.

Muggah, R. (2005) No magic bullet: a critical perspective on disarmament, demobilization and reintegration. *Round Table: Commonwealth Journal of International Affairs* 94(379): 239–52.

Mulligan, J. (2002) On land, in the air this war is different. *Providence Journal*, 10 March: http://www.globalsecurity.org/org/news/2002/020310-attack01.htm (18 March 2008).

Münkler, H. (2005) *The New Wars*. Cambridge: Polity.

Murithi, T. (2005) *The African Union: Pan-Africanism, peacebuilding and development*. Aldershot: Ashgate.

Nader, L. (1997) Controlling processes: tracing the dynamic components of power. *Current Anthropology* 38(5): 711–38.

Nayani, S. (2006) Peacebuilding and the Sri Lankan peace process. Unpublished PhD thesis, University of York.

Newman, E. (2004) The 'new wars' debate: a historical perspective is needed. *Security Dialogue* 35(2): 173–89.

Nordstrom, C. (1999) Girls and war zones: troubling questions. In Indra, D. (ed.) *Engendering Forced Migration: Theory and practice*. New York: Berghan.

Nordstrom, C. (2004) *Shadows of War: Violence, power, and international profiteering in the twenty-first century*. Berkeley, CA: University of California Press.

Nordstrom, C. (2008) Casting long shadows: war, peace and extralegal economies. In Darby, J. and Mac Ginty, R. (eds) *Contemporary*

*Peacemaking: Conflict, peace processes and post-war reconstruction.*
Basingstoke: Palgrave, pp. 289–99.

Nye, J. (2005) *Soft Power: The means to success in world politics.* New York:
Public Affairs.

Oberschall, A. (2007) *Conflict and Peace Building in Divided Societies:
Responses to Ethnic Violence.* London: Routledge.

OECD (2007) *Handbook on 'Security Sector Reform'.* Paris: OECD.

Orenstein, C. (1997) Fantasy Island: Royal Caribbean parcels off a piece of
Haiti. *The Progressive*: http://findarticles.com/p/articles/mi_m1295/
is_n8_v61/ai_19622661/pg_1?tag=artBody;col1 (accessed 21 July 2008).

Ottaway, M. (2007) Is democracy the answer? In Crocker, C.A., Hampson, F.O.
and Aall, P. (eds) *Leashing the Dogs of War: Conflict management in a divided
world.* Washington, DC: United States Institute of Peace Press, pp. 603–18.

Ozerdem, A. (2008) *Becoming Civilian: Disarmament, demobilisation and
reintegration.* London: I.B. Tauris.

Paris, R. (2004) *At War's End: Building peace after civil conflict.* Cambridge:
Cambridge University Press.

Perlez, J. and Rohde, D. (2007) Pakistan attempts to crush protests by lawyers.
*New York Times*, 6 November.

Peters, K. (2007) Reintegration support for young ex-combatants: a right or a
privilege? *International Migration* 45(5): 35–59.

Pirouz, R. and Nautré, Z. (2005) *An Action Plan for Iraq: The perspective of
Iraqi civil society.* London: Foreign Policy Centre.

Pitkin, H.F. (1967) *The Concept of Representation.* Berkeley, CA: University
of California Press.

Pollard, S. (1997) *The International Economy since 1945.* London: Routledge.

Posen, B. (1993) The security dilemma and ethnic conflicts. In Brown, M.E. (ed.)
*Ethnic Conflict and International Security.* Princeton, NJ: Princeton
University Press, pp. 103–24.

Potter, A. (2008) Women, gender and peacemaking in civil wars. In Darby, J.
and Mac Ginty, R. (eds) *Contemporary Peacemaking: Conflict, peace
processes and post-war reconstruction*, 2nd edn. Basingstoke: Palgrave,
pp. 105–19.

Pruitt, D.G., Bercovitch, J. and Zartman, I.W. (1997) A brief history of the Oslo
talks. *International Negotiation* 2(2): 177–82.

Prunier, G. (1995) *The Rwanda Crisis: History of a genocide.* New York:
Columbia University Press.

Prusher, I. (2003) Iraq's new challenge: civil society. *Christian Science Monitor*,
8 October.

Pugh, M. (1997) *The UN, Peace, and Force.* London: Routledge.

Pugh, M. and Cooper, N., with Goodhand, J. (2004) *War Economies in a
Regional Context: Challenges of transformation.* Boulder, CO: Lynne Rienner.

Putnam, R. (2000) *Bowling Alone: The collapse and revival of American
community.* New York: Simon & Schuster.

Quinn, A. and Cox, M. (2007) For better, for worse: how America's foreign
policy became wedded to liberal universalism. *Global Society* 21(4):
499–519.

Raiffa, H. (1982) *The Art and Science of Negotiation*. Cambridge, MA: Harvard University Press.

Ramsbotham, O., Woodhouse, T. and Miall, H. (2005) *Contemporary Conflict Resolution: The prevention, management and transformation of deadly conflicts*, 2nd edn. Cambridge: Polity.

Rawls, J. (1999) *A Theory of Justice*. Oxford: Oxford University Press.

Rehn, E. and Johnson Sirleaf, E. (2002) *Women, War, Peace: The independent experts' assessment of the impact of armed conflict on women and women's role in peace building*. New York: UNIFEM.

Reilly, B. (2003) Democratic validation. In Darby, J. and Mac Ginty, R. (eds) *Contemporary Peacemaking: Conflict, violence and peace processes*. Basingstoke: Palgrave, pp. 174–83.

Reno, W. (1997a) War, markets, and the reconfiguration of west Africa's weak states. *Comparative Politics* 29(4): 493–510.

Reno, W. (1997b) African weak states and commercial alliances. *African Affairs* 96: 165–85.

Richani, N. (2002) *Systems of Violence: The political economy of war and peace in Colombia*. New York: State University of New York Press.

Richards, P. and Vincent, J. (2008) Sierra Leone: the marginalization of the RUF. In de Zeeuw, J. (ed.) *From Soldiers to Politicians: Transforming rebel movements after civil war*. Boulder, CO: Lynne Reinner, pp. 81–102.

Richardson, L.F. (1950) *The Statistics of Deadly Quarrels*. Pittsburgh, PA: Boxwood.

Richmond, O. (2005a) *The Transformation of Peace*. London: Palgrave.

Richmond, O. (2005b) The dilemmas of subcontracting the liberal peace. In Richmond, O. and Carey, H. (eds) *Subcontracting Peace: The challenges of NGO peacebuilding*. Aldershot: Ashgate, pp. 19–35.

Richmond, O. and Carey, H. (eds) (2005) *Subcontracting Peace: The challenges of NGO peacebuilding*. Aldershot: Ashgate.

Richmond, O. (2006a) The problem of peace: understanding the 'liberal peace'. *Conflict, Security and Development* 6(3): 291–314.

Richmond, O. (2007) *The Transformation of Peace*. Basingstoke: Palgrave.

Richmond, O. and Franks, J. (2007) Liberal hubris? Virtual peace in Cambodia. *Security Dialogue* 38(1): 27–48.

Rigby, A. (2001) *Justice and Reconciliation: After the violence*. Boulder, CO: Lynne Reinner.

Riungu, E. (n.d.) Impact of small arms and light weapons on women and children amongst the Pastoralists of North East Africa. Unpublished PhD thesis, St Andrews University.

Robbins, P. (2003) *Stolen Fruit: The tropical commodities disaster*. London: Zed Books.

Roeder, P.G. and Rothchild, D. (eds) (2005) *Sustainable Peace: Power and democracy after civil wars*. Ithaca, NY: Cornell University Press.

Rogers, P. (2000) *Losing Control: Global security in the twenty first century*. London: Pluto.

Rooney, A. (2000) *My War*. New York: PublicAffairs.

Ross, M. (2003) The natural resource curse: how wealth can make you poor. In Bannon, I. and Collier, P. (eds) *Natural Resources and Violent Conflict*. Washington, DC: World Bank, pp. 17–42.

Rostow, W. (1960) *The Stages of Economic Growth: A non-communist manifesto*. Oxford: Oxford University Press.

Rotberg, R.I. and Thompson, D. (eds) (2000) *Truth v. Justice: The morality of truth commissions*. Princeton, NJ: Princeton University Press.

Roth, A. (2002) Lord Bauer: Thatcher's rightwing economist opposed to third world aid. *Guardian*, 6 May.

Ruthven, M. (2003) Edward Said: controversial literary critic and bold advocate of the Palestinian cause in America. *Guardian*, 26 September.

Sachs, J. (2005) *The End of Poverty*. London: Penguin.

Sachs, J. (2007) Economic solidarity for a crowded planet. *Reith Lectures 2007*: www.bbc.co.uk/radio4/reith2007/lecture4.shtml (accessed 4 November 2008).

Sachs, J. (2008) Promises, promises. *Developments* 40: 6.

Sachs, J. (n.d.) *Full Bio*: www.earth.columbia.edu/articles/view/1770 (accessed 4 November 2008).

Sands, P. (2003) *From Nuremberg to the Hague: The future of international criminal justice*. Cambridge: Cambridge University Press.

Sanyal, P. (2006) Credit, capital and collective action: microfinance and pathways to women's empowerment. Paper presented at the annual meeting of the American Sociological Association, Montreal Convention Center, Montreal, Quebec, Canada.

Saunders, H. (1999) *A Public Peace Process: Sustained dialogue to transform racial and ethnic conflict*. Basingstoke: Palgrave.

Schnabel, A. and Carment, D. (eds) (2004) *Conflict Prevention from Rhetoric to Reality: Volume 1: Organizations and Institutions; Volume 2: Opportunities and Innovations; Volume 3: Pacific Settlement of International Disputes*. Lanham, MD: Lexington.

Schofield, J. (2007) Now we have 1.6 mobile phones each. *Guardian*, 14 September 2007: www.guardian.co.uk/technology/blog/2007/sep/14/nowwehave16mobilephonese (accessed 25 November 2008).

Scholey, P. (2006) Peacebuilding research and north–south research relationships: perspectives, opportunities and challenges. In MacLean, S., Black, D. and Shaw, T. (eds) *A Decade of Human Security: Global governance and new multilateralisms*. Aldershot: Ashgate, pp. 179–92.

Schwab, P. (2004) *Designing West Africa: Prelude to 21st century calamity*. Basingstoke: Palgrave.

Seligson, M. (2003) The dual gaps: an overview of theory and research. In Seligson, M. and Passé-Smith, J. (eds) *Development and Under-Development: The political economy of global inequality*, 3rd edn. Boulder, CO: Lynne Rienner, pp. 1–6.

Semmel, B. (1970) *The Rise of Free Trade Imperialism: Classical political economy, the empire of free trade and imperialism 1750–1850*. Cambridge: Cambridge University Press.

Sen, A. (2006) *Identity and Violence*. New York: Norton.

Shaw, T. and Mbabazi, P. (2007) Two Ugandas and a liberal peace? Lessons from Uganda about conflict and development at the start of a new century. *Global Society* 21(4): 567–78.

Shaw, T., MacLean, S. and Black, D. (2006) Introduction: a decade of human security. What prospects for global governance and new multilateralisms? In Shaw, T., MacLean, S. and Black, D. (eds) *A Decade of Human Security: Global governance and new multilateralisms*. Aldershot: Ashgate, pp. 3–18.

Shutt, H. (1998) *The Trouble with Capitalism: An enquiry into the causes of global economic failure*. London: Zed Books.

SIDA (2006) *Microfinance and Women's Empowerment: Evidence from the self-help group bank linkage programme in India*. Stockholm: SIDA.

Silke, A. (2000) Drink, drugs, and rock'n'roll: financing loyalist terrorism in Northern Ireland – part two. *Studies in Conflict and Terrorism* 23(2): 107–27.

Simmel, G. (1955) *Conflict: The web of group affiliations*. New York: Free Press.

Slim, H. (1998) Sharing a universal ethic: the principle of humanity in war. *International Journal of Human Rights* 2(4): 28–48.

Slim, R. and Wolpe, H. (1996) Managing conflict in divided societies: lessons from Tajikistan. *Negotiation Journal* 12: 31–46.

Slomp, G. (2008) On sovereignty. In Salmon, T. and Imber, M. (eds) *Issues in International Relations*. London: Routledge.

Smith, A. (1776) *An Inquiry into the Nature and Causes of the Wealth of Nations*. London.

Solomon, R.H. (2007) Foreword. In Crocker, C.A., Hampson, F.O. and Aall, P. (eds) *Leashing the Dogs of War: Conflict management in a divided world*. Washington, DC: United States Institute of Peace Press, pp. ix–xi.

Southeast Asian Press Alliance (SEAPA) (2006) Cambodian editor harassed for linking Hun Sen nephew to land grab. *Southeast Asian Press Alliance*, 29 June: http://seapa.wordpress.com/2006/06/29/editor-harassed-for-linking-hun-sen-kin-to-land-grab/ (accessed 15 August 2008).

Spearin, C. (2008) Private, armed and humanitarian? States, NGOs, international private security companies and shifting humanitarianism. *Conflict, Security, Development* 39(4): 363–82.

Stedman, S. (2007) UN transformation in an era of soft balancing. *International Affairs* 83(5): 933–44.

Stiglitz, J. (2003) *Globalization and its Discontents*. New York: Norton.

Stiglitz, J. with Bilmes, L.J. (2008) *The Three Trillion Dollar War: The true cost of the Iraq conflict*. New York: Norton.

Stiglitz, J. and Charlton, A. (2005) *Fair Trade for All: How trade can promote development*. Oxford: Oxford University Press.

Straus, S. (2007) Origins and aftermaths: the dynamics of genocide in Rwanda and their post-genocide implication. In Pouligny, B., Chesterman, S. and Schnabel, A. (eds) *After Mass Crime: Rebuilding states and communities*. Tokyo: United Nations Press, pp. 122–41.

Sutton, F.X. (2006) Nation-building in the heyday of the classic development ideology: Ford Foundation experience in the 1950s and 1960s. In Fukuyama, F. (ed.) *Nation-Building: Beyond Afghanistan and Iraq*. Baltimore, MD: Johns Hopkins University Press, pp. 42–63.

Tajfel, H. (1978) Social categorisation, social identity and social comparison. In Tajfel, H. (ed.) *Differentiation between Social Groups: Studies in the social psychology of intergroup relations*. London: Academic Press.

Taylor, I. (2005) *NEPAD: Towards Africa's development or another false start?* Boulder, CO: Lynne Rienner.

Thomas, A. (2006) Reflections on development in a context of war. In Yanacopulos, H. and Hanlon, J. (eds) *Civil War, Civil Peace*. Oxford: James Currey, pp. 185–205.

Thornhill, R. and Palmer, C.T. (2000) *A Natural History of Rape: Biological bases of sexual coercion*. Cambridge, MA: MIT Press.

Tickner, A. (2001) *Gendering World Politics: Issues and approaches in the post-Cold War era*. Columbia, New York: Columbia University Press.

Tilly, C. (1985) War making and state making as organized crime. In Evans, P., Rueschemeyer, D. and Skocpol, T. (eds) *Bringing the State Back In*. Cambridge: Cambridge University Press, pp. 169–91.

Tilly, C. (2002) Violent and non-violent trajectories in contentious politics. In Ungar, M., Bermanzohn, S. and Worcester, K. (eds) *Violence and Politics: Globalization's paradox*. New York: Routledge, pp. 13–31.

Tisdall, S. (2007) Iran's secret plan for summer offensive to force US out of Iraq. *Guardian*, 22 May.

Touval, S. (1982) *The Peace Brokers: Mediators in the Arab–Israeli conflict, 1948–1979*. Princeton, NJ: Princeton University Press.

Traynor, I. (2003) The privatisation of war. *Observer*, 10 December.

Turner, J.C., Hogg, M., Oakes, P., Reicher, S. and Wetherell, M. (1987) *Rediscovering the Social Group: A self-categorization theory*. Oxford: Blackwell.

Turshen, M. and Twagiramariya, C. (1998) *What Women Do in Wartime: Gender and conflict in Africa*. London: Zed Books.

Underhill, G. (2001) The public good versus private interests and the global financial and monetary system. In Drache, D. (ed.) *The Market or the Public Domain: Global governance and the asymmetry of power*. London: Routledge, pp. 274–95.

United Nations (1992) Report of the Secretary-General, *An Agenda for Peace*. New York: UN.

United Nations (1995) Boutros Boutros-Ghali, *An Agenda for Peace*, 2nd edn. New York: UN.

United Nations (2000) *Report of the Panel on Peacekeeping Operations* (Brahimi Report). New York: UN: www.un.org/peace/reports/peace_operations/.

United Nations Development Programme (UNDP) (1994) *Human Security Report 1994*. New York: UNDP.

United Nations Development Programme (1997) *Human Development Report 1997: Human development to eradicate poverty*. New York: UNDP.

United Nations Development Programme (2006) *Human Development Report 2006: Beyond scarcity – Power, poverty and the global water crisis*. New York: UNDP.

United Nations Institute for Disarmament Research (UNIDR) (1996–8) Various titles, Disarmament and Conflict Resolution Series. Geneva: UN.

United Nations Mission in Kosovo (UNMIK) (2004) Condemning violence in Kosovo, Security Council demands return to rule of law. UNMIK Online: at www.unmikonline.org (accessed 18 March 2008).

van de Walle, N. (2001) *African Economies and the Politics of Permanent Crisis, 1979–1999*. Cambridge: Cambridge University Press.

Vayrynen, T. (2001) *Culture and International Conflict Resolution*. Manchester: Manchester University Press.

Wainwright, E. (2003) Responding to state failure: the case of Australia and the Solomon Islands. *Australian Journal of International Affairs* 57(3): 485–93.

Wake, C. (2008) An unaided peace? The (unintended) consequences of international aid in the Oslo peace process. *Conflict, Security and Development* 8(1): 109–31.

Wallensteen, P. (2007) *Understanding Conflict Resolution*, 2nd edn. London: Sage.

Waltz, K. (2001) *Man, the State and War*. New York: Columbia University Press.

Webb, K. (1978) *The Growth of Nationalism in Scotland*. London: Harmondsworth.

Webb, K., Walters, M. and Koutrakou, V. (1996) The Yugoslavian conflict, European mediation and the contingency model. In Bercovitch, J. (ed.) *Resolving International Conflicts: The theory and practice of mediation*. Boulder, CO: Lynne Rienner, pp. 171–89.

Weiss, T. and Daws, S. (eds) (2007) *The Oxford Handbook of the United Nations*. Oxford: Oxford University Press.

Whittaker, D.J. (1999) *Conflict and Reconciliation in the Contemporary World*. London: Routledge.

Widner, J. (2005) *Constitution Writing and Conflict Resolution*, WIDER Research Paper; 2005/51: www.wider.unu.edu/publications/working-papers/research-papers/2005/en_GB/rp2005-51/.

Wierda, M. (2006) Transitional justice in Sierra Leone. In de Zeeuw, J. and Kumar, K. (eds) *Promoting Democracy in Post-Conflict Societies: Views and lessons from Africa, Asia and Central America*. Boulder, CO: Lynne Rienner, pp. 183–207.

Williams, A. (1992) *Many Voices: Multilateral negotiations in the world arena*. Boulder, CO: Westview.

Williams, A. (1998) *Failed Imagination? New world orders of the twentieth century*. Manchester: Manchester University Press.

Williams, A. (2005) 'Reconstruction' before the Marshall Plan. *Review of International Studies* 31: 541–58.

Williams, A. (2006) *Liberalism and War: The victors and the vanquished*. London: Routledge.

Williams, A. (2007a) *Failed Imagination? The Anglo-American new world order from Wilson to Bush*, 2nd edn. Manchester: Manchester University Press.

Williams, A. (2007b) Reconstruction: the bringing of peace and plenty or occult imperialism? *Global Society: Journal of Interdisciplinary International Relations* 21(4): 539–51.

Williams, M. (1994) *International Economic Organisations and the Third World*. New York: Harvester Wheatsheaf.

Wilmer, F. (2002) *The Social Construction of Man, the State, and War: Identity, conflict, and violence in the former Yugoslavia*. London: Routledge.

Win, E. (2007) Not very poor, powerless or pregnant: the African woman forgotten by development. In Cornwall, A., Harrison, E. and Whitehead, A. (eds) *Feminisms in Development: Contradictions, contestations and challenges*. London: Zed Books, pp. 79–85.

Winn, N. (ed.) (2004) *Neo-Medievalism and Civil Wars*. London: Frank Cass.

Winter, J. (1995) *Sites of Memory, Sites of Mourning: The Great War in European cultural history*. Cambridge: Cambridge University Press.

Winter, J. (2000) The generation of memory: reflections on the 'Memory Book', Contemporary Historical Studies. *German Historical Institute Bulletin*, Fall: 69–92.

Wolfsfeld, G. (2003) The role of the news media in peace negotiations: variations over time and circumstance. In Darby, J. and Mac Ginty, R. (eds) *Contemporary Peacemaking: Conflict, violence and peace processes*. Basingstoke: Palgrave, pp. 87–99.

Wright, Q. (1942) *A Study of War*. Chicago, IL: University of Chicago Press.

Wulf, H. (ed.) (2000) *Disarmament and Conflict Prevention in Development Cooperation*. Bonn: BICC.

Yoshida, T. (2007) Advancing or obstructing reconciliation: changes in history education and disputes over history textbooks in Japan. In Cole, E.A. *Teaching the Violent Past: History, education and reconciliation*. Lanham, MD: Rowman & Littlefield.

Young, C. (2003) Explaining the conflict potential of ethnicity. In Darby, J. and Mac Ginty, R. (eds) *Contemporary Peacemaking: Conflict, violence and peace processes*. Basingstoke: Palgrave Macmillan, pp. 9–18.

Zartman, I.W. (1985) *Ripe for Resolution: Conflict and intervention in Africa*. New York: Oxford University Press.

Zartman, I.W. (2005) Need, greed and creed in intrastate war. In Arnson, C. and Zartman, I.W. (eds) *Rethinking the Economics of War: The intersection of need, greed and creed*. Baltimore, MD: Johns Hopkins University Press, pp. 256–84.

Zaum, D. (2006) The authority of international administrations in international society. *Review of International Studies* 32(3): 455–73.

Zeeuw, J. de (ed.) (2008) *From Soldiers to Politicians: Transforming Rebel Movements after Civil War*. Boulder, CO: Lynne Reinner.

# Index